Austrian Seven Years War
Infantry and Engineers

UNIFORMS, ORGANISATION AND EQUIPMENT

COMPLETELY REVISED
2ND EDITION

No. 2   No. 31   No. 52

Dr Stephen Summerfield

KEN TROTMAN PUBLISHING

Published in 2014 by Ken Trotman Publishing.
Booksellers & Publishers
P.O. Box 505
Godmanchester
Huntingdon PE29 2XW
England
Tel: 01480 454292
Fax: 01480 384651
www.kentrotman.com

ISBN:
978-1-907417-52-8

Preface

It has been a pleasure to completely revise this book since it was first published four years ago. The original 270 illustrations of the first edition have been digitally enhanced. The chapter on the history or the Seven Years War has been cut to make room for the additional 445 mainly contemporary illustrations, uniforms, equipment details, maps and flags. All the order of battles have been retained and can be found in the appendix.

- The regiments have been organised by province instead of the 1769 regimental number and 12 new maps have been added.
- The chapters on uniforms and equipment have been enhanced by a further 170 uniform/equipment details in addition to the original 60 as well as 58 contemporary illustrations from the Austrian 1749 Drill book was courtesy of Dr. J. Sissak.
- Details of the flags used during the War of Austrian Succession and the early part of the Seven Years War have been added (34 illustrations).
- The author has attempted to reconcile the conflicting evidence concerning the uniforms for the infantry and the uniform changes brought about by reforming regiments and the need for economy by dating the illustrations. The 320 uniform illustrations are dated to 1757 according to Wrede modifying the Brauer plates, 1760 using the Donath (1970) plates and the contemporize Albertini and Bautzener plates of 1762. These show a reduction of the use of dyed cloth.
- It should be remembered that the men would have worn their uniform and equipment as long as it was serviceable so there was great variation even within companies. The new recruits would normally be wearing the newest issue uniforms. Hence, coloured or white turnbacks and waistcoats would have co-existed for some time. It is likely that the expensive white metal buttons and braid were transferred to the new uniforms. Drummers in reversed colours persisted to about 1760 despite the order of 1755 for white coats. It was not until 1767, after the Seven Years War that the uniforms were reformed and standardised.
- The complex and confusing uniform of the *Grenzer* has now been updated by the addition of 36 illustrations by Bautzener (1762), Ottenfeld (1895), and Donath (1970) illustrations plus notes from the Raspe (1762) and Knötel (c1900) plates. Alas dating the uniform has not been possible due to the rotation system of the battalions.

At the start of the Seven Years War most infantry regiments had waistcoats the same colour as their facings and the drummers were often in reversed colours. Later in the Seven Years, these distinctions had disappeared probably due to the needs of economy and cost of the dyed cloth. Only the Hungarian regiments retained coloured waistcoats.

Most of the 19th and early 20th century illustrations follow those of either Albertini, Bautzen Manuscript and Raspe Manuscript both dated as 1762 which differ considerably at times in the details especially the Grenzer. Hence it is not surprising that none of the German Infantry show colour waistcoats.

The age of the prints has meant that there may have been changes in the shade especially of the greens and the reds and the yellowing of the paper. The illustrations in this book have been colour corrected. The facings of the regiments changed a number of times between 1740 and 1763. These have been summarised in a table and colour swatches for the colour have been given from a 19th Century Manuscript. The exact shade of blue, green or red is still difficult to determine with the distance of time. The precise details of uniforms are difficult to sort out and these have been highlighted rather than reconciled by the works of Pengel and Hurt (1982 and 1983).

The Albertini (1762)[1] (also spelt Albertina) were first reproduced in 1873 by Kornauth and these delightful full length plates are considered the most reliable by both Pengel (1982)[2] and Duffy (2000). However, the colour has suffered over the last two and a half centuries. A great deal of care has been made by the author to digitally enhance the colour of all the illustrations.

The complete Bautzen Manuscript (1762)[3] was reproduced by Thümmler (1993).[4] They are charming in their naive simplicity but have suffered considerably with age and the yellowing of the paper.

The Brauer Plates (c1930)[5] and the work by Herbert Knötel[6] were based upon the Raspe Manuscript (1762)[7] with some differences. The excellent research of Donath (1970) is more faithful to the Raspe Manuscript (1762) and these have been redrawn by the author to fill out areas that have not been covered by Albertini (1762) or Brauer (c1930). It was felt unnecessary to show examples directly from the Raspe Manuscript as these were well represented by Brauer (c1930) and Donath (1970).[8]

---

[1] Albertini (1762) *Dessins des Uniformes des Troupes I.I. et R.R. de l'Année 1762,* Vienna (Reproduced in Kornauth, Friedrich (1873) *Das Heer Maria Theresias Faksimile-Ausgabe der Albertina-Hanschrift "Desins des Uniformes des Troupes I.I et R.R. de l'Annee 1762,* Vienna – This shows 102 different uniforms and considered the most reliable of the contemporary sources.)

[2] Pengel R.D. and Hurt G.R. (1982) *Austro-Hungarian Infantry 1740-1762,* On Military Matters.

[3] Bautzen Manuscript (1762) *Die Bautzener Bilderhanschrift aus dem Jahre 1762.*

[4] Thümmler, Lars-Holger (1993) *Die Österreichische Armee im Siebenjährigen Krieg Die Bautzener Bilderhandschrift aus dem Jahre 1762,* Berlin

[5] Brauer, Hans (1926-62) *Heeres-Uniformbogen,* Uniformbogen No. 7 and No. 23, Heere und Tradition, Berlin. (By Herbert Knötel)

[6] Knötel, Herbert (1890-1921) *Uniformkunde,* Plates: IV:43; V:51; VI:12; VI:13, VI:44; XII:4 and XIV:59.

[7] Raspe Manuscript (1762) *Der sämtlichen Kayserlich Koeniglichen Armee zur eigentlichen Kentnis der Uniform von jedem Regimente. Nebst beygefügter Geschichte, worinne von der Stiftung, denen Chefs, der Staercke, und den wichtigsten Thaten jedes Regiments Nachricht gegeben wird.,* Nürnberg. (Brauer and the Knötel plates are based upon the Raspe Manuscript)

[8] Donath, Rudolf (1970) *Die Kaiserliche und Kaiserlich-Königliche Österreichische Armee 1618-1918,* Simbach (These follow mainly the Raspe Manuscript and more faithfully than Knötel.)

The rarely seen pen and ink drawings have been reproduced from Ottenfeld (1895 rp2003) *Die Österreichische Armée von 1700 bis 1867*[9] by the kind permission of Richard Brown of Ken Trotman Ltd who produced an excellent facsimile in three volumes.

The list of *Inhaber* and regimental histories has been derived mainly from Thürheim (1880) and Wrede (1898-1905)[10] with additional material from Duffy (2000 & 2008)[11] and Thümmler (1993).[12]

This is the companion volume to Summerfield *Austrian Seven Years War Cavalry and Artillery*. The following conventions have been followed:

- Austrian rank titles and names have been preserved as far as possible.
- The Austrian Infantry Regiments have been numbered IR1-IR57 in accordance to the infantry regimental numbers that were given in 1769. The gaps in the sequence have been noted in the text. Although this was not done in the period, it was considered necessary to show the continuity of the regiments through the changing of their *Inhaber*. This convention is also used by Pengel (1982) and Duffy (2000 and 2008).
- The Grenz Infantry Regiments are according to their precedence in 1761. The Regimental Index gives a cross reference of Inhaber.
- The Cuirassier (KR), Dragoon (DR), Hussar (HR) and Grenz Hussar (GHR) have been assigned by their seniority in 1761. See Summerfield *Austrian Seven Years War Cavalry and Artillery* for more details.
- The Regimental Index in this Volume 2 gives a cross reference to the 1769 Cavalry Numbers used by Pengel (1982) and Duffy (2000 and 2008).
- The Austrians used their own measurements throughout the period and these have been converted to metric.
- The more familiar caisson has been used instead of ammunition wagon, *Munitionwagen* or *Kugelwagen*.

Dr Stephen Summerfield
Loughborough University
1 August 2014

---

[9] Ottenfeld, Rudolf von and Teuber, Oscar (1895 rp 2003) *Die Österreichische Armee von 1700 bis 1867*, Verlag von Emil Berte, Vienna (reprint by Ken Trotman Ltd)

[10] Wrede, Alphons Freiherr von (1898-1905), *Geschichte der K. und K. Wehrmacht. Die Regimenter, Corps, Branchen und Anstalten von 1618 bis Ende des XIX. Jahrhunderts*, Volume I-V, Vienna

[11] Duffy, Christopher (2000) *Instruments of War* Volume I of the Austrian Army in the Seven Years War; Emperor's Press. Duffy, Christopher (2008) *By Force of Arms*, Volume II of the Austrian Army in the Seven Years War, Emperor's Press.

[12] Thürheim, Andreas (1880) *Gedenkblätter aus der Kriegsgeschichte der k. k. Österreichischen Armee*, Vol I-II, Vienna

Acknowledgements

The informative books of Christopher Duffy upon the Austrian and Prussians Armies have been an inspiration to me. These I would recommend to compliment to this book.

The comments and enhancement of the second edition was made much easier by the kind assistance of Dr Jiří Sissak. The proof-reading of Mark Webb and Richard Brown have been invaluable to get this book to its final form. The editorial comments of Dal Gavin have been as ever of great assistance. In addition, this work would have been much harder to put together without the wonderful contributors to the *Seven Years War Project* (www.kronoskaf.com/syw) and Lars-Holger Thümmler of *Generalstad* (www.kuk-wehrmacht.de). I wish also to thank Hans Karl Weiss, Christian Rogge, Digby Smith and Steven H. Smith for their kind assistance.

I wish to thank NGA Archive, Markus Stein, Dr Jiří Sissak and Dave Hollins for their kind permission to reproduce illustrations from their extensive collections. Especially, I wish to acknowledge the kind permission to reproduce the fine illustrations from their edition of Ottenfeld and Teuber (1898 rp2003) of Ken Trotman Ltd. I wish to thank the British Library, *Heeresgeschichtliches Museum* (HGM) in Vienna, the *Landes und Universitatsbibliotek* in Darmstadt, Loughborough University Library, New York Public Library, the Royal Engineers Library and the Royal Armouries at Fort Nelson for their kind assistance.

Austrian Fusilier
1749 Drill Book courtesy of Dr. J. Sissak

Contents

Maps

Tables

Order of Battles

The Treaty of Dresden (13 September 1745) ended the Second Silesian War between Austria, Saxony, and Prussia. Maria Theresa recognised Frederick's sovereignty over Silesia in return for Prussian recognition of Francis as Holy Roman Emperor. The Austro-Russian Treaty of the Two Empresses of 1746 renewed the alliance that had been first concluded 20 years before.[19] The Treaty of Aix-la-Chapelle (18 Oct 1748) finally ended the War of Austrian Succession.

The Peace of Hubertusburg was signed on 15 February 1763. This restored the boundaries of Prussia, Austria and Saxony as they had been before the war started. This left Frederick as master of Silesia much to the frustration of Maria Theresa. The Austrians lost 303,595 men with 32,622 killed in action and 93,404 men dead of disease or wounds. A total of 89 infantry colours, 23 cavalry standards, 397 cannon, 46 howitzers, 31 mortars and 554 caissons had been captured by the Prussians during the war.[20]

In 1765, Emperor Francis Stephen died and was succeeded by Joseph II, Maria Theresa's eldest son, who became joint ruler with her until 1780 when she died.

1757

IR4 Deutschmeister Grenadier
Pokorny (2001), courtesy of Dr S. Sissak

---

[19] Scott (2000) 167
[20] Woods (2008) 14

The Army

In 1649, Emperor Ferdinand III (1608-57) established a permanent military of nine *Regimenter zu Fuss* and ten *Regimenter zu Pferd*. The first regular Austrian standing army was created in 1669 by Italian born General Raimondo Graf Montecúccoli (1608-80) who was president of the *Hofkriegsrat* from 1668 until his death in 1680. There was never enough money to fund the army from the estates, imperial diet and other revenues.[21]

**Old soldiers salute
Eugene of Savoy (1663-1736)**

The Austrian Army had since the death of Eugene of Savoy undergone a severe decline in quality. At the end of the Turkish War of 1737-39, the regular army had 52 infantry regiments and 40 cavalry regiments with paper strength of 160,000 men. The severe financial difficulties led to much discussion in reducing its size but little had been done by the death of Charles VI in October 1740. The army now had at the start of the Austrian War of Succession only 107,892 men under arms instead of 141,880. This increased to almost 200,000 by 1743 and sunk to 171,616 in 1748. The effective strength was 40-50,000 men below this mark.[22]

Austrian finances were in a very poor state after the defeats in the War of Polish Succession (1733-35) and Turkish War of 1737-39 in alliance with Russia where Vienna had to cede some of their gains from the Treaty of Passarowitz (21 July 1718).[23] The War of Austrian Succession cost 185.85 million florins which were more than eight times the annual state revenue. The occupation of Bohemia and Silesia lost 8 million florins or two thirds of the state revenue.[24]

The Army was known as the *Kaiserliche Armee* (Imperial Army) then on 21 October 1740 it was renamed *Königlich Ungarisch-Böhmische Armee* and then finally on 14 September 1745, the name became the *Kaiserlich-Königliche Armee*.

---

[21] Grant (1987) 114
[22] Hochedlinger (2003) 297
[23] Scott (2000) 160
[24] Hochedlinger (2003) 234 and 280-2

Even the most conservative elements at the court realised that there needed to be reform. In 1749, Maria Theresa started the much needed reform of the administration, finances of the state and the army. The principle architect of the civilian and financial reform was led by Friedrich Wilhelm Graf von Haugwitz (1702-65). In 1744, he led the government of unconquered Austrian Silesian. At this time he became aware that the Prussians raised 7 million florins in taxes from their newly conquered province of Silesia whereas the Habsburgs had only been able to raise 2.1 million florins. His work continued when he transferred to Inner Austria in 1747. In 1749, his reforms were implanted throughout the Habsburg lands except for Hungary, Lombardy and the Netherlands. In May 1749, the Austrian and Bohemian Chancelleries were replaced by the *Directorum in publicis et cameralibus* modelled upon the Prussian General Directory. This was chaired by Haugwitz. In 1757, the special councils of the Austrian Netherlands and Lombardy were incorporated into the State Chancellery.[25]

FM Leopold Daun was tasked with the improvement of the infantry and cavalry who established greater uniformity in drill and discipline. A new supply system, a drill book for the whole army and the command language was only German. Prince Liechtenstein undertook the staggering improvement in the Artillery that more than made up the shortfall in quality in the rest of the army.[26]

The transformation of the Habsburg state had only just started. The problems of lack of geographical continuity, a common language, laws or culture had not been overcome. The lands and provinces could only be governed by consent of the powerful established landowners. This also meant that the Army had to be divided among the divided territories. The husband of Maria Theresa was the Holy Roman Emperor so also could call upon the services of the *Reichsarmee* (the Army of the Empire), although this was a fairly small force composed of contingents from a variety of the small (and smaller) entities within Germany.

The much needed Haugwitz financial reforms of 1748-49 would produce 110,000 regulars from Austro-Bohemia and Hungary with another 25,000 each from the Netherlands and Italian provinces. This made a total of 160,000 men excluding the Grenz and Technical troops.

Austria started mobilising on 18 June 1756 but there was a severe lack of men, horses and ordnance. About one third of the infantry were quartered in Bohemia and Moravia but only 9% of the regular cavalry with over 70% quartered in Hungary and distant Transylvania. The contract for the Artillery horses was only signed on 24 July.[27] Finding suitable men for the army was always a problem for Austria. Daun estimated that even before the outbreak of the Seven Years War, there was a 38,000 man deficit in infantry in 1755. By June 1756, this deficit had been reduced to 10,000 men.

The paper strength at the start of the Seven Years War was 156,750 rising to 197,518 men in 1757. In October 1761, the regular army was reduced to 177,497 men and further to 153,164 at the end of the war in 1764. [28]

---

[25] Hochedlinger (2003) 269-270
[26] Duffy (2008) 11-12
[27] Duffy (2008) 15
[28] Hochedlinger (2003) 298-300

OOB 1: Number of regiments in the Austria Army, 1756[29]

56 Infantry Regiments, 18 Cuirassier Regiments,
14 Dragoon Regiments,
11 Hussar Regiments
9 Grenz Infantry and 4 Grenz Hussar detachments.
1 German and 1 Netherlands Artillery Corps with miners
1 Engineer Corps, 1 Pontoneer Corps

OOB 2: Austrian Army in 1756[30]

Infantry

44 Infantry Regiments with 2,408 men each	105,952 men	
10 Infantry Regiments with 2,000 men each	20,000 men	
1 Infantry Battalion	658 men	126,610 men
With Grenz Infantry Regiments	15,600 men	15,600 men
		142,210 men

Cavalry and Hussars

18 Cuirassier Regiments with 818 troopers each	14,724 men	
12 Dragoon Regiments with 817 troopers each	9.804 men	
10 Hussar Regiments with 615 hussars	6,150 men	30678 men
With Grenz Hussars	1,000 men	1,000 men
		31,678 men

Technical Troops

24 German Artillery Companies	2,304 men	
8 Netherlands Artillery Companies	768 men	
2 Miner Companies	238 men	
2 Pontoneer Companies	246 men	3,556 men

TOTAL	177,444 men

OOB 3: Newly raised Infantry Regiments, 1756-58.

Newly Raised Infantry Regiments	
IR39 Johann Pálffy (raised 1756-7)	2,000
Newly raised Dragoon Regiments (No Grenadier company)	
DR6 Löwenstein Chevauleger (raised 1759)	800
Staff Regiments (for the protection of the HQ)	
IR Stabs-Infanterie-Regiment (raised 1758)	2,732
DR Stabs-Dragoner-Regiment (raised 1758)	465

---

[29] Generalstab (1901) I: 130
[30] Generalstab (1901) I: 133

Recruiting

This was the responsibility of each regiment. It was not until 1766 that recruiting districts (*Cantons*) on the Prussian model were introduced. Only the Hungarian Infantry and Hussars recruited from within a particular area. The other regiments, termed as "German", recruited throughout Europe especially within the Holy Roman Empire. This is extensively explored by Duffy (2000).

Regimental recruiting parties gave cash bounties to men 18-40 years old and over 5 *Fuss* 3 *Zoll* / 5 foot 5 inches (Imperial/US) / 166 cm who chose to enlist.[31] From 13 December 1758, this minimum height was increasingly unofficially relaxed in the search for healthy recruits. The infantry preferred taller recruits who could easier handle the long muskets. The cavalryman received double the bounty of the infantryman. Voluntary enlistment was supplemented by a limited conscription in Austria and Bohemia. Enlistment was for life. In May 1757, limited service of six years or the duration of the war was introduced. By the end of the war about a third of the army were enlisted under limited service.

Inhaber

Each regiment had an *Inhaber* (colonel-proprietor or *Chef*) who gave his name to the Regiment. It was not until 1769 that regimental numbers supplemented the name. He enjoyed almost complete control of the finances, discipline, training, uniform and the selection of company grade officers. The latter was normally delegated to the colonel who commanded the regiment. The Inhaber was normally a general or a member of the royal family and many used it as a source of revenue. Considerable differences in spelling of Inhaber names especially of Hungarian or Italian origin can be found.

Officers

Despite generous incentives from Vienna, Austria lacked the native nobility to serve in the officer corps unlike Britain, France, Prussia and Russia. The Austrian officer corps remained heterogeneous and cosmopolitan as ever. From 1757, deserving officers with thirty years good service were granted nobility. As this did not come with land, the officer class were even tighter associated with the monarch.[32]

Most officers joined their regiments as cadets and received training within the regiment before being promoted to *Fähnrich* in the infantry or *Cornet* in the cavalry. In 1752, education of young cadets was improved by the opening of the Military Academy at Wiener Neustadt for sons of officers, impoverished nobles or civil servants. The first director was FM Leopold Daun. This was able to supply a third of the newly commissioned officers. Half the Academy was made up of sons of distinguished officers or officials and the other half from the nobility. The latter had many social advantages and so were fortunate in swifter promotions.

Company officers were promoted by their regimental *Inhaber* and senior ranks by the *Hofkriegsrat* (Council of War) who demanded a payment from the officer for each promotion. There was also an unofficial system of purchase that meant that younger officers could buy out long-serving or wounded officers.

---

[31] Duffy (2000) p198. (Austrian Vienna *Fuss* = 31.6cm = 12.44 Imperial inches and Vienna *Zoll* = 2.634cm = 1.037 Imperial inches.)
[32] Hochedlinger (2003) 305-6

Table 2: Austrian, British and French officer ranks.

Austrian Army	Prussian Army	British Army
Generale	**Generale**	**Generals**
General-Feldmarschall (FM)[33]	*Feldmarschall* (FM)	*General or Field Marshal*
Feldzeugmeister (FZM)[34]	*General der Infanterie* (GdI)	*Lieutenant General*
General de Cavallerie (GdC)[35]	*General der Kavallerie* (GdK)	*Lieutenant General*
Feldmarschall-Lieutenant (FML)	*General-Lieutenant* (GL)	*Major General*
Generalfeldwachtmeister (GFWM)[36]	*General-Major* (GM)	*Brigadier General*
Ober-Offizier	**Stab-Offizier**	**Staff Officers**
Obrist[37]	*Oberst*	*Colonel*
Obrist-Lieutenant (Obrist-Lt)[38]	*Oberst-Leutnant* (Oberst-Lt)	*Lieutenant Colonel* (Lt Col)
Obrist-Wachtmeister[39]	*Major*	*Major*
		Company Officers
Hauptmann / Rittmeister[40]	*Hauptmann / Kapitän*	*Captain*
Kapitänleutnant[41]	-	*2nd Captain*
Oberlieutenant	*Premierleutnant*	*1st Lieutenant*
Unterlieutenant[42]	*Sekondeleutnant*	*2nd Lieutenant*
Fähnrich[43] / *Fahnen-Kadetten*[44]		*Ensign / Cornet*
Kadetts		
K.K. Kadetten-Ordinäres[45]		*Cadet*
Privat-Kadetten[46]		*Cadet*
Unter-Offiziere	**Unter-Offizier**	**NCOs**
Feldwebel / Wachtmeister		*Sergeant Major*
Führer		*Colour Sergeant*
Furier		
Feldscher		
Musterschreiber		*Clerk*
Corporal	*Korporal*	*Corporal*
Mannschaft	**Mannschaft**	**Men**
Gefreiter	*Gefreiter*	*Lance Corporal*
Gemeine	*Gemiene*	*Soldier*

---

[33] *Generalleutnant* was the highest ranking general in the Austrian Army. Only Margraf Ludwig Wilhelm von Baden-Baden (1655-1707), Prinz Eugen von Savoy (1663-1736), Francis Stephen of Lorraine (1708-65) and Charles Alexander of Lorraine (1712-80) obtained this rank in the 18th century.

[34] *Obrist-General-Feldzugmeister* until 1750.

[35] *Obrist-General-Feldzugmeister* until 1750.

[36] *Obristfeldwachtmeister* until 1740 and then in 1771, renamed Generalmajor.

[37] *Oberst* from 1771.

[38] *Oberstleutnant* from 1776.

[39] *Major* from 1769.

[40] *Hauptmann* (Infantry) and *Rittmeister*. Renamed *Fuhrwesen* in 1771.

[41] *Zeite-Rittmeister* from 1771

[42] *Lieutenant* until 1748.

[43] Cuirassier and Hussars.

[44] Same rank as *Faunrich* in the infantry. Abolished in 1798.

[45] Had the equivalent rank as *Feldwebel*.

[46] Usually a son of a serving soldier.

Chapter 2
Regular Infantry

In 1718, the *Regimenter zu Fuss* were renamed *Infanterie-Regiment*. The Hungarian regiments were known as *Haydukenregimenter*.

Upon the accession of Maria Theresa in 1740, there were 51 infantry regiments of which three were Hungarian, two Italian, three Walloon from the Netherlands and one Tyrolean (Battalion). The remainder drew recruits from the other Habsburg territories including Austria, Bohemia, Moravia, and Austrian Silesia plus other states in the Holy Roman Empire. Each regiment had three battalions of five companies plus two grenadier companies.[47]

Table 3: Austrian Infantry 1741-64[48]

Year	Infantry Regiments	Nationality
1741	51	43 German, 3 Hungarian, 2 Italian and 3 Walloon
1742	59	43 German, 9 Hungarian, 2 Italian and 5 Walloon
1742	60	43 German, 9 Hungarian, 3 Italian and 5 Walloon
1748	54	39 German, 9 Hungarian, 2 Italian and 4 Walloon
1750	56	39 German, 11 Hungarian, 2 Italian and 4 Walloon
1757	56	39 German, 11 Hungarian, 2 Italian and 4 Walloon
1764	57	39 German, 11 Hungarian, 2 Italian and 5 Walloon

Table 4: Organisation of Austrian Infantry 1741-64[49]

Year	Fusilier Bns	Coys of men	Grenadier Coys	Total Coys	Regimental Strength
1740					2,016
1741-43	3 Bns	5 coys of 120	2 coys of 100	17	2,007
1744-48					2,307
1749-55	4 Bns	4 coys of 136	2 coys of 100	18	2,408
1756	2 Field Bns / 1 Garrison Bn	6 coys of 136 / 4 coys of 136	2 coys of 100	18	2,408
1757	2 Field Bns / 1 Garrison Bn	6 coys of 140 / 4 coys of 140	2 coys of 100	18	2,693
1758-61	3 Field Bns	6 coys of 140	2 coys of 100	20	2,760
1762-63	4 Field Bns	4 coys of 140	2 coys of 100	18	2,427
1764-67	2 Field Bns / 1 Garrison Bn	6 coys of 116 / 4 coys of 116	2 coys of 100	18	2,080
1768-74	2 Field Bns / 1 Garrison Bn	6 coys of 113 / 4 coys of 113	2 coy of 113	18	2,080

---

[47] Ottenfeld (1895) 117-8
[48] Hochedlinger (2003) 301
[49] Hochedlinger (2003) 302

In 1748, this was increased to four battalions of four companies plus two grenadier companies. Each Regiment had sixteen fusilier companies (136 all ranks) and two grenadier companies (106 all ranks). In peacetime, this was formed into four battalions of fusiliers (about 550 men each) and two companies of grenadiers (100 all ranks) giving an authorized total of 2,408 men.

The first company was known as the *Leib-Companie* or *Inhaber-Companie*. All companies were divided to three to six *Corporalschaften* of 1-2 Corporals, 3-4 *Gefreiter* and 24-28 men. *Corporalschaft* was divided into four *Cammeratschaften* (6-7 men) commanded by Corporal, *Gefreiter* or old soldier (*alte Gemeine*).[50]

IR4 Deuschmeister presenting arms, 1756
Photograph by Charles Srolik, 1896

In 1756, there were 33 German, 2 Italian, 4 Walloon and 16 Hungarian Infantry Regiments. In summer of 1756, two 6-company field battalions of 18 officers and 798 men each were mobilised. The *Garrnison* (Garrison) Battalion of four companies with 12 officers and 532 men remained as the regimental reserve. The two grenadier companies were formed into independent Grenadier Battalions. The eighteen regiments including the two national-Italian regiments in Italy and the four Walloon regiments in the Netherlands both had a lower establishment due to lack of recruits. Their fusilier company mustered only 3 officers and 113 men for a total of 18 officers and 678 men per battalion.[51]

---

[50] *Reglament und Ordnung* 1749, Part II, p16
[51] Generalstab (1901) I: 144

In spring of 1758, each fusilier company establishment was increased to 140 officers and men. Each regiment now had three fusilier battalions of 6 companies giving a total of 24 officers and 816 men per battalion. The two grenadier companies were still combined into Grenadier Battalions. This 1758 organisation remained unaltered until the end of the war. The exception was the four Walloon (Netherlands) regiments organised in 3 battalions with 4 companies each. Severe campaign losses caused out of necessity the field of a reduced number of battalions.

Note

IR5 (1st Garrison Regt) and IR6 (2nd Garrison Regt) were raised in 1766 and 1767 respectively so are outside our period of interest.

In 1767, the Austrian infantry received a new uniform. In 1769, the regimental numbers were introduced and these have been used for clarity in this work as it permits tracing the lineage of the regiments to 1918. The exception being the Netherlands (Walloon) Regiments of IR38 and IR55 in 1796, German Regiments of IR13, IR23, IR43, IR45, IR46 and IR50 were disbanded in 1809, and the Italian regiment of IR44 disbanded in 1809 with these regiments being replaced at a later date.[52]

Table 5: Regimental Staff in 1748 (8 officers and 15 NCOs)

	Austrian Ranks	Notes
Officers (6 officers 1748-56 and 7 officers 1757-69)		
1	*Obrist*	Colonel
1	*Obrist-Lieutenant*	Lieutenant colonel
1	*Obristwachtmeister*	Raised to two per regiment in 1757. Officially renamed *Major* in 1769
1	*Regiments-Proviantmeister*	Regimental Provision-master
1	*Regiments-Quartiermeister*	Regimental Quartermaster who ranked as lieutenant
1	*Regiments-Feldscherer*	Regimental Surgeon
Civilian		
	Auditor and Secretari	Regimental Clerks
NCO		
1	*Wachtmeister Lieutenant*	Regimental Sergeant-Major
1	*Caplan*	Chaplain
1	*Regiment-Tambour*	Drum-Major,
1	*Büchsenmeister*	Armourer
3	*Fahnenführer / Führer*	Colour Sergeant
8	*Cadetten*	Officer Cadet
1	*Regiment-Wagonmeister*	Regimental wagon-master appointed in wartime
1	*Profoss*	Provost who was normally a retired NCO

---

[52] Pengel (1982b) 1

Table 6: Fusilier Company organisation in 1748.

3 officers, 6 NCOs, 4 Musicians 1 Pioneer, and 99 Grenadiers

	Austrian Rank	Notes
Officers		
1	*Hauptmann / Capitän-Lieutenant*	Captain / 2nd Captain
1	*Oberlieutenant*	1st Lieutenant
1	*Fähnrich / Unterlieutenant*	Ensign / 2nd Lieutenant
NCOS (7 NCOs)		
1	*Feldwäbel*	Sergeant-major
1	*Führer*	Colour Sergeant
4	*Corporal*	Corporal
1	*Furier*	Company clerk (civilian)
Men (133 men)		
10	*Gefreiter*	Lance-corporals
110	*Gemeine*	Men
2	*Fourierschützen*	Officer's servants (batmen)
2	*Tambour*	Drummers
2	*Pfeifer*	Fifers
1	*Zimmerleute*	Pioneer/Sapper

Garrison Bns

During 1757, many Garrison Battalions were formed into converged 6-company battalions in response to the Prussian invasion of Bohemia. For example, III/IR13 (Moltke) was formed by four companies of IR13 (Moltke) and two companies of IR49 (Kheul). In spring 1758, the Garrison Battalions serving with the field army were re-raised and organised into six company battalion. In 1760, the garrison regiments were established. These were deployed to escort the transports and other rear activities. In winter 1761-62, overall strength of the regiments had to be reduced as a result of Austria's dwindling financial resources. Each regiments IIIrd (Garrison) Battalion was reduced to four companies to reduce costs.

Depot Bns

In the winter 1757-58, each infantry regiment raised a depot of 1-2 officers and a 100-200 NCOs to operate in the rear areas where the spare regimental baggage was also located. By September 1758, the Depots of 43 regiments had more than 6,900 men located at Prague.

Infantry Tactics

In 1748, the Austrian *Militärkommission* concluded that the superiority of the Prussian infantry in discipline, firepower and drill was the major cause for the victories of Frederick in the two Silesian Wars. As a result, the new drill was introduced in 1749. The new large formation manoeuvres was tested in the summer training camps. However, only in *Reglement 1749* was there a written summary of all innovations issued to the army.

Movement was regulated at the 'ordinary', 'medium', or at the 'double' pace. The latter could also be employed for the attack before closing to small arms fire distance.

Deployed in line of battle, the battalions aligned with 6 pace intervals, with grenadiers present, they likewise formed up with 6 paces intervals with each 1 company deployed on either flank of the regiment.

Fusiliers were deployed in 4 ranks up to the battle of Kolin (18 June 1757) and thereafter in 3 ranks. The regular six company field-battalion was formed in six divisions and the four company Walloon battalions formed into four divisions. The battalion was furthermore divided into 12 (or 8) half-divisions and 24 (or 16) pelotons. Each peloton had 7-8 files if deployed in 4 ranks and 9-10 files if deployed in 3 ranks. Each 3-pdr battalion gun was placed within the battalions intervals.

The battalion could deploy with closed files (touching shoulders) or open files by doubling the intervals (an arms distance). To turn to flank was done by the wheeling of pelotons/half-divisions/divisions or alternatively turning left/right in ranks then marching off. This method was often employed on the battlefield. The extended lines of multiple battalions altered a change of their front by wheeling round their axis.

Deployment from column into line was done by the ordinary quarter wheels of a battalion's sub-divisions (*Einschwenken*) as customarily practiced by basically all contemporary armies. With the deployment, an inversion of the order of ranking was not permitted with the regulations.

The young Comte Gisors, son of French Marshal Belle-Isle attended a training camp near Kolin in 1754 as part of the staff of Emperor Francis Stephen and Maria Theresa. He observed the troops being well disciplined and well-clad, but found training of the rank and file rather uneven, the marching step was too short or slow, and pacing was found ill-timed in general. The troops would avoid advancing with extended front but preferred the column, and more often the simple movement by ranks.[53]

---

[53] Rousset (1868) 83

Musket drill from 1749 Drill Manual

Austrian regulations provided a multitude of fire procedures. Musket drill emphasised both speed and aimed fire. The most common was fire by divisions, half-divisions, or pelotons starting from the flanks to the centre. The entire first rank, the two colour pelotons in the centre of the battalion fired only when ordered to do so by the battalion commander. Fire was conducted invariably at the halt, but the regulations permitted fire during a slow advance. A general battalion discharge was recommended only to hasten the retiring or routing opponent during the pursuit.

IR4 Deuschmeister marching in 1756 uniform
Photograph by Charles Srolik, 1896

By the Seven Years War, the Austrian Infantry had matched the Prussian for speed of fire. The Austrian veteran officer Cogniazzo of IR2 Erzherzog Karl noted that only when a recruit could perform the musket drill 5 times per minute without powder or word of command would he be permitted to join the *Peloton* or company drill.[54] A rate of fire of 2 rounds per minute was considered excellent by both the Austrians and Prussians.

Cogniazzo (1780) states that fire by *Pelotons* (platoons) was suitable when employed in open terrain, while fire by divisions was capable of creating veritable breeches within the opponent's ranks. He considered firing while advancing by divisions let alone *pelotons* to be unfeasible because they were too apt to lose their distances, hence cause nothing but confusion and disorder within the formation. This observation implies that the Austrian infantry were less capable than the highly practiced Prussians in advancing while firing.

With the bayonet charge, only the first rank levelled their muskets and would fire just before closing with the enemy.

---

[54] Cogniazzo (1780)

Chapter 3
German Infantry Uniforms

There were considerable differences in detail within companies and between regiments. This is clearly shown by differences shown in the sources. The Inhaber had control over the design of the uniforms throughout the period. The 1720 Regulations stated stipulated, "A coat made of good, durable cloth. Well lines with baize or linen, with waistcoat of the same; a pair of good leather breeches; a strong pair of strong woollen stockings; a pair of shoes made of Russian leather with good soles; a good durable hat; two shirts; two neckcloths or silk cravats; a good knapsack; a pouch with belt attached; a sword and bayonet."[55]

According to the order dated 18 December 1748, the white coat was made of *"weissperlfarbe"* (unbleached white) wool cloth from the Moravian town of Jihlava (now in the Czech Republic). The first order for all uniforms and military economy was made on 5 June 1755.[56]

In 1757, Maria Theresa made an attempt to standardise uniforms throughout the army and on 16 August, the highest order instructed that all infantry should have white coats with red facings and brass buttons. However, on 27 October 1757 this order was overturned and she ruled that "we should proceed no further with the standardisation, at least as long as the existing uniforms last out."[57] This decision increased the variation in uniform within companies. New recruits wore white lining jackets and waistcoats with brass buttons. This resulted in part of the regiment in coloured waistcoats and others in white. Even the button colour varied with part in brass and part in white metal. During the war, there was no money. General *Reglement* wrote, "The uniform is good, when it covers three quarters of the body of a soldier." On 1 November 1757, the complicated *Intercalar Systeme* changed the authorised the soldier's deduction for uniforms and permitted the regiments to purchase the cloth as well as the tailoring.

From 10 July 1758, the materials to produce the uniforms were supplied by supplied central warehouse (*Montoursmagazin*) in Vienna all from deposit in Vienna. The tailoring was commissioned by each regimental Inhaber. The new *Oeconomie Systeme* of 1 November 1758 set the authorised deductions for uniforms and that the cloth would be obtained from state magazines.[58] The tailoring was still commissioned by each regimental *Inhaber*.

On 1 November 1761, the army reverted to the system of 1748 where the state controlled the supply of uniforms. In 1765, the design of uniforms was removed from Inhaber and given to the eight *Montours Commision* (Outfit Commission).

---

[55] Knotel et al (1980) *Uniforms of the World 1700-1937.* p13-1414
[56] Order (5/6/1755), *Ordnung nach welcher sich die kaiser. königl. Infanterie-Regimenter in Friedenzeiten in der Montirung und sonstigen oekonomischen Punkten zur Erzielung deren Ersparungskassen zu achten haben."* (Dr. J. Sissak (2014) *Private communication*)
[57] Duffy (2000) p312.
[58] Duffy (2000) p318.

German Fusilier Uniforms

HEADGEAR: Black tricorn laced white and black cockade on the left. Only IR3, IR21, IR26, IR28, IR29, IR36, IR41 and IR54 had scalloped hat lace. The sprig of green leaves was normally worn on campaign as the field sign in summer and corn stalks in winter.

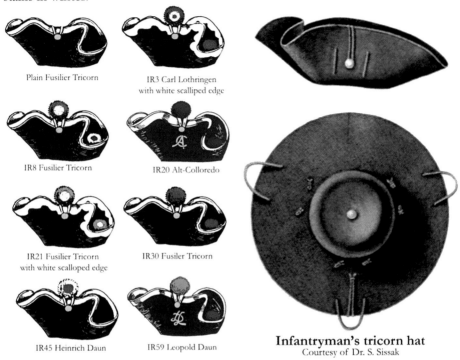

Plain Fusilier Tricorn

IR3 Carl Lothringen with white scalliped edge

IR8 Fusilier Tricorn

IR20 Alt-Colloredo

IR21 Fusilier Tricorn with white scalloped edge

IR30 Fusiler Tricorn

IR45 Heinrich Daun

IR59 Leopold Daun

Infantryman's tricorn hat
Courtesy of Dr. S. Sissak

POM-POMS: Some regiments had pom-poms. At the rear corners were bobs that often followed the facing colour according to Albertini (1762).

Table 7: Pom-poms

Pom-pom	Regiment	Pom-pom	Regiment
No pom-poms:	IR4, IR8-IR9, IR11, IR13-IR14, IR16, IR18, IR23-IR27, IR29, IR35, IR38, IR43-IR44, IR48-IR50, IR57.	Blue and white:	IR56
		Blue-white-blue:	IR12
		Blue-yellow-blue:	IR10
		Green-white-red:	IR28
		Green-yellow-white:	IR41
		Green and white:	IR21
		Mixed red-black-yellow:	IR1
		Red-white-red-white:	IR15
		Red and yellow:	IR7, IR36
		Red-yellow-blue:	IR3
Black:	IR55	White and blue:	IR40
Dark blue:	IR20	Yellow and blue:	IR42
Green:	IR46, IR59	Yellow and red:	IR45
Red:	IR30	Yellow-red-white:	IR22
Yellow:	IR47, IR54	Yellow-red-yellow:	IR17

FORAGE CAP: Simple cloth forage cap made from old waistcoats was worn for manual work.

HAIR: The hair was dressed at the side in double locks and extended down the back in a military pigtail that reached as far as the waist according to the order of 16 March 1754. Moustaches were worn by some soldiers.

STOCK: A red or a black stiff fabric stock. For parades the regimental commanders agreed before on the colour of the neck-stocks. According to Schirmer, all German Infantry Regiments had red stocks except IR8, IR21 and IR26.

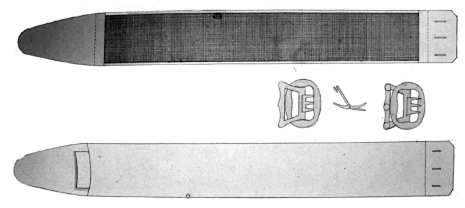

Neck stock

FACING COLOURS: Over the period of 1750-67, the facing colours on the lapels and cuffs were reasonably consistent. The lack of regimental numbers until 1769 sometimes causes confusion so some references differ in the colour. The shade of the facing colour varied over the period.

Table 8: Facing colours and button for the German Infantry.

In 1757 facings had 24 red, 16 blue, 3 green, 1 rose-pink and 1 black.
In 1762 facings had 23 red, 17 blue, 3 green, 1 rose-pink and 1 black

	1757 (Wrede)		1762 (Schirmer)	
	Brass	White metal	Brass	White metal
Red	1, 8, 15, 26, 30, 35, 41, 43, 44, 45, 46, 57, 59	3, 10, 11, 17, 18, 22, 25, 49, 50, 54, 55	1, 3, 8, 10, 15, 17, 18, 22, 25, 26, 35, 41, 43, 44, 45, 46, 54, 55, 57, 59	11, 49, 50[59],
Blue	4, 12, 13, 16, 21, 56	7, 20, 23, 24, 27, 29, 36, 40, 42, 47	4, 7, 12, 13, 16, 20, 21, 23, 24, 29, 30, 40, 42, 47, 56	27, 36
Green	9, 48	28	9, 28, 48	NONE
Rose-pink	NONE	38	NONE	38
Black	14	NONE	14	NONE
TOTAL	22 brass	23 white metal	39 brass	6 white metal

---

[59] The red lapels had 7 lace buttonholes and the cuffs had 3 lace buttonholes.

COAT: The coat was made of *"weissperlfarbe"* (unbleached) white wool cloth from the Moravian town of Jihlava and from 1758, it was supplied central warehouse in Vienna.[60] The collarless coat had lapels and large square cuffs in the facing colour. Normally the lapels had nine buttons arranged in three groups of three. The horizontal pockets and cuffs had three buttons. On 16 March 1754, the *Hofkriegsrat* attempted to impose uniformity. This stipulated that the coat would be long enough to be two finger widths (about 4cm) clear of the ground when the man was kneeling, generous enough for the lapels to be buttoned across and the cuffs could be pulled down to protect the fingers against the cold and the musket lock against damp.[61]

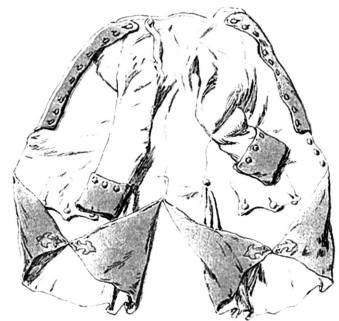

1735-1767

WORKING COAT:

Austrian working coat
Contemorary drawing courtesy of Dr. S. Sissak

BUTTONS: In 1757 according to Wrede (1898), half the German Infantry Regiments had white metal buttons (22 out of 45) and by 1762 this had reduced to only IR11, IR27, IR36, IR38, IR49, and IR50 according to Schirmer.

---

[60] Dr. J. Sissak (2014) *Private communication*
[61] Duffy (2000) p244

Table 9: German Infantry facings, 1740-62.

	Est.	1740	1743	1748	1757 (Wrede)	1762 (Albertini)
IR1	1716	Red from 1726				
IR3	1715	Red				
IR4	1696	Blue				
IR7	1691	Blue (1730	Red	Blue		
IR8	1647	Scarlet				
IR9	1725	Green				
IR10	1715	Red				
IR11	1619	Red	Blue	Red		
IR12	1702	Blue				
IR13	1642	Red	Blue			Light blue
IR14	1733	Light blue		Black		
IR15	1716	Blue			Red	
IR16	1703	Blue				
IR17	1632	Red				
IR18	1682	Red				
IR20	1681	Blue	Red		Blue	
IR21	1733	Light blue				
IR22	1709	Red				
IR23	1673	Blue				
IR24	1632	Blue				
IR25	1672	Red	Blue (1742)	Red from 1751		
IR26	1717	Blue	Red			
IR27	1682	Light blue				
IR28	1698	Green	Red	Green		
IR29	1709	Red		Blue		
IR30	1725	Blue		Red (1753-57)		Blue (1758)
IR35	1682	Blue		Red		
IR36	1630	Light blue				Blue
IR38	1725	Rose-pink				
IR40	1733	Blue	Dark Red	Blue		
IR41	1701	Light blue	Red			
IR42	1674	Blue	Dark Red		Light Blue	
IR43	1715	Blue	Orange			
IR44	1744			Red from 1744		
IR45	1682	Dark Red				
IR46	1745		Red from 1745			
IR47	1682	Blue	Red		Blue	
IR48	1721	Green				
IR49	1715	Red				
IR50	1629	Dark Red with white Litzen				
IR54	1620	Red				
IR55	1742		Red from 1742			
IR56	1684	Red	Blue from 1741			
IR57	1688	Blue				Red
IR59	1682	Red				

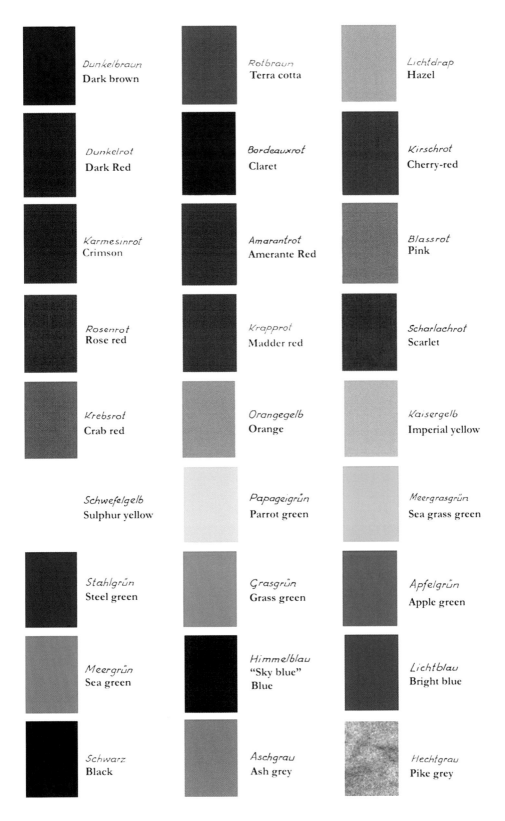

Dunkelbraun Dark brown	*Rotbraun* Terra cotta	*Lichtdrap* Hazel
Dunkelrot Dark Red	*Bordeauxrot* Claret	*Kirschrot* Cherry-red
Karmesinrot Crimson	*Amarantrot* Amerante Red	*Blassrot* Pink
Rosenrot Rose red	*Krapprot* Madder red	*Scharlachrot* Scarlet
Krebsrot Crab red	*Orangegelb* Orange	*Kaisergelb* Imperial yellow
Schwefelgelb Sulphur yellow	*Papageigrün* Parrot green	*Meergrasgrün* Sea grass green
Stahlgrün Steel green	*Grasgrün* Grass green	*Apfelgrün* Apple green
Meergrün Sea green	*Himmelblau* "Sky blue" Blue	*Lichtblau* Bright blue
Schwarz Black	*Aschgrau* Ash grey	*Hechtgrau* Pike grey

TURNBACKS: About half the German Infantry Regiments had coloured turnbacks at the start of the Seven Years War (21 in 1757) and this had reduced to only 3 by 1762.

Table 10: The colour of turnbacks in 1757, 1758 and 1762

	1757 [Wrede (1898)]	1758 [Schirmer]	1762 [Albertini]
Blue	4, 12, 23, 24, 27, 29, 42, 47	4, 12, 23, 24, 27, 29, 30, 42, 47	27 (light blue)
Red	1, 3, 8, 17, 18, 22, 26, 30, 46, 50, 55	1, 3, 8, 17, 18, 22, 26, 46, 50, 55	26, 50
Green	9, 48	48	None
White	7, 10, 11, 13-16, 20, 21, 25, 28, 35, 36, 38, 40, 41, 43-45, 49, 54, 56, 57, 59	7, 9-11, 13-16, 20, 21, 25, 28, 35, 36, 38, 40, 41, 43-45, 49, 54, 56, 57, 59	1, 3, 4, 7-18, 20-25, 28-30, 35, 36, 38, 40-49, 54-57, 59

TURNBACK TAB: Many of the German Infantry regiments had a distinctive turnback tab. However there is a great deal of conflict between sources.[62] The IR8-IR14, IR28, IR30, IR41, IR44, IR48, IR55, and IR56 do not seem to have turnback tabs.

SHOULDER STRAP: The shoulder strap was on the left shoulder only. There is great variation in the colour and design of these according to the literature.[63]

Table 11: Shoulder strap colour and design according to Donath (1970) and Albertini (1762).

	Infantry Regiment
White	4, 7, 8, 9, 11, 13, 22, 23, 24, 26, 35, 40, 41, 44, 45, 48, 49
Blue	16, 20, 27, 29, 47, 56
Red	10, 18, 43, 46, 50, 57
Rose pink	38
Black	14
White with black-red-white border	30
White with blue border and central wavy line	42
White with light blue border and central wavy line	36
White with green border and wavy stripe	28
White with red border	3, 26, 55, 57
White with red zigzag border	54
Blue with white border	23
Blue with wavy white border	21
Blue with white border and central wavy stripe	42
Red with white border	25
Red with red and white border	15, 17
Yellow with red border	3

[62] Pengel (1982) 46-47
[63] Pengel (1982) 40-44

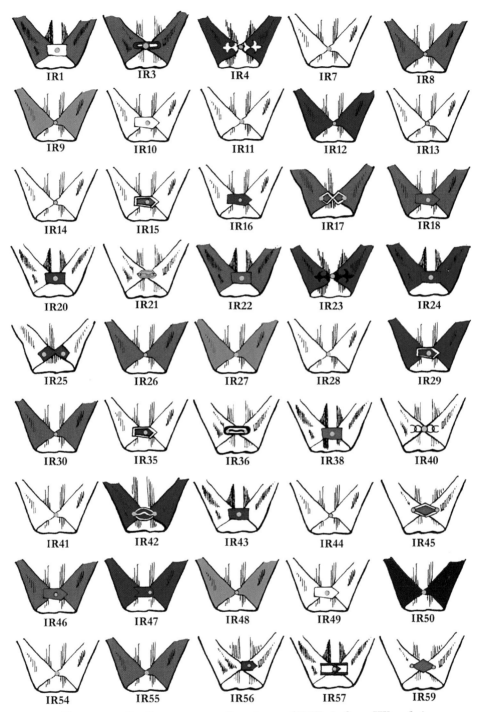

German Infantry turnbacks, c1757 (after Wrede)

WAISTCOAT: White long skirted waistcoat with buttons either in a single or double row. Before 1760 the waistcoat was often in the regimental facing colour. By 1762, all waistcoats were white.

Table 12: The colour of waistcoats in 1757, 1758 and 1762.

	1757 [Wrede (1898)]	1758 [Schirmer]	1762 [Albertini]
White	7, 13-15, 18, 20, 21, 24-28, 35, 36, 38-45, 49, 54, 56, 57, 59	7, 9, 13-15, 18, 20, 21, 24-28, 35, 36, 38-45, 49, 50, 54, 56, 57, 59	All white
Blue	4, 12, 22[64], 23, 29, 47	4, 12, 22[64], 23, 29, 30, 47	
Red	1, 3, 8, 17, 30, 46, 50, 55	1, 3, 7, 17, 46, 55	
Green	9, 48	48	

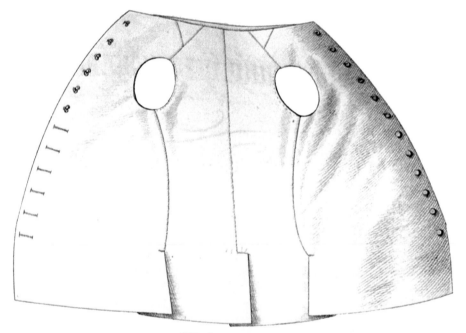

Waistcoat

In 1760, the regulations were enforced and these became all white.[65]

> 28 regiments with double row of yellow buttons (*IR1, IR4, IR9, IR12-IR18, IR20, IR21, IR23, IR24, IR25, IR30, IR35, IR40-IR48, IR54, IR56, and IR57*).
> 3 regiments with single row of yellow buttons (*IR3, IR26* and *IR55*)
> 1 regiment with double row of white buttons (*IR11*)
> 2 regiments with single row of white buttons (*IR27* and *IR38*)

---

[64] Despite having red facings.
[65] According to Pengel (1982b: 24).

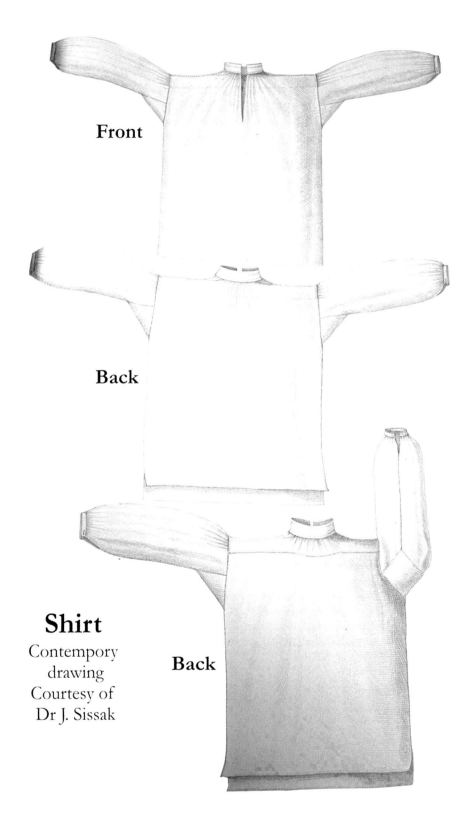

Front

Back

Shirt
Contempory
drawing
Courtesy of
Dr J. Sissak

Back

LEGWEAR: White tightly cut breeches and white gaiters. From 1754, Prussian style black gaiters were worn in the field. The white gaiters were now reserved for formal parades.

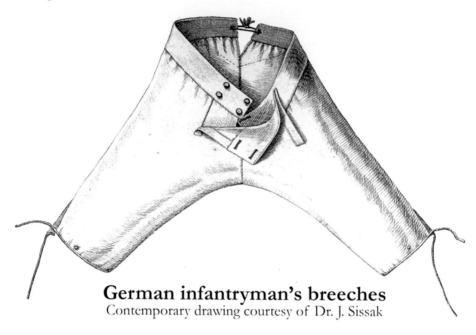

German infantryman's breeches
Contemporary drawing courtesy of Dr. J. Sissak

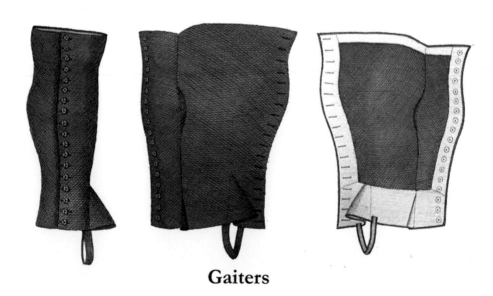

Gaiters

FOOTWEAR: The leather soled shoes were made of thick black leather and good waxed thread. They were waxed and polished regularly. The left and right shoe was not differentiated. It was common practice to alternate the wearing of the shoes each day to even out the wear. The working boots (clogs) had a wooden sole.

German infantryman's shoe
Contemporary drawing courtesy of Dr. J. Sissak

Working clog

EQUIPMENT: The knapsack made of ticking (a tightly woven linen cloth) carried a spare shirt, gaiters, cleaning materials and other small items. A narrow white belt was worn over the right shoulder and hung in the small of the back. An order of 5 June 1755, permitted the knapsack to be made of unshaven calfskin.

Austrian Knapsack
Courtesy of Dr. J. Sissak

The bread ration was carried in a separate linen bag. The characteristic Austrian drum or egg shaped canteen had a brown leather strap.

White leather belt over the left shoulder carrying a black cartridge box with a small brass plate carrying the initials "MT" was worn on the right hip. A white waist-belt carrying the bayonet was worn under the coat.

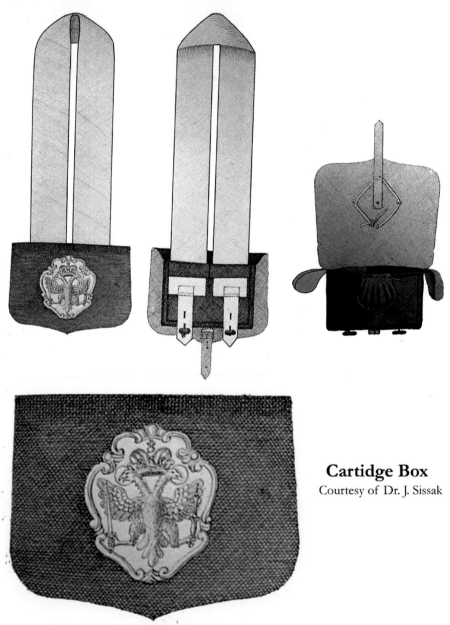

Cartidge Box
Courtesy of Dr. J. Sissak

SIDEARMS: The M1745 musket for fusiliers with bayonet until they were replaced by the M1754 musket.

Fusilier NCO Uniform

HEADWEAR: Sergeants (*Feldwebel* and *Führer*) had gold or silver hat lace depending upon the regimental button colour. Corporals had white or yellow hat lace to their black tricorns depending upon the regimental button colour.

UNIFORM: As Fusiliers. Some regiments had the cuffs and/or the lapels were edged in gold or silver braid according to button colour.

POLEARMS: Until 1759, sergeants carried the halberd and corporals the half pike. These were then replaced by muskets.

SIDEARMS: Sergeants had a Hazelwood cane suspended coat button by an 18mm leather strap and grenadier sabre. Corporals only had a grenadier sabre.

IR4 NCOs in 1756 uniform
Photograph by Charles Srolik, 1896

Officer Uniform

Fusilier saluting a captain, c1749
Courtesy of Dr. J. Sissak

HEADWEAR Tricorn laced gold or silver hat lace depending upon button colour.

STOCK: White cloth neck stock.

COAT: Similar cut to the other ranks but with finer cloth and no turnbacks. No shoulder strap.

WAISTCOAT: The waistcoat was in the colour as the rest of the regiment.

The rank was distinguished by braid edging depending upon the button colour.

Obrist - three braid

Obrist-Lt - two braid

Obristwachtmeister - one braid

No braid for the rank of Hauptmann and below.

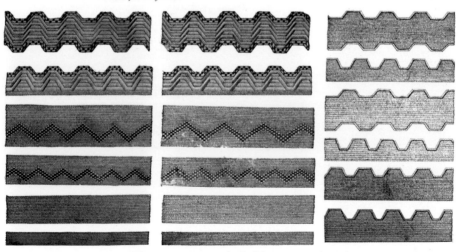

Examples of Officer's Braid

IR1 Kaiser   **IR20 Alt-Colleredo**   **IR28 de Ligne**   **IR47 Harrach**

SASH: Yellow and black woollen sash for lieutenants. Yellow and black silk sash were worn by majors and above.

POLEARMS: Up to 1759, partisans were carried by officers. This was replaced by a musket with brass fittings.

SIDEARMS: Fusilier officers carried straight bladed swords.

SWAGGER STICKS: Carried by officers to identify their ranks.

Obrist **(Colonel)** long rush stick with a golden knob

Obrist-Lt **(Lt-Col)** long rush stick with a larger silver knob without chain

Obristwachtmeister (renamed Major in 1756) long rush stick with a silver knob and a small silver chain

Hauptmann **(Captain)** long rush stick with a bone knob

Auditor, Adjutant, *Wagenmeister* etc. had a Spanish reed stick banded in brass and top brass.

Lieutenant had a Spanish reed without knob

Lieutenant's cane

Captain, c1748
J. Brermann & Sohn.

Musician Uniform

Up to 1760, the 1755 regulations that stipulated that musicians would wear white coats with swallow nest in facing colour bordered with lace in button colour was generally ignored. Table 12 gives some known examples where the regimental facing colour was used for the coat colour with white lapels, and turnbacks. The swallow nest often had lace in the silver or gold button colour. After 1760, the 1755 regulations were strictly enforced. Musicians did not carry a musket or cartridge box. The brass drum was decorated with arms or the Inhaber or the Imperial arms. The rims were decorated with diagonal stripes, flames or triangles. The bandolier was white and facing colour or white and button colour. This was often covered with white cloth.

Drum used by Infantry

German Infantry Drummer, c1760
Lithograph by F. Gerasch. Courtesy of Dr. J. Sissak

Table 13: Pre-1760 facing colours for German Infantry musicians[66]

Coat	Facings	Infantry Regiment
Black coat	White	IR14
Blue coat	White	IR4, IR16, IR24, IR30, IR36, IR40, IR56
Green coat	White	IR9, IR28, IR48
Red coat	White	IR3, IR8, IR15, IR22, IR26, IR41, IR43, IR44, IR55, IR57
Rose-pink	White	IR38
White coat	Blue	IR21, IR27, IR47, IR56

Drum and drummer's bandoleer
Contemporary drawing courtesy of Dr. J. Sissak

Flute and case

German Infantry Drummers of IR4-IR26

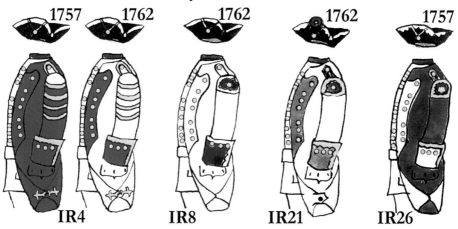

1757 1762 1762 1762 1757

IR4 IR8 IR21 IR26

[66] Pengel (1982b) 53-54 and Donath (1970)

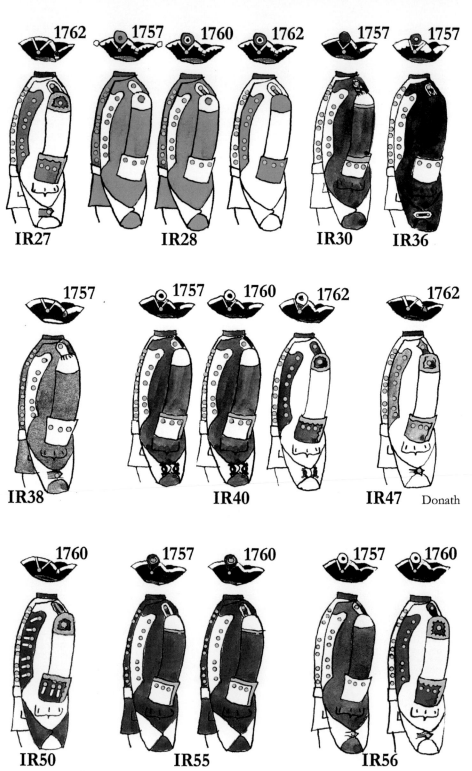

German Infantry Drummers of IR27-IR56

After Donath (1970) and Pengel (1982)

~ 46 ~

Drummers from the 1749 Drill Book
Courtesy of Dr. J. Sissak

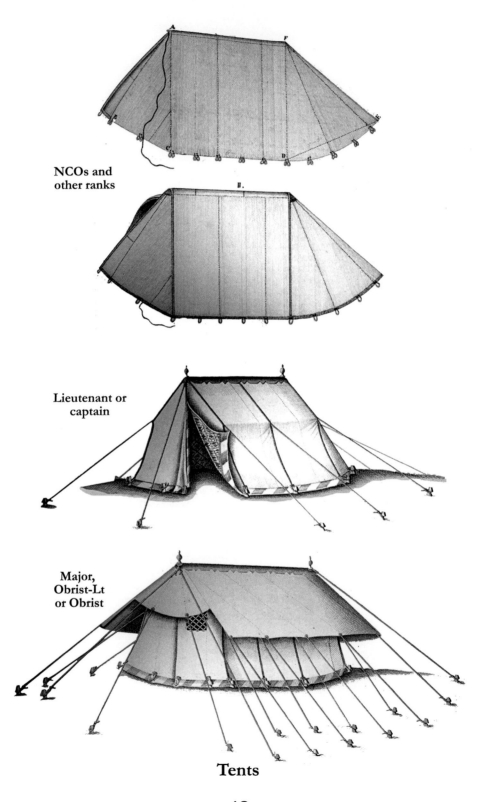

NCOs and
other ranks

Lieutenant or
captain

Major,
Obrist-Lt
or Obrist

Tents

~ 48 ~

Chapter 4
Lower Austria (*Niederösterreich*)

The Archduchy of Lower Austria was the most prosperous of the German Hereditary Lands benefiting from Vienna being its capital and water routes from Germany, Poland, Hungary, Turkey and Italy.

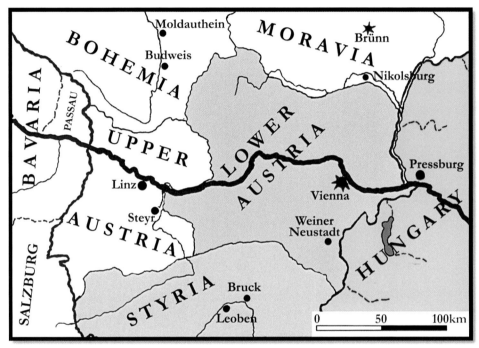

Map 2: Lower Austria
Stephen Summerfield, 2014

OOB 4: Regiments in Lower and Upper Austria, June 1756.

ARCHDUCHY OF AUSTRIA

Infantry Regiments (I-II, Grenadiers and Garrison Bn)

IR35 Waldeck	2,354	
IR49 Kheul	2,416	
IR59 Leopold Daun	<u>2,401</u>	7,172
Cuirassier Regiments		
KR1 Erzherzog Leopold	<u>809</u>	809
TOTAL		7,980

IR3 Carl Lothringen

Raised in 1715 and was also known as Jung-Lothringen. The hardest fighting regiment of the army losing 51.6% in action.[67] In 1918, IR3 Erzherzog Carl.

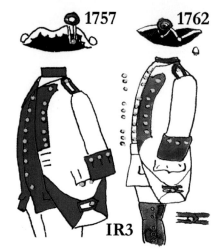

1757 1762 IR3

HEADWEAR: White scalloped lace on tricorn and red with white centre pom-pom.
COAT: Red cuffs, lapels and turnbacks with white centre. White turnbacks with yellow turnback tab from c1762.
WAISTCOAT: Red waistcoat then white c1762.
BUTTONS: White metal the brass by 1762.
SHOULDER STRAP: White edged red.

Inhaber
1715 *Carl Ignaz von Lothringen und Bar*
1726 *Leopold Graf Ligneville* (d. 1734)
1734 *Gottfried Ernst Frhr. von Wuttgenau*
1736 *Carl von Lothringen*[68]

Commanders
1750 *Christian Frhr. von Vogelsang*
1758 *Joseph Graf Ferraris*
1761 *Carl Maximilian Freiherr von Schorlemmer*

Garrison
1752 Brussels, 1759 Ghent and 1763 Brussels.

Campaigns[69]
War of Austrian Succession: Fought at Mollwitz (10 Apr 1741). In 1742, a Bn was at the siege of Glatz, the grenadiers were at Chotusitz (17 May) then the siege of Prague. In 1744 it was on the Rhine then Bohemia. In 1745 it was present at Hohenfriedberg (4 June) and Trautenau (30 Sept). In 1746, in the Netherlands at Rocoux and Lawfeld (2 July 1747).

Seven Years War In 1757, fought at Prague (6 May), the storm of Gabel (14-15 July), Breslau (22 Nov) and Leuthen (5 Dec) where it suffered the second highest regimental loss in the retreat. At Hochkirch (14 Oct 1758), under Obrist Graf Ferrarus captured an 18-pdr battery. In 1759 it was in Saxony and Silesia without participating in any major actions. In 1760, at the siege of Dresden, performed very well in O'Kelly's counterattack at Torgau (3 Nov) and covered the subsequent retreat. Part of Loudon's storm of Schweidnitz (1 Oct 1761).

1762
Albertini

IR3

---

[67] Duffy (2008) 429
[68] Brother of the Emperor who died on 4 July 1780 in Brussels.
[69] Thürheim (1880) I: 12

IR4 Deutschmeister

The regiment was formed in 1696 by Grand Master Franz Ludwig of Pfalz Neuberg. The name of Hoch und Deutschmeister was after the Grand Master (*Hochmeister*) of the Teutonic Order. Recruits came from the Rhineland, Palatinate and the Teutonic Order's numerous dominions in Southern Germany including Swabia. It suffered the third highest infantry desertion of 1169 men.[70]

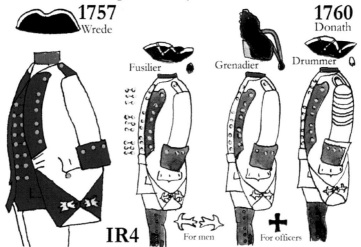

COAT: Blue cuffs, lapels and turnbacks with yellow turnback tab. In c1760, the turnbacks became white with yellow turnback tab.
WAISTCOAT: Blue waistcoat became white in 1760.
BUTTONS: Brass
SHOULDER STRAP: Blue

Inhaber
Grand Master of the Teutonic Order
1696 *Franz Ludwig, Duke of Neuburg*
1732 *Clemens August von Wittelsbach, Elector of Cologne,*
1761 *Carl Duke of Lorraine* (d. 1780)
1780 *Maximilian, Elector of Cologne*

Commander
1756 *Carl Mohr v. Wald* (killed at Kolin),
1757 *Franz Graf Callenberg*
1760 *Johann Christoph v. Meichsner zu Adelshofen*

[70] Duffy (2008) 429

Garrison

In 1754 Offen. In 1756 Budapest in Hungary. In 1763: Mons in the Austrian Netherlands.

1760

IR4 Deutschmeister
Pokorny (2001), courtesy of Dr S. Sissak

Campaigns[71]

War of Austrian Succession: In 1741-42, part of *Traun's Army.* Fought at Campo Santo (8 Feb 1743) where it captured the standard of the Irlanda Regiment. In 1744, took part in the invasion of Naples and the siege of Genoa (1746-47).

Seven Years War In 1756, the regiment assembled around Königgrätz as part of Corps Piccolomini. In 1757 it distinguished itself at Kolin (18 June) where Major Johann Graf Soro who commanded a Grenadier Bn was awarded the first knights cross of the Military Order of Maria-Theresa. The grenadiers took part in the storming of Gabel (15 July). A detachment was in Corps Nádasdy at the storming of the Silesian fortress of Schweidnitz (18 Nov). One Bn fought at Breslau (22 Nov) and Leuthen (5 Dec). In 1758, Hochkirch (14 Oct). The III (Garrison) Bn was with Corps de Ville in Moravia and later formed part of the garrison of Olmütz (27 May-2 July). In 1760, the regiment was part of Loudon's Army at the stormed of Hirschberg at Landeshut (23 June) and Liegnitz (15 Aug). Detachments were part of the defence of Schweidnitz (8 Aug - 9 Oct 1762).

---

[71] Thürheim (1880) I: 18; Wrede I: 138

IR23 Baden-Baden

Formed in 1673 and disbanded in 1809. The regiment was re-raised in 1814 in Lombardy.

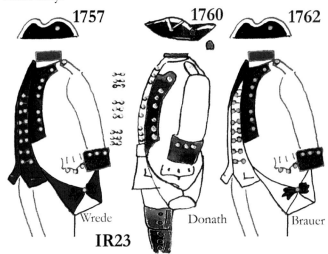

POM-POM: None.
COAT: Blue cuffs, lapels and turnbacks with blue trefoil turnback badge. In 1760, plain white turnbacks.
WAISTCOAT: Blue then white by 1760.
BUTTONS: White metal then brass by 1762.
SHOULDER STRAP: White

Inhaber
1672 *Ferdinand Ludwig Frhr. Wopping*
1674 *Hermann Markgraf Baden-Baden*
1676 *Ludwig Wilhelm Markgraf Baden-Baden*
1707 *Georg Ludwig Markgraf von Baden-Baden*
1761 *August Georg Simpert Markgraf Baden-Baden*
1771 *Joseph Heinrich Frhr. von Reid*

Commanders
1748 *Philipp Frhr. von Müffling*
1757 *Franz Dimpfel*
1758 *Alois Graf Harrach*
1764 *Peter Frhr. von Mac-Elligot*

Garrison:
Slovenia (1756).

Campaigns
War of Austrian Succession: In 1741, at Mollwitz. In 1742 with the Main Army at the siege of Prague. In 1743-44, in Bavaria at the sieges of Straubing and Ingolstadt. In 1745, in Bohemia at Hohenfriedberg and Soor.

Seven Years War In 1757, present at Kolin (18 June), Breslau (22 Nov) and Leuthen (5 Dec). In 1758, part of Corps Durlach. In 1759 it fought at Kunersdorf (12 Aug) where it suffered heavy losses. In 1760, the regiment fought at Landshut, Liegnitz and the storm of Glatz. In 1761, two battalions participated in the storm of Schweidnitz. In 1762, a battalion was distinguished at Burkersdorf and a detachment was present at the defence of Schweidnitz.

IR24 Starhemberg

Raised in 1632 and was the third oldest infantry regiment in the Austrian army. In 1918, IR24 Ritter von Kummer.

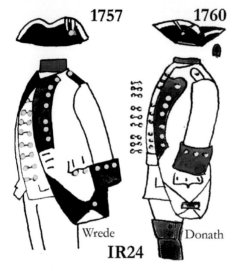

1757   1760

Wrede   Donath

IR24

COAT: Blue cuffs, lapels and turnbacks. In c1762, white turnbacks with dark blue turnback tab.
WAISTCOAT: White.
BUTTONS: Yellow
SHOULDER STRAP: Dark blue

Inhaber
1632 *Philipp Graf Mannsfeld* (d. 1657)
1657 *Lucas Frhr. von Spieck*
1665 *Jakob Graf Leslie*
1675 *Heinrich Franz Fürst Mannsfeld-Fondi*
1702 *Jakob Ernst von Ghelen*
1703 *Graf Max Adam Starhemberg* (d. 1741)
1741 *Emanuel Michael Graf Starhemberg*
1771 *Johann Peter Frhr. von Preiss* (d. 1797)

Commander
1756 *Sylvester Ferdinand von Alemann* (killed at Kolin (18 June 1757))
1757 *Guido Graf Starhemberg*
1763 *Peter Freiherr von Creutz*

Garrison
1756 Lombardy (Como, Mantua, San Martino); 1763 Pavia.

Campaign[72]
War of Austrian Succession: In 1742, at Chotusitz (17 May) then the siege of Prague. In 1744, a Bn was present at the siege of Freiburg. In 1745, the regiment was at Trautenau before transferring to Italy. In 1746 it was at Piacenza and Rottofreddo then the expedition to Provence. In 1747 it was present at the siege of Genoa.

Seven Years War In 1757, fought at Reichenberg, a Bn at Prague (6 May) and 2 Bns at Kolin (18 June). In 1758 it actively participated in the Domstadtl ambush and the battle of Hochkirch. In 1760, fought at Landshut (23 June), storm of Glatz (26 July) and reduced to a single battalion due to heavy losses after Liegnitz (15 Aug). A detachment was present at the defence of Schweidnitz.

1762
Albertini

IR24

---

[72] Thürheim (1880) I: 149-150

IR49 Angern

Raised in 1715 by the Margrave of Baden-Durlach for Imperial Service and in 1724 became part of the Austrian Army.

POM-POM: None.
COAT: Red collar and cuffs with white turnback with white tab.
BUTTONS: White.
SHOULDER STRAP: White.

Inhaber

1715 *Markgraf Carl von Baden-Durlach* (d. 1738)
1724 *Otto Graf Walsegg* (d. 1743)
1743 *Johann Leopold Frhr. von Bärnklau* (d. 1746)
1747 *Carl Gustav Freiherr von Kheyl* (d. 1758)
1758 *Ludwig Frhr. von Angern*
1767 *Carl Graf Pellegrini* (d. 1796)

Commanders

1751 *Jakob Graf Molza*
1762 *Christian Eichholz*

Garrison

Wels in the Archduchy of Austria (1754); Carlsberg (1763)

Campaigns[73]

War of Austrian Succession: In 1742-5, campaigned in Bavaria and along the Rhine. In 1746, transferred to Italy where it fought at Piacenza, Rottofreddo, siege of Genoa and the invasion of Provence. In 1747 took part in the siege of Genoa.

Seven Years War In 1756, fought at Lobositz (1 Oct). In 1757 it was distinguished at Prague (6 May), Breslau (22 Nov) where its *Inhaber* Graf Kheul was killed and Leuthen (5 Dec). In 1758 it was part of the ambushes at Gundersdorf and Domstadtl, Olmütz (28 May-2 July) and Hochkirch (14 Oct). In 1759, at Pretzch, Maxen (20 Nov), Meissen. In 1760, at Landeshut (23 June), distinguished at Liegnitz (15 Aug). In 1761 it participated in Loudon's storm of Schweidnitz. In 1762, the regiment was at Burkersdorf (20-21 July).

1762
Albertini

IR49

---

[73] Thürheim (1880) I: 325

Chapter 5
Upper Austria (*Oberösterreich*)

This was strictly the "Austria" territory, the only province populated entirely by Germans. The Archduchy of Upper Austria (*Oberösterreich*) extended west on both sides of the Danube towards Bavaria and the independent Bishoprics of Salzburg and Passau. It was predominately agricultural with the export of iron goods and a growing woollen trade.

The capital of **Linz** had the two suburbs of Margarethen and Kalvarienwand.

Traun Steyr was founded around 980 at the confluence of the rivers Enns and Steyr, by the Otakars, margraves and later Dukes of Styria, as the Styraburg. It had two suburbs Steyersdorf and Ennsdorf (the two rivers).

Mühl was the area between the Danube and the Bavaria (north).

The Dukes of Babenberg founded the free commercial city of **Freystadt** in 1220 (Frienstatt: free city).

Other important towns of the Circle were **Grein** and **Steyereck**.

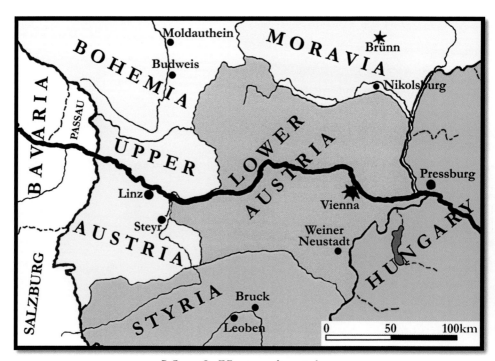

Map 3: Upper Austria
Stephen Summerfield, 2014

IR14 Salm

The regiment was raised in 1733. In 1754, there were 69% of the regiment recruited from the Holy Roman Empire outside the Habsburg lands and was considered the most German regiment due to the influence of the Inhaber. This was reduced during the course of the war. It suffered the largest infantry desertion of 1,779 men due to hard outpost duty in Saxony, the recruitment of prisoners and retention of short-service soldiers.[74]

1757

POM-POM: None.
COAT: Light blue (1740) then in 1748 black cuffs and lapels with white turnbacks.
WAISTCOAT: White.
BUTTONS: Brass.
SHOULDER STRAP: White then black by 1762.

Inhaber
1733 *Nicolaus Leopold Rheingraf von Salm* (d. 1770)
1770 *Franz Joseph Graf Ferraris*

Commander
1752 *Adam Ferdinand Freiherr von Kammer-Obereck*
1757 *Maximilian Prinz zu Salm*
1758 *Christian Freiherr von Bettendorf*
1762 *Maximilian August Zorn von Blowsheim*

IR14

Garrison
1748 Antwerp; 1763 Roermond

Campaigns
War of Austrian Succession: In 1743, present at Dettingen (27 June). In 1745, the regiment was in Graf Traun's Army on the Main. In 1747 it fought at Lawfeld (2 July) and Bergen op Zoom (18 Sept). A detachment was in Luxembourg.

Seven Years War
In 1918, IR14 Ernst Ludwig von Hessen. In 1757, distinguished at Kolin (18 June) where it suffered 20 officers and 400 men lost mainly from heavy artillery fire and at Moys (7 Sept). In 1760, the Grenadiers were at Landeshut (23 June) and the regiment was present at Loudon's storm of Glatz (26 July). In 1761-2, the regiment campaigned in Saxony and was distinguished at Freiberg (29 Oct 1762).

1762
Albertini

IR14

---

[74] Duffy (2008) 430: Duffy (2000) 446

IR50 Harsch

Raised in 1629 and was the oldest infantry regiment in the Austrian Army. Considered the model for uniform and drill for the rest of the army.[75] Lost in 1809 to the Duchy of Warsaw.

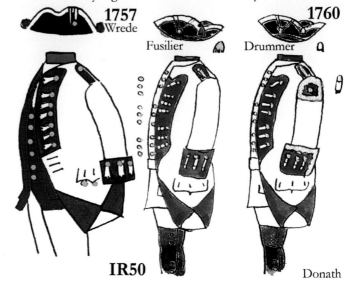

1757 Wrede

Fusilier

1760 Drummer

IR50

Donath

COAT: Dark red with white buttonholes loops and red turnbacks.
WAISTCOAT: Dark red then white in 1760.
BUTTONS: White metal
SHOULDER STRAP: Red
POM-POM: None

Inhaber
1691 *Leopold Graf Herberstein*
1740 *Casimir Heinrich Graf Wurmbrand-Stuppach*
1749 *Ferdinand Philipp Graf Harsch*
1766 *Andreas Fürst Poniatowski*

Commander
1754 *Nicolaus Freiherr von Weichs*
1758 *Andreas Graf Poniatowski*
1760 *Richard Chevalier d'Alton*

Garrison
1749 Eger; 1756 in Bohemia; 1763 Vienna.

Campaigns
War of Austrian Succession: In 1742, part of the garrison of Prague. In 1743 it was in Corps Batthyany. In 1744, the I-II Bn was on the Rhine while the III Bn was besieged in Prague. In 1745, one Bn was at Hohenfriedberg and Trautenau and two Bns were at Kesseldorf. In 1746, transferred to the Netherlands and fought at Rocoux. In 1747 it fought at Lawfeld.

Seven Years War In 1756, fought at Lobositz (1 Oct) and one Bn in Passberg Fortress. In 1757, at Prague (6 May), Breslau (22 Nov). In 1758, at Hochkirch (14 Oct). In 1759 it was with the main army at Maxen (20 Nov). In 1760 it was distinguished at Torgau (3 Nov) and one Bn present at the defence of Dresden. In 1762 it was in Silesia at Pretzschendorf.

1762 Albertini

IR50

[75] Duffy (2008) 437

IR59 Leopold Daun

The regiment was raised on 30 January 1682 in Upper and Lower Austria by patent. Suffered above average losses in action and deserters.[76]

1757 Wrede

1760

IR59

Donath

POM-POM: White.
COAT: Red cuffs and lapels. White turnbacks with red tab.
WAISTCOAT: White.
BUTTONS: Brass.
SHOULDER STRAP: Red

Inhaber
1682 *Melchior Leopold Frhr. van der Bück* (d. 1693)
1693 *Ludwig Ferdinand Conte Marsigli* (d. 1730)
1704 *Anton Aegydius Frhr. Jorger von Tollet* (d. 1716)
1716 *Ottokar Graf Starhemberg*
1731 *Franz Wenzel Graf Wallis*
1740 *Margraf Leopold Joseph Daun, Fürst von Thiano*
1766 *Franz Graf Daun, Fürst von Thiano* (d. 1771)

Commander
1749 *Johann Wolf*
1757 *Carl Graf Pellegrini*
1759 *Franz Graf Daun*

Garrison:
1755 Vienna; 1763 Vienna

Campaigns[77])
War of Austrian Succession: In 1741, at Neisse (22 May). In 1742, it was at Chotusitz (17 May) and the siege of Prague. In 1743, at Simbach (9 May). In 1744 it was at Lautenberg (3 July). In 1745 it was at the siege of Amberg, a Bn at Habelschwert (14 Feb), at Hohenfriedberg lost 9 officers and 380 men and Soor (30 Sept). In 1746 it was in Italy and participated in the invasion of Provence. In 1747 it blockaded Genoa and was at Bisagno (13-14 June).

Seven Years War: In 1757, fought at Reichenberg (21 Apr), Kolin (18 June) and Gabel. One battalion participated in Hadik's raid on Berlin and the other at the storming of Schweidnitz. I-III Bns were present at Breslau (22 Nov) and Leuthen (5 Dec). In 1758, at Hochkirch (15 Oct). In 1759, at Maxen (20 Nov). In 1760 it was part of Lacy's expedition to Berlin and at Torgau (3 Nov). In 1761 it was in Saxony. In 1762, the regiment was at Burkersdorf (20-21 July). It was distinguished in the defence of Schweidnitz.

1762 Albertini

IR59

[76] Duffy (2008) 438
[77] Thürheim (1880) I: 412-3

Chapter 6
Inner Austria

Created in 1564 included the diverse territories of *Styria, Carinthia, Carniola, Görg,* and *Gradisca* plus the Austrian Littoral of *Trieste, Istria* and *Fiume* sprawled across the Alps from the borders of Lower and Upper Austrian, and Hungary to the plains of the Po and the Adriatic coast.

Map 4: Inner Austria

Stephen Summerfield, 2014

The **Duchy of Styria**[78] is located in modern-day southern Austria and northern Slovenia. It was well known for the quality of the iron throughout Europe and was considered to be superior to Swedish iron. The provincial capital of Graz with its Zeughaus (Arsenal) contained a large number of obsolete weapons due to its decline in military importance. These were lost to Bavaria in 1809.

The **County of Görz and Gradisca**[79] was based around Gorizia in Friuli-Venezia Giulia is in current north-eastern Italy was acquired in 1518. They spoke mostly Slovenian or Italian.

The **Duchy of Carinthia (Kärnten)**[80] in southern Austrian and parts of northern Slovenia was bordered to the north by the *Hohe Tauern* (the highest range in the Alps east of the Brenner Pass) and the *Niedere Tauern* (in Central Eastern Alps in Austria) ranges and to the south by the *Carnic Alps* in Eastern Tyrol and *Karawanken*

---

[78] German: Herzogtum Steiermark; Slovene: Vojvodina Štajerska; Hungarian: Stájerország
[79] German: Grafschaft Görz; Italian: Contea di Gorizia; Slovenian: Goriška grofija
[80] German: Herzogtum Kärnten; Slovene: Vojvodina Koroška

(mountain range between Austrian and Slovenia). The *Lower Carinthian Plain* surrounds the provincial capital of *Klagenfurt*. It was a large exporter of wool and mining. From 976 it was part of the Holy Roman Empire and a Habsburg land from 1335.

The **Duchy of Carniola (Krain/Crain)**[81] is a traditional and historical region of Slovenia and was particularly exposed to Turkish incursions from the first invasion in 1415. It supplied a large number of the miners, pioneers, and sappers due to their strong mining background despite mining being a reserved occupation. As part of Austria-Hungary, the region was a crown land officially known as the Duchy of Carniola until 1918. Its capital was Ljubljana.

OOB 5: Regiments in Inner Austria, June 1756.

CARNIOLA
Infantry Regiments (I-II, Grenadiers and Garrison Bn)

IR36 Browne	2,444	2,444

CARINTHIA
Infantry Regiments (I-II, Grenadiers and Garrison Bn)

IR47 Harrach	2,371	2,371

STYRIA (AUSTRIAN ALPS)
Infantry Regiments (I-II, Grenadiers and Garrison Bn)

IR13 Moltke	2,372	
IR21 Arenberg	2,469	4,841

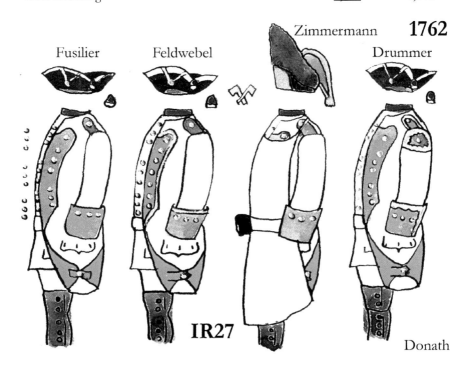

Fusilier Feldwebel Zimmermann **1762** Drummer

IR27

Donath

---

[81] Slovenian: Vojvodina Kranjska, German: Herzogtum Krain

IR16 Königsegg

It was formed on 23 June 1703 from a cadre of three IR4 Deutschmeister companies, two IR28 Thürheim companies and new drafts.[82] In 1760, Major Graf Königsegg was dismissed for corruption.[83] In 1918, IR16 Freiherr von Giesl.

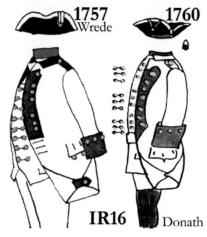

1757 Wrede **1760**

IR16 Donath

POM-POM: None
COAT: Blue cuffs and lapels. White turnbacks with blue dart-shaped turnback tab.
WAISTCOAT: White.
BUTTONS: Brass.
SHOULDER STRAP: Blue.

Inhaber
1703 *Damian Hugo Graf Virmond* (d. 1722)
1722 *Alois Graf von Livingstein*
1741 *Christian Moritz Graf Königsegg-Rothenfels*
1778 *Ludwig Frhr. Terzy* (d. 1800)

Commander
1756 *Franz Graf Königsegg-Aulendorff*
1762 *Joseph Freiherr de Vins*

Garrison
1756 Bozzolo in Mantua; 1763 Como in Lombardy

Campaigns[84]
War of Austrian Succession. In 1742, in the Winter Expedition in Upper Austria and Bavaria before joining the main army in Bohemia fighting at Chotusitz (17 May) and at the Siege of Prague. In 1746, in Italy at the battles of Piacenza and Rottofreddo, siege of Genoa and the invasion of Provence. In 1747, present at the siege of Genoa.

Seven Years War In 1757, fought at Hirschfeld (20 Feb), Reichenberg, one Bn at Prague (6 May), Moys (7 Sept), and Breslau (22 Nov). In 1758, fought at Hochkirch (14 Oct). In 1759 it received heavy losses at Sebastiansberg (31 July). Later fought at Pretzch (29 Oct 1759), Landeshut (23 June 1760) and Liegnitz.

1762 Albertini

IR16

---

[82] Thürheim (1880) I: 93
[83] Duffy (2008) 431
[84] Thürheim (1880) I: 94

IR26 Puebla

Formed in 1717. A good combat record.[85] Lost to France in 1809 and regained in 1815. In 1918, IR26 Schreider.

HEADWEAR: Tricorn with white hat lace and white pom-pom. By 1762, hat had scalloped white lace.
COAT: Red cuffs, lapel & turnbacks.
STOCK: Red
BUTTONS: Yellow
SHOULDER STRAP: Red or white outlined red.

Inhaber
1717 *Friedrich Wilhelm Markgraf von Brandenburg-Ansbach* (d. 1723)
1724 *Heinrich Frhr. Müffling* (d. 1737)
1737 *Nikolaus Franz Graf Grünne*
1751 *Anton Graf Puebla, Conde de Portugallo* (d. 1776)
1776 *Franz Carl Frhr. von Reise* (d. 1786)

Commanders
1752 *Carl Frhr. von Würzburg*
1758 *Ferdinand Graf Grünne*
1762 *Franz Xavier Graf Harrach*
1771 *Franz Frhr. von D'Armont*

Garrison:
Transylvania (1756).

Campaign[86]
War of Austrian Succession: In 1741, at Mollwitz (10 Apr). In 1742, the regiment fought at Chotusitz (17 May) and siege of Prague. In 1744 it campaigned in Rhine and Bohemia. In 1745, the regiment was at Habelschwert. At Hohenfriedberg (4 June), the Bayreuth Dragoons rode down the regiment and it lost 23 officers and it later participated at the battle of Trautenau. In 1746 it was in Italy. In 1747 it participated in the siege of Genoa.

Seven Years War In 1757, present at Kolin (18 June), Schweidnitz, Breslau (22 Nov), Leuthen (5 Dec). In 1758, distinguished at Hochkirch (14 Oct), Dommitzch, distinguished at Dresden where it captured a Prussian battery and at Burkersdorf. The regiment took part in the disastrous first counterattack at Torgau (3 Oct) where it lost 900 men and all it flags. In 1762, a detachment participated in the defence of Schweidnitz.

85 Duffy (2008) 432
86 Thürheim (1880) I: 166

IR27 Baden-Durlach

Raised by the patent of Emperor Leopold I dated 3 February 1682. In 1918, IR27 Albert König der Belgier (King Albert of Belgium).

1757
Brauer

POM-POM: None
COAT: Light blue cuffs, lapels and turnbacks.
WAISTCOAT: White
BUTTONS: White
SHOULDER STRAP: Light blue

Inhaber

1682 *Octavio Graf Nigrelli*
1703 *Johann H. Frhr. von Zum-Jungen* (d. 1732)
1732 *Max Prinz Hessen-Kassel* (d. 1763)
1753 *Christof Prinz von Baden-Durlach* (d. 1789)
1791 *Leopold Graf Strasoldo* (d. 1809)

IR27

Commanders

1753 *Ferdinand von Chukelsky* (Killed at Prague)
1757 *Carl Freiherr von Bülow*
1757 *Rudolph Felix Freiherr von Stein*

Garrison

1754 Pisek; 1756 in Lombardy with the Garrison Bn in Hungary and in 1763 Gent.

Campaign[87]

War of Austrian Succession. In 1742, at Chotusitz then the siege of Prague. In 1744, campaigned on the Rhine and in Bohemia. In 1745, at Hohenfriedberg (4 June) and Trautenau (30 Apr).

Seven Years War In 1756, fought at Lobositz (1 Oct). In 1757, Prague (6 May), Schweidnitz, Breslau (22 Nov) and at Leuthen (5 Dec) it suffered total losses of 30 officers and 900 men of which many were captured. A detachment was captured when Dresden surrendered on 19 Dec. In 1758, the re-constituted regiment fought at Hochkirch (14 Oct). In 1759 it was present at Maxen (20 Nov). In 1760, defence of Dresden and at Torgau (3 Nov). In 1761 it participated in the storm of Schweidnitz and at the battle of Leutmannsdorf. In 1762, one battalion was distinguished at Burkersdorf and another in the defence of Schweidnitz.

1762
Albertini

IR27

---

[87] Thürheim (1880) I: 171

IR43 Platz

The regiment was raised in 1715. It suffered the second highest desertion of 1656 men exceeded by IR14 Salm. In 1762, Obrist Carl Vernada attributed this heavy desertion rate to laborious outpost duty and absorbing large numbers of foreigners and Prussian deserters.[88] Disbanded in 1809.

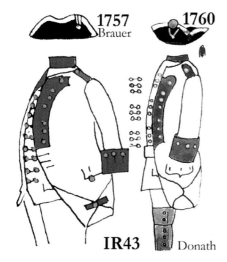

1757
Brauer

1760

IR43 Donath

POM-POM: None
COAT: Red collar and cuffs. White turnbacks with red tab.
BUTTONS: Brass.
SHOULDER STRAP: Red.

Inhaber
1723 *Erasmus Graf Stahemberg*
1730 *Johann Adrian von Lochstädt*
1732 *Bartholomäus Valparalso, Marchese D'Andia*
1734 *Matthias Heinrich Frhr. von Wuschletitz*
1737 *Johann Anton Graf Platz*
1768 *Ludwig Graf Buttler*

Commander
1748 *Carl Freiherr von Guldenhof*
1757 *Johannes Freiherr von Hussey*
1761 *Carl Graf Verneda*

Garrison
1748 Luxemburg; 1763 Lodi

Campaigns
War of Austrian Succession: In 1741-42, one Bn in Bavaria and the other was in Transylvania. In 1743-4 it was in Corps Batthyányi. In 1745, the regiment fought at Soor and Trautenau. In 1747, the regiment fought at Lawfeld.

Seven Years War In 1757, two Bns and the grenadiers were in Bohemia and at Kolin (18 June) where it suffered heavy losses. The grenadiers were at Moys (7 Sept). In 1758 it was present at the siege of Neisse. In 1759, at Krakau (Cracow) (23 Nov). In 1760, the regiment was in Corps Loudon, where it was distinguished at Landeshut (23 June) and Liegnitz (15 Aug). One Bn was stationed at Königgrätz. In 1761, one Bn took part in the storming of Schweidnitz. In 1762, the regiment was with the Army in Silesia. One Bn and a grenadier coy under Captain Carl Frhr. von Sterndahl was besieged in Schweidnitz.

---

[88] Duffy (2000) 446 and Duffy (2008) 436

IR45 Heinrich Daun

An excellent record recruited from Bohemia, Upper and Lower Austria just like IR47 Harrach.[89] Lost to France in 1809.

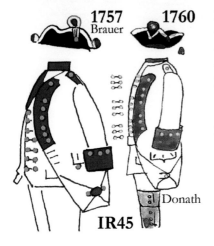

POM-POM: Yellow with red centre or red with yellow centre.
COAT: Red cuffs and lapels. White turnbacks with red tab.
BUTTONS: Brass.
SHOULDER STRAP: Red

Inhaber
1682 *Joachim Sigmund Graf Trautmansdorff*
1711 *Heinrich Graf Daun*
1761 *Wilhelm Frhr. von O'Kelly*
1767 *Friedrich Frhr. von Bülow*

Commanders
1740 *Joseph Kager von Stampach*
1746 *Frhr. von Chevereuil*
1750 *Rudolf Carl Graf Gaisruck*
1758 *Zorn von Blowsheim*
1759 *Leopold von Frankendorf*
1771 *Ellis Schwarz Elder von Scharzsculen*

Garrison:
Transylvania (1756).

Campaigns
Seven Years War In 1757, present at Breslau (22 Nov) and Leuthen. In 1758, the regiment fought at Hochkirch. In 1760 it participated in Lacy's raid on Berlin. Distinguished in the counterattack at Torgau (3 Nov). In 1762, the regiment was distinguished again at Teplitz (2 Aug).

[89] Duffy (2008) 436

Chapter 7
Austrian Littoral of Northwestern Italy

The Austrian Littoral comprised the provinces of *Trieste, County of Istria* (1382), and *Fiume* (1466) provided very few men for the Austrian Army.

The **County of Istria** is the largest peninsula in the Adriatic Sea located at the head of the Adriatic between the Gulf of Trieste and the Bay of Kvarner. It had been part of the Holy Roman Empire from the late 11th century and a Habsburg possession from 1382. In 1797, with the Treaty of Campo Formio, the Venetian parts of the peninsula passed to the Holy Roman Empire. In 1806, Istria became part of the Kingdom of Italy (1806–1810) and then part of the Illyrian Provinces (1810–1813) before being returned to Austria in 1815.

The **Free Port of Fiume** (now *Rijeka*) became a Habsburg possession in 1466 and was created as a Free Port in 1723.

The **Free Port of Trieste** is in north-east Italy almost surrounded by the Slovenian border at the head of the Gulf of Trieste on the Adriatic Sea. After two centuries of war against the Republic of Venice, the major citizens of Trieste petitioned *Leopold III of Habsburgs Duke of Austria* to become part of his domains which was signed in October 1382. Trieste became an important port and trade hub. In 1719, *Emperor Charles VI* made it a free port within the Habsburg Empire. It was annexed by the French as the Illyrian Provinces (1809-13) before being returned to the Austria in 1815.

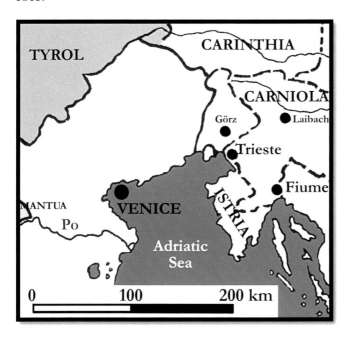

Map 5: Austrian Littoral of North-western Italy
S. Summerfield, 2014

IR13 Moltke

The regiment was raised in 1642 as Adam Ernst von Traun Regiment. Lost to Bavaria in 1809 and replaced by a new IR13 in 1814.

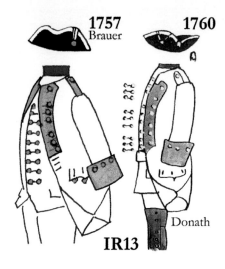

1757 Brauer   **1760**

Donath

IR13

POM-POM: None.
COAT: Light blue cuffs and lapels with white turnbacks.
BUTTONS: Brass.
SHOULDER STRAP: Light blue

Inhaber
1737 *Philipp Ludwig Freiherr von Moltke,*
1780 *Zettwitz*

Commanders
1756 *Vinzenz Graf Migazzi,*
1757 *Ludwig Graf Attems*
1760 *Wolfgang Graf Rindsmaul*

Garrison
Graz in Styria (1752); Austrian Alps (Steyr) in 1757; Weisskirchen (Neisse) in Hungary (1763)

Campaign
Seven Years War In 1757, I-III Bns were present at Kolin (18 June). I Bn surrendered at Breslau (22 Nov). II-III Bns fought at Leuthen (5 Dec). In 1758, the II Bn was part of the garrison of Schweidnitz that surrendered. The III Bn garrisoned Olmütz. In 1760, the reformed I-III Bns fought at Hochkirch, at Landeshut (23 June) and at Liegnitz (15 Aug). III Bn participated in Loudon's storm of Glatz (26 July). In 1761, the regiment took part in the second storming of Schweidnitz (1 Oct 1761) and in its subsequent defence (8 Aug-9 Oct 1762).

1762
Albertini

IR13

Chapter 8
Tyrol and Vorlande

Mountainous Tyrol along with the scattered enclaves in southern Germany situated between the Rhine, the Danube and Lake Constance. This region was administered from Innsbruck.

Map 6: Tyrol, Vorarlberg, and Vorder-Österreich (Outer Austria)
Stephen Summerfield, 2014

Outer Austria (*Vorder-Österreich*) included the Habsburg possessions in the Black Forest and the small possessions along the southern Rhine and Habsburg Alsace.

Swabian Austria (*Schwäbische Österreich*) centred on Markgraf of Burgau.

County of the Tyrol was raised to a county in 1504. Under *Maria Theresa* (r. 1740–1780) it was governed from Vienna.

Vorarlberg: a mountainous region separated *Vorlande* from the Tyrol.

OOB 6: Regiments in Tyrol and Vorlande, June 1756.

TYROL
Infantry Regiments (I-II, Grenadiers and Garrison Bn)

IR46 Maguire	<u>2,322</u>	2,322

IR41 Bayreuth

Raised in 1701 by Markgraf of Brandenburg-Bayreuth. It suffered the fourth highest infantry desertion of 1,125 men.[90]

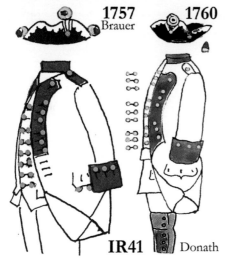

1757 Brauer

1760

IR41 Donath

POM-POM: Light blue-red, blue-yellow-red or yellow-white-red pom-pom
COAT: Red cuffs and lapels. White turnbacks.
WAISTCOAT: White.
BUTTONS: Brass.
SHOULDER STRAP: Red.

Inhaber

1701 *Christian Markgraf von Brandenburg-Bayreuth*
1704 *Georg Wilhelm Prinz Brandenburg-Bayreuth*
1727 *Wilhelm Ernst Prinz Brandenburg-Bayreuth*
1734 *Friedrich Markgraf von Brandenburg-Bayreuth*
1763 *Thomas Graf Plunquet* (d. 1770)
1770 *Josef Wenzel Fürst zu Fürstenberg-Stuhlingen*

Commander

1755 *Franz Felix*
1758 *Carl Freiherr von Kavanagh*
1763 *Heinrich Graf O'Donnell*

Garrison

1749 and 1763 Luxemburg

Campaigns[91]

War of Austrian Succession: In 1742, part of the winter expedition to Upper Austria and Bavaria. In 1743 it blockaded Braunau. In 1744, a Bn was at the siege of Freiburg. In 1745 it fought at Trautenau (30 Sept) before transferring to the Netherlands. In 1746, at Rocoux (4 Oct). In 1747 it was present at Lawfeld. In 1748, the regiment participated in the siege of Maastricht.

Seven Years War: In 1757, fought at Prague (6 May), at Moys where it received heavy losses and at the siege of Schweidnitz. In 1758, a Bn was at the siege of Neisse. In 1760, the regiment fought at Kunersdorf and was captured at Torgau (3 Nov) by the Prussian Bayreuth Dragoons. In 1761, the regiment was re-raised by taking its III (garrison) battalion from Luxembourg. In 1762 it was present at Burkersdorf (20-21 July) and a detachment was at the defence of Schweidnitz.

1762 Albertini

IR41

[90] Duffy (2000) 446
[91] Thürheim (1880) I: 276

IR46 Maguire

It was originally raised in 1745 as the *Tiroler Land- and Feld-Regiment* from the *Tiroler Land-Bataillon* that had been formed in 1703. Recruiting within the Tyrol was not very easy with only 20% from that area according to the returns for 24 May 1759. High proportion of recruits in 1761 and suffered from heavy desertion in 1762.[92] Disbanded in 1809.

1757 Wrede

1760

Donath

IR46

POM-POM: Green or yellow.

COAT: Red cuffs, lapels and turnbacks with red turnback tab. In 1760 white turnbacks.

WAISTCOAT: Red then white in 1760.

BUTTONS: Brass.

SHOULDER STRAP: Red.

Inhaber
1745 *Spauer*,
1748 *O'Gilvy*,
1751 *Sincère*,
1752 *Johann Sigmund Graf Maguire*
1764 *Migazzi*

Commander
1755 *Anton Freiherr von Kottwitz*
1760 *Aeneus Graf Caprara*

Garrison
Innsbruck in Tyrol (1745 and 1763).

Campaign
Seven Years War
In 1757 it fought at Prague (6 May), Moys (7 Sept), Schweidnitz, Breslau (22 Nov) and Leuthen. In 1760, participated in the defence of Dresden and then covered the retreat after Torgau.

1762 Albertini

IR46

[92] Duffy (2008) 436

Chapter 9
Kingdom of Bohemia

In 1515, *Charles* (1500-58), who became King of Spain in 1516 and Holy Roman Emperor in 1519, married the heir to the Kingdom of Bohemia. As a result on October 1526, *Charles* was elected Kings of Bohemia. King of Bohemia included *Bohemia (Böhmen), Moravia (Mähren)*, and *Silesia (Schlesien)*. Most of the latter was conquered by the Prussians in 1740 and ultimately retained by them.

Bohemia was in decline disordered by religious intolerance and exploited by German speaking absentee landlords.[93]

Map 7: Bohemia
Stephen Summerfield, 2014

---

[93] Durant (1965) IX: 431

OOB 7: Regiments in the Kingdom of Bohemia, June 1756.

BOHEMIA

Infantry Regiments

IR1 Kaiser	2,392	
IR8 Hildburghausen	2,408	
IR10 Ludwig Jung-Wolfenbüttel,	2,406	
IR11 Wallis	2,395	
IR17 Kollowrat	2,395	
IR18 Marschall	2,389	
IR20 Alt- (Anton) Colloredo,	2,391	
IR27 Baden-Durlach	2,342	
IR29 Carl Alt-Wolfenbüttel	2,382	
IR50 Harsch	2,367	
IR33 Nicolaus Esterhazy	1,652	
IR37 Joseph Esterhazy	1,652	27,171

Cavalry Regiments

KR2 Erzherzog Ferdinand	824	
KR15 Ansbach-Bayreuth	754	
DR1 Erzherzog Joseph Dragoons	815	
DR3 Batthyány Dragoons	813	3,206

TOTAL	30,377

Austrian Fusiliers employing Chevaux de Frise
Austrian drill book c1740

IR10 Jung (Ludwig) Wolfenbüttel[94]

The regiment was raised on 14 October 1715 as the "Prinz Heinrich von Württemberg" Regiment. Recruiting area was southwest Holy Roman Empire.

POM-POM: Light blue with white centre.
COAT: Red cuffs and lapels. White turnbacks with white turnback tab.
WAISTCOAT: White.
BUTTONS: White then brass by 1760.
SHOULDER STRAP: White.

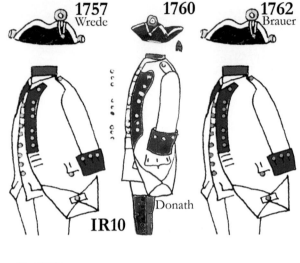

1757 Wrede   1760   1762 Brauer

Donath

IR10

Inhaber
1715 *Heinrich Friedrich Prinz Württemberg*
1717 *Friedrich Ludwig Prinz von Württemberg*
1734 *Georg Anton Frhr. Lindermann* (d. 1739)
1740 *Ernst Ludwig von Braunschweig-Wolfenbüttel*
1790 *Carl Frhr. Kheul* (d. 1798)

Commanders
1756 *Carl Graf Alemsloe*
1759 *Friedrich Ferdinand Graf Pappenheim*

Garrison
Pilsen in Bohemia (1752); Pisek (1763).

Campaigns[95]
War of Austrian Succession: In 1743, fought at Dettingen (27 June). In 1745, part of Traun's Army. In 1746, in the Netherlands at Rocoux (11 Oct) and Lawfeld (2 July 1747).

Seven Years War Fought at Lobositz (1 Oct 1756). In 1757, at Prague (6 May), Breslau (22 Nov), Leuthen (5 Dec). In 1758, the regiment fought at Hochkirch. In 1759 it was present at Meissen (2-3 Dec). In 1760, one Bn under Obrist-Lt Frhr. Hasslinger in the siege of Dresden, at Torgau (3 Nov) where it suffered severely under artillery fire and part of Lacy's raid on Berlin. In 1761 it was in Saxony. In 1762, at Pretzschendorf, and performed very well at Spechtshausen in Saxony where three battalions were present.

1762 Albertini

IR10

---

[94] Known as *Jung-Wolfenbüttel* to distinguish it from IR29 *Alt-Wolfenbüttel*. In 1918, IR10 Gustav von Schween der Goten und Wenden.
[95] Thürheim (1880) I: 52-53

IR11 Wallis

Very old regiment raised in 1619 by Wallenstein. In 1918, IR11 Georg Prinz Sachsen.

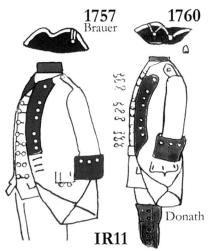

1757
Brauer

1760

Donath

IR11

1774 *Michel Graf Wallis* (d. 1798)

POM-POM: None
COAT: Red cuffs and lapels. White turnbacks.
WAISTCOAT: White
BUTTONS: White
SHOULDER STRAP: White

Inhaber
1619 *Rudolf Frhr. von Teuffenbac* (d. 1653)
1640 *Ludwig Frhr. von Steinachier* (d. 1673)
1673 *Jobst Hilmar Frhr von Knigge*
1684 *Philipp Emerich Graf Metternich*
1698 *Heinrich Tobias Frhr. von Hasslinger*
1717 *Heinrich Wilhelm Graf Wilczek*
1739 *Franz Wenzel, Graf von Wallis* (d. 1774)

Commander
1756 *Philipp Graf Browne de Camus*
1758 *Michael Graf Wallis*
1761 *Michael Ritter von Jeschek*

Garrison
Prague in Bohemia (1754); Kolin (1763)

Campaigns[96]
War of Austrian Succession: Fought at siege of Prague (1742), at Ingolstadt (1743). In 1746 it transferred to Italy, fighting at Rottofreddo, invasion of Provence and in 1747 at the siege of Genoa.

Seven Years War: Fought at Lobositz (1 Oct 1756). In 1757, suffered heavy losses at Prague (6 May), one Bn at Breslau (22 Nov) and Leuthen (5 Dec) where most of the regiment was captured. Distinguished at Hochkirch (14 Oct 1758). In 1760, fought at Landeshut (23 June), Liegnitz (15 Aug) and 3 Bns at the siege of Glatz. In 1761, the regiment was in Saxony. In 1762 it fought at Burkersdorf (20-21 July) and Liegnitz.

1762
Albertini

IR11

---

[96] Thürheim (1880) I: 59-60

IR15 Pallavicini

Raised in 1701 for the duration of the War of Spanish Succession and joined Austrian service in 1716. The regiment had rather a poor reputation.[97] In 1918, IR15 Freiherr von Georgi.

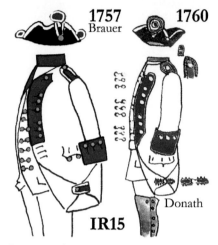

1757 Brauer **1760**

Donath

IR15

POM-POM: Red-white-red pom-pom.
COAT: Red cuffs and lapels. White turnback with red turnback tab edged white.
WAISTCOAT: White.
BUTTONS: Brass.
SHOULDER STRAP: Red with white edge.

Inhaber
1701 *Carl Josef Ignaz Prinz von Lothringen*
1716 *Carl Alexander Prinz von Lothringen*
1736 *Giovanni Lucas Conte die Pallavicini*
1773 *Dominico St Tomiotti de Fabris, Conte di Cassano*

Commander
1755 *Johann Frhr. von Tillier*
1758 *N. von Graevenitz*
1759 *Adolph von Rolshoffen*

Garrison
1752 Como (Lombardy); 1763 Chrudim in eastern Bohemia.

Campaign[98]
War of Austrian Succession: In Khevenhüller Corps and in 1742 participated in the Winter Expedition into Upper Austria and Bavaria. In 1743, the regiment was on the Rhine before transferring to Italy where it fought at Rottfredo (1746) and the siege of Genoa. In May 1747, a Bn under *Major Allemann* blockaded Massone Castle.

Seven Years War: In 1757, fought at Prague (6 May), Breslau (22 Nov) and Leuthen (5 Dec). In 1758, a Bn was at the siege of Neisse and all three Bns were present at Hochkirch. In 1759, at Maxen (20 Nov). In 1760 it participated in numerous actions in Saxony including Torgau (3 Nov). In 1762, one battalion was distinguished at Teplitz (2 Aug) and the whole regiment was present at Freiberg (29 Oct).

1762 Albertini

IR15

---

[97] Duffy (2008) 431
[98] Thürheim (1880) I: 88

IR17 Kollowrat

The regiment was raised in 1632. During the Seven Years War it suffered the fifth highest infantry desertion of 1099 men.[99] In 1918, IR17 Ritter von Milde

1757 Wrede

1760

IR17   Donath

POM-POM: Yellow with red centre
COAT: Red cuffs, lapels and turnbacks. In 1760, white with red tab.
WAISTCOAT: Red then white in 1760.
BUTTONS: White then brass in 1760.
SHOULDER STRAP: Red.

Inhaber
1632 *Melchior Graf Hatzfeld* (d. 1658)
1659 *Antonio Graf Collalto* (d. 1675)
1675 *Friedrich Frhr. von Stadel* (d. 1694)
1694 *Carl Efon Graf Fürstenberg von Mösskirch*
1702 *Carl Emanuel Fürst von Langerval Graf von Buquoi*
1703 *Carl Alexander Prinz Seit.*
1733 *Herzog von Württemberg* (d. 1737)
1737 *Cajetan Graf Kollowrat-Krakowski* (d. 1769)
1769-73 Vacant

Commander
1747 *Franz Aulock*
1759 *Lorenz Freiherr von Rasp*

Garrison
1756 Pilgram (Pelhřimov), Bohemia; 1763 Saaz (Žatec)

Campaigns[100]
War of Austrian Succession: In 1741, at Mollwitz (10 Apr) and the siege of Prague. In 1744, the regiment was on the Rhine then Bohemia. In 1745, at Habelschwert, Hohenfriedberg (4 June) and Trautenau (30 Sept).

1762 Albertini

IR17

Seven Years War In 1756, fought at Lobositz (1 Oct) then on Browne's relief expedition to Saxony. In 1757 it took heavy losses at Prague and Breslau. At Leuthen (5 Dec) the regiment lost the highest percentage of prisoners and missing in the army. In 1758 it fought at Domstadtl (30 June) and was distinguished at Hochkirch. In 1760 it was distinguished at Landeshut (23 June). Also present later that year at Liegnitz (15 Aug) and Torgau (3 Nov). In 1761, participated in Loudon's storm of Schweidnitz (1 Oct).

---

[99] Duffy (2000) 446
[100] Thürheim (1880) I: 101

IR18 Marschall

The regiment was raised by Patent of 16 April 1682 from five Tyrolean companies and drafts from disbanded regiments. In 1918, IR18 Leopold Salvator.

1757 Wrede
1760
IR18   Donath

POM-POM: None.
COAT: Red cuffs, lapels and turnbacks. Then in 1760, white turnbacks with red tab.
WAISTCOAT: White.
BUTTONS: White metal then brass in 1760.
SHOULDER STRAP: Red.

Inhaber
1682 *Leopold Herzog von Lothringen*
1698 *Josef Herzog von Lothringen*
1705 *Johann Adam Frhr. von Wetzel*
1707 *Franz Xaver Graf Sonnenberg* (d. 1731)
1714 *Damian Frhr. von Sickingen*
1716 *Johann Hermann Franz Graf zu Nesselrode*
1719 *Friedrich Heinrich Frhr. Graf Seckendorf*
1742 *Ernst Friedrich von Marschall auf Burgholzhausen*
1773 *Jacob Friedrich Frhr. von Brinken* (or *Brincken*)

Commander
1755 *Carl Ludwig Freiherr von Seckendorff*
1759 *Christian Friedrich Freiherr von Leubelfink*

Garrison
1752 Linz; 1756 Bohemia; 1763 Jung-Brunzlau (Mladá Boleslav)

Campaigns[101]
War of Austrian Succession: In 1742, fought at Chotusitz (17 May) and the Siege of Prague. In 1743 it was at Simbach. In 1744 it fought at Philipsburg, Germersheim, Lautenberg, Mosheim and the III Bn at the capitulation of Freiburg. In 1745 it fought at Hohenfriedberg and Trautenau (30 Sept). In 1747-48, the regiment was in Italy.

Seven Years War In 1756, the grenadiers fought at Lobositz (1 Oct). In 1757 it was present at Prague (6 May) and Bamberg. In 1758, the III Bn was besieged in Olmütz. In 1759, the regiment was in the *Reichsarmee*, fought at Meissen and notable for its lone stand at Löthain (Korbitz) (21 Sept) and one Bn was present at Maxen (20 Nov). In 1760 it participated at Landshut (23 June), in the storming of Glatz (26 July), at Liegnitz (15 Aug) and the siege of Kosel. In 1761 it was in Saxony. In 1762, the regiment was at Fischerberg. A detachment was besieged in Schweidnitz.

1762 Albertini

IR18

---

[101] Thürheim (1880) I: 110-111

IR21 Arenberg

Raised in 1733 at the cost of the *Obrist Graf Colmerero* of IR24. In 1918, IR21 Graf von Arenberg und Traun.

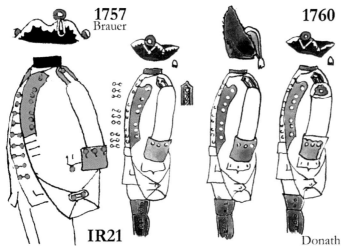

1757 Brauer

1760

IR21

Donath

HEADWEAR: Tricorn with white scalloped lace and green with white centre pom-pom.
COAT: Light blue cuffs and lapels. White with light blue tab edged white.
WAISTCOAT: White.
BUTTONS: Brass.
SHOULDER STRAP: White edged light blue.

Inhaber
1733 *Ludwig Graf Colmenero de Valderlos*
1734 *Ludwig Ferdinand Graf Schulenburg-Oynhausen*
1754 *Carl Raymond Duke von Arenberg* (d. 1778)
1778 *Sigmend Frhr. von Gemmingen-Hornberg*

Commanders
1756 *Silvius Lindainer von Rosen*
1763 *Ernst Freiherr von Normann*

Garrison:
1755 Marburg an der Drau (now Maribor) in Slovenia; 1763 Königgrätz

Campaigns
War of Austrian Succession: Winter 1742 campaign in Upper Austria and Bavaria. In 1743 it was in Bavaria. In 1746 it was in Italy at Piacenza and Rottofreddo then the siege of Genoa. The regiment was recruited from throughout the entire Holy Roman Empire. A report in 1755 stated that the regiment suffered from a high desertion rate due to harsh discipline and drunkenness. The regiment was considered a good fighting regiment.

Seven Years War In 1757, fought at Kolin (18 June), Schweidnitz, Breslau (22 Nov) and Leuthen (5 Dec). In 1758 participated in the successful defence of Olmütz (28 May-2 July) then fought at Hochkirch (14 Oct). In 1759, the regiment was distinguished at Kunersdorf. In 1760, the regiment

1762 Albertini

IR21

excelled at Torgau (3 Nov) where it covered the retreat of the army with IR3 Carl Lothringen and IR12 Botta. In 1761 it participated in the second storming of Schweidnitz (1 Oct) and in 1762 at Freiberg (29 Oct).

IR25 Piccolomini

The Regiment was raised in 1672. In 1918, IR25 Edler von Pokorny.

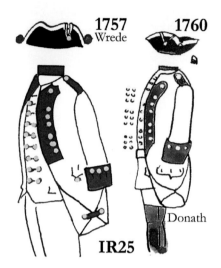

1757 Wrede

1760

Donath

IR25

POM-POM: None
COAT: Red cuffs and lapels. White turnbacks with red turnback tab.
WAISTCOAT: White
BUTTONS: White metal then brass in 1760.
SHOULDER STRAP: Red.

Inhaber
1672 *Johann Carl Graf Serenyi* (d. 1691)
1691 *Franz Christof Frhr. von Amenzaga* (d. 1693)
1693 *Scipio Graf Bagni* (d. 1721)
1721 *Philipp Frhr. Langlet* (d. 1727)
1727 *Marquis Mathew de Luciny* (d. 1729)
1731 *Carl Franz Frhr. von Wachtendonk* (d. 1741)
1741 *Octavio Fürst Piccolomini d'Aragona*
1757 *Franz Ludwig Graf Thürheim* (d. 1782)
1783 *Ludwig Graf Brechainville* (d. 1799)

Commander
1752 *Marchese Vittelleschi*
1758 *Franz Wocher*

Garrison:
1753 Brünn; 1756 Moravia; 1763 Linz

Campaigns[102]
War of Austrian Succession: In 1743, fought at Campo Santo (8 Feb). In 1744 it participated in the expedition to Naples. In 1746, the regiment was at Piacenza (16 June) and Genoa (1 Sept).

Seven Years War In 1757, fought at Kolin (18 June), one Bn at the siege of Schweidnitz, Breslau (22 Nov) where 3 Bns were distinguished and at Leuthen where a whole battalion and a grenadier company was captured on 9 Dec. In 1758, lost 7 officers and 312 men captured at the surrender of Schweidnitz (16 Apr), distinguished at Hochkirch (14 Oct). In 1759, the grenadiers were at Frauenwald (4 Mar), Kulmbach and Bamberg (14-16 May), Trachtenberg (5 Sept) and Meissen (21 Sept). In 1760, the regiment was part of Lacy's raid on Berlin and at Torgau (3 Nov). In 1761 it campaigned in Saxony. In 1762, the regiment fought at Freiberg (15 Oct). A detachment was present at the capitulation of Schweidnitz (9Oct).

1762 Albertini

IR25

---

[102] Thürheim (1880) I: 158

IR28 Wied-Runkel

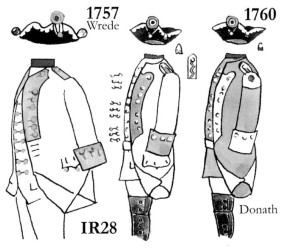

1757 Wrede

1760

Donath

IR28

It was raised in 1698. In 1915, IR28 Viktor Emmanuel III König von Italien when it was disbanded.

HEADWEAR: Tricorn with scalloped lace and green with red centre pom-pom.
COAT: Green cuffs and lapels. White turnbacks.
WAISTCOAT: White.
BUTTONS: **White then brass in 1760**.
SHOULDER STRAP: Green.

Inhaber
1698 *Franz Sebastian Graf Thürheim* (d. 1726)
1713 *Friedrich Ludwig von der Lanken* (d. 1716)
1716 *Leopold Philipp Dueg von Arenberg* (d. 1754)
1754 *Leopold Frhr. Scherzer* (d. 1754)
1754 *Friedrich Georg Graf Weid-Runkel* (d. 1779)
1779 *Wilhelm Graf Wartensleben* (d. 1798)

Commander
1755 *Sigmund Freiherr von Burmann*
1759 *Sigmund Freiherr von Gemmingen auf Hornberg und Teschklingen*

Garrison
1754 Antwerp; 1763 Nikolsburg (Mikulov)

Campaign[103]
War of Austrian Succession: In 1743, at Dettingen. In 1745 it was part of Traun's army on the Main. In 1746, the regiment fought at Rocoux. In 1747 it was at Lawfeld and in 1748 participated in the siege of Maastricht.

Seven Years War In 1757, distinguished with heavy losses at Prague (6 May), at Breslau (22 Nov) and captured at the surrender of the city (19 Dec). Raised again in 1758, a Bn was at the siege of Neisse and the regiment fought at Hochkirch (14 Oct). In 1759 it was distinguished at Maxen (20 Nov). In 1760 it suffered heavy losses including 24 officers at Torgau (3 Nov). In 1761 it was in Saxony. In 1762, a battalion was captured at Freiberg (15 Oct).

1762 Albertini

IR28

---

[103] Thürheim (1880) I: 181

IR35 Waldeck

The regiment was raised in 1682.

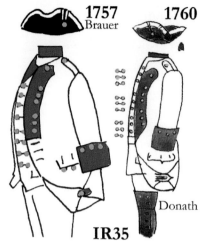

1757 Brauer

1760

Donath

IR35

COAT: Red cuffs and lapels. White turnback with red tab edged white.
WAISTCOAT: White.
BUTTONS: Yellow
SHOULDER STRAP: White

Inhaber
1682 *Georg Friedrich Herzog von Württemberg-Stuttgart* (d. 1685)
1685 *Ulysses Marchese de Spinola* (d. 1686)
1688 *Guidobald Graf Starhemberg* (see IR13)
1688 *Carl Ludwig Archinto Conte de Tayna*
1693 *Johann Martin Geschwind Frhr. von Pöckstein*
1721 *Johann Daniel Graf Fürstenbusch* (d. 1738)
1739 *Carl August Fürst Waldeck* (d. 1763)
1763 *Johann Sigmund Graf Maguire* (d. 1767)
1767 *Ludwig IX, Landgraf von Hessen-Darmstadt*

Commander
1756 *Philipp Wilhelm Freiherr von Biela*
1759 *Anton Freiherr von Formentini* (Killed at Liegnitz)
1760 *Josias Bellizari*
1763 *Christian Graf Erbach*

Garrison:
Vienna (1755); Prague (1763)

Campaigns[104]
War of Austrian Succession: In 1742, part of the winter expedition in Upper Austrian and Bavaria then at Chotusitz and siege of Prague. In 1743, the regiment fought in Bavaria. In 1744 it was in Bohemia. In 1745, a Bn was at Habelschwert and Trautenau. The regiment was at Kesseldorf. In 1746 it was at Rocoux. In 1747 it was at Lawfeld. In 1748, at Rosendahl.

Seven Years War In 1756, fought at Lobositz (1 Oct). In 1757, Prague (6 May), Breslau (22 Nov) and Leuthen (5 Dec) where it received very heavy losses. In 1758, the reformed regiment fought at Hochkirch (14 Oct). In 1759, at Kunersdorf (12 Aug). In 1760, Landeshut and Liegnitz. In 1761, a Bn was present at Loudon's storm of Schweidnitz. In 1762, at Leitmannsdorf, Burkersdorf (21 July) and a detachment was present at the siege of Schweidnitz.

1762
Albertini

IR35

---

[104] Thürheim (1880) I: 232-3

IR36 Browne

Raised in 1630 and the second oldest infantry regiment in the Austrian Army. Disbanded in 1915 when it was known as IR36 Reichsgraf Browne.

1757 Wrede **1760**

IR36 Donath

POM-POM: White with red centre then in 1760 red with yellow centre.
COAT: Blue cuffs and lapels. White turnback with blue tab.
WAISTCOAT: White.
BUTTONS: White metal.
SHOULDER STRAP: Blue

Inhaber
1683 *Jakob Graf Leslie* (d. 1692)
1692 *Philipp Erasmus Fürst zu Liechtenstein*
1704 *Max Ludwig Graf Regal* (d. 1717)
1718 *Franz Paul Graf Wallis* (d. 1737)
1737 *Max Ulysses Graf Browne de Camus* (d. 1757)
1757 *Joseph Graf Browne* (d. 1759)
1759 *Johannes Freiherr von Tillier* (d. 1761)
1761 *Franz Ulrich Graf Kinsky* (d. 1792)
1792 Vacant

Commander
1756 Joseph Graf Browne de Camus
1758 Johann Freiherr von Koch
1763 Wenzel Graf Herberstein

Garrison:
1752 Laibach (Ljubljana) in Slovenia; 1756 Carniola (Slovenia); Prague (1763)

Campaign[105]
War of Austrian Succession: In 1741, at Mollwitz (16 Apr), a Bn & grenadiers in the siege of Brieg Fortress that surrendered on 4 May. In 1742, the regiment was at Sahay and the siege of Prague. In 1744, I-II Bns & grenadiers were on the Rhine and in Bohemia. The III Bn as garrison of Freiburg fortress. In 1745, at Hohenfriedberg (4 June) and Trautenau (30 Sept). In 1746, at Rocoux (11 Oct). In 1747, at Lawfeld (2 July). In 1748, a Bn was at the siege of Maastricht.

Seven Years War In 1756, fought at Lobositz (1 Oct). In 1757, the regiment was at Prague (6 May), Schweidnitz, Breslau (22 Nov), and Leuthen (5 Dec) with heavy losses. In 1758, the regiment was distinguished at Hochkirch (14 Oct) and Maxen. In 1760, at Kunzendorf (17 Sept) and distinguished at Torgau (3 Nov). In 1762, present at Burkersdorf (20-21 July).

1762 Albertini

IR36

---

[105] Thürheim (1880) I: 240-1

IR42 Gaisruck

Raised on 21 February 1674 by Bishop Johann Hartmann von Würzburg and Bamberg for Emperor Leopold I. The regiment entered Austrian service in 1685. According to FM Daun, this regiment was made up mainly of recruits. It had a good record.[106]

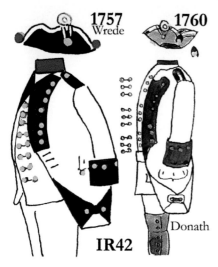

1757 Wrede

1760

Donath

IR42

POM-POM: Yellow with white centre.
COAT: Blue cuffs and lapels. White turnbacks with blue tab.
WAISTCOAT: White.
BUTTONS: Brass.
SHOULDER STRAP: Blue.

Inhaber
1683 *Hans Carl Thüngen*
1694 *Leopold Frhr. Von Thavonat* (d. 1694)
1694 *Wenzel Graf Guttenstein*
1706 *Franz Josef Frhr. von Wetzel* (d. 1720)
1720 *Philipp Ludwig Frhr. von Bettendorf* (d. 1733)
1734 *Alexander Graf O'Nelly* (d. 1743)
1743 *Franz Sigmund Graf Gaisruck* (d. 1769)
1769 *Reinhardt Frhr. von Gemmingen auf Hornberg und Treschklingen* (d. 1775)

Commander
1755 *Jacob Freiherr von Brinken*
1758 *Joseph Ittner* (killed on 3 Nov 1760 at Torgau)
1760 *Eustachius von Wieder*

Garrison
1754 Leipnik (Lipník nad Bečvou) with Garrison Bn in Erfurt (1756); 1763 Eger

Campaigns
War of Austrian Succession: In 1743, at Dettingen (27 June). In 1744, I-II Bn was at the siege of Antwerp and Dendermonde. III Bn and Grenadiers fought at Kronweissenburg (6 July). In 1746, a Bn at Rocoux (11 Oct). In 1747, at Lawfeld (2 July).

Seven Years War In 1757, very distinguished at Kolin (18 June), Breslau (22 Nov) and Leuthen (5 Dec 1757) with heavy losses. In 1758, the regiment was distinguished at Hochkirch (14 Oct). In 1760 it was distinguished at the defence of Dresden, Torgau (3 Nov) where it received the second highest regimental losses. In 1762 it fought Burkersdorf (20-21 July).

1762 Albertini

IR42

---

[106] Duffy (2008) 435

IR47 Harrach

The regiment was raised in 1682 raised in Silesia. A reliable regiment recruited in Bohemia, Upper and Lower Austria.[107]

POM-POM: Yellow
COAT: Blue cuffs, lapels and turnbacks. In 1760, white turnbacks.
TURNBACKS: White.
BUTTONS: Brass.
SHOULDER STRAP: Blue

Inhaber
1682 *Georg Frhr. von Wallis*
1689 *Franz Helfried Graf Jörger de Tollet*
1691 *Notger Wilhelm Graf Ottingen-Baldern*
1694 *Lorenz Graf Solari* (d. 1704)
1704 *Joseph Philipp Graf Harrach zu Rohrau*
1764 *Margraf von Brandenburg-Bayreuth*

Commander
1753 *Karl Graf Engelhaussen*
1757 *Ferdinand Freiherr von Baumbach*
1760 *Paul Graf Seriman*

Garrison
Villach in Carinthia (Slovenia) in 1750; Marburg (1763)

Campaigns[108]
War of Austrian Succession: In 1741m at Mollwitz (10 Apr). In 1742, at Chotusitz (17 May). In 1744 it campaigned on the Rhine and Bohemia. One Bn was at the siege of Freiburg. In 1745, the regiment fought at Hohenfriedberg (4 June) and Trautenau (30 September).

Seven Years War Fought at Lobositz (1 Oct 1756), distinguished at Prague (6 May 1757), Moys, Kolin (18 June 1757), Breslau (22 Nov 1757), Leuthen, Hochkirch (14 Oct 1758) and Bamberg. In 1760, part of the *Reichsarmee* and was distinguished with heavy losses at Torgau (3 Nov 1760). One battalion was at the storm of Schweidnitz in 1761. The regiment fought at Reichenbach.

1757 Wrede

1760

Fusilier   Officer   Drummer

IR47

Donath

1762
Albertini

IR47

---

[107] Duffy (2008) 436
[108] Thürheim (1880) I: 308-9

IR54 Sincère

Raised in 1620 by Adam Wilhelm Schellhardt in the *Reich* and joined Austrian service in 1661.

POM-POM: Yellow
COAT: Red cuffs and lapels. White turnbacks.
WASTCOAT: White.
BUTTONS: White metal then brass in 1760
SHOULDER STRAP: Red.

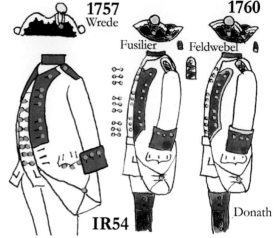

1757 Wrede — 1760 Fusilier / Feldwebel — Donath

IR54

Inhaber

1620 *Adam Wilhelm Schellhardt*
1627 *Johann Frhr. von Aldringer*
1634 *Johann Franz Frhr. Barwitz von Fernamont*
1649 *Otto Christoph Graf Sparre*
1669 *Ernst Rüdiger Graf Starhemberg*
1701 *Georg Friedrich Frhr. von Kreichbaum*
1710 *Bertrand Frhr. von Wachtendonk* (d. 1720)
1720 *Lothar Graf Königsegg-Rothenfels* (d. 1751)
1751 *Claudius Frhr. von Sincère* (d. 1769)
1769 *Carl Graf Callenberg* (d. 1800)

Commander

1754 *Christoph Freiherr von Bibow*
1758 *Jakob Graf Nugent*
1760 *Johann Graf Annoni*
1760 *Ferdinand Graf Kokorzowa*

Garrison:

1754 Znain; 1763 Pilsen

Campaigns[109]

War of Austrian Succession: In 1742-3 in Bavaria. In 1744 it was in Bohemia. In 1745, the regiment was at Hohenfriedberg (4 June) and Trautenau (30 Sept) before transferring to the Netherlands. In 1746, at Rocoux (11 Oct). In 1747, at Lawfeld (2 July).

Seven Years War: In 1757, fought at Reichenberg, Prague and a detachment participated in Hadik's raid on Berlin. In 1759 it was present at Maxen. In 1760, suffered the sixth highest losses at Torgau (3 Nov). It was still unfit for action in 1761 stationed in Saxony. The regiment participated in the battles of Burkersdorf and Reichenbach. A detachment distinguished itself during the defence of Schweidnitz.

1762 Albertini

IR54

---

[109] Thürheim (1880) I: 367

IR57 Andlau

The regiment was raised on 9 December 1688.

POM-POM: None.
COAT: Red cuffs and lapels. White turnbacks with white edged red tab.
WAISTCOAT: White/
BUTTONS: Brass.
SHOULDER STRAP: White edged red

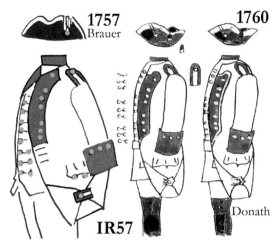

Inhaber

1688 *Albrecht III von Sachsen-Coburg*
1699 *Carl Sebastian Frhr. von Kratze*
1704 *Johann Damian von Sickingen*
1713 *Johann Hannibal Frhr. zu Wallenstein*
1715 *George Graf Browne* (d. 1729)
1731 *Patrik Frhr. von Oneullau* (d. 1734)
1734 *Sigmund Adam Frhr. von Thüngen*
1745 *Joseph Freiherr von Andlau* (d. 1767)
1769 *Graf Joseph Colloredo-Waldsee* (d. 1818)

Commanders

1756 *Franz Chevalier de Perelli*
1757 *Otto Heinrich von Rath*

Garrison

1756 Cremona; 1757 Milan; 1763 Klagenfurt

Campaigns[110]

War of Austrian Succession: In 1741, at Mollwitz (10 Apr). In 1742, the regiment fought at Chotusitz (17 May) and siege of Prague. In 1743 it was in Bavaria. In 1744 it was present at the siege of Olmütz then Silesia. In 1745 it was at Hohenfriedberg (4 June) where it lost 789 men. The III Bn was at Jägersdorf and the storm of Kosel. In 1746 it was in Italy at Piacenza, siege of Gavi and on 5 December Obrist Frhr. Buttler was murdered during the revolt in Genoa. In 1747, the regiment was at the siege of Genoa.

Seven Years War In 1757, I Bn & the grenadiers were at Prague (6 May), a detachment at Moys (7 Sept), Breslau (22 Nov), Leuthen (5 Dec). In 1758, Hochkirch (14 Oct). In 1759 it was captured at Sebastiansberg (15 April). The III Bn joined the main army from Italy and the reconstituted regiment fought in 1760 at Landshut (23 June), Liegnitz (15 Aug). In 1762 it was at Burkersdorf (20-21 July). A detachment of 208 men under *Major Graf Berchtold* was part of the defence of Schweidnitz.

---

[110] Thürheim (1880) I: 393-4

Chapter 10
Moravia and Austrian Silesia

Moravia[111]

This is now in the east of the Czech Republic taking its name from the Morava River that rises in the northwest of the region. The Moravians are Slaves that speak various Czech dialects.

Until 1641, the Moravian capital was the centrally-located at **Olmütz** (*Olomouc* in Czech) surrounded by marshy land on the Morava river, but after its capture by the Swedes it moved to the larger city of Brünn (*Brno* (Czech)) at the confluence of the Svitava River with the Svratka River and resisted the invaders successfully. The town is and was protected (westwards) by the strong fortress of the Spielberg Castle.

**Map 8:
Moravia and
Austrian Silesia**
S. Summerfield, 2014

Iglau (Czech: *Jihlava*) was a Royal fortified town on the bohemian border. Its name is derived from the German word for hedgehog. An old Slavic settlement upon a ford was moved on a nearby hill where the mining town was founded (ca. 1240) by king Václav I, in the Middle Ages inhabited mostly by Germans (coming mostly from Northern Bavaria and Upper Saxony).

Mährische Schönberg (Czech: *Šumperk*) close to the Silesian border was founded by German colonists in 1269 on a trade route and profited from the copper mines. The German name Schönberg means "beautiful hill". **Kremsier** (Czech: *Kroměříž*) with the territories of Prerau (Czech: *Prerov*) was one of the oldest towns in Moravia.

Ungarische Hradische (Czech: *Uherské Hradiště*) was founded in 1257 by the Czech King Otakar II and was the earliest known Jewish community dated from 1592.

---

[111] Morava (Czech) Mähren (German)

Znaim (Czech: *Znoymo*) or Znaym, Znogma was a Royal town settled on the top of a rough hill over the river Thaya.

Austrian Silesia[112]

The Duchy of Upper and Lower Silesia was inherited by the Habsburgs as part of the Kingdom of Bohemia upon the death of the King Louis II of Bohemia in October 1526. The two main cities were Teschen and Troppau (now Opava). In 1742, Lower Silesia and most of Upper Silesia was lost to Prussia. Maria Theresa fought three wars in an attempt to recover Silesia. The last was the Seven Years War. This was only a small part of Upper Silesia and did not contain any part of Lower Silesia within its borders. The capital of Austrian Silesia was Troppau (Opava) on the Oppa (Opava) River.

Teschen (Czech: *Těšín*) also Telling (Latin *Tessinum*) was a former Principality of Albert the Duke of Saxony consisting many of Poles. **Troppau** (Czech: *Opava*), also Oppain (Latin *Oppavia* or *Troppavia*) on the river Opa was the capital of the Silesian Principality and was surrounded by a tall wall.

Austrian Camp c1757

OOB 8: Regiments in Moravia and Silesia, June 1756.

MORAVIA
Infantry Regiments (I-II, Grenadiers and Garrison Bn)

IR12 Botta	2,388	
IR25 Piccolomini	2,383	
IR31 Haller	1,840	
IR42 Gaisruck (Gaisrugg)	2,383	
IR53 Simbschen (initially only I Bn)	671	
IR54 Sincère	2,379	12,044

SILESIA
Infantry Regiments (I-II, Grenadiers and Garrison Bn)

IR7 Neipperg	2,393	2,393
		14,437

---

[112] *Österreichisch Schlesien* (German); *Rakouské Slezsko* (Czech); *Śląsk Austriacki* (Polish)

IR1 Kaiser

It was raised in 1716. In 1918, IR1 Kaiser.

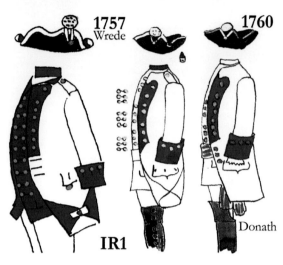

1757 Wrede

1760

Donath

IR1

POM-POMS: Yellow speckled black.

COAT: Red collar, cuffs, lapels and turnbacks (from 1726). In 1760, the turnbacks became white with white turnback tab.

WAISTCOAT: Red then white in 1760.

BUTTONS: Brass.

SHOULDER STRAP: White.

Inhaber
1726 *Crown Prince Francis Stephen Lorraine Duke of Lorraine* (1729), and *Emperor Francis I* (1745).
1765 *Emperor Joseph II*

Commanders
1752 *Leopold Freiherr von Lagelberg*
1758 *Engelberg Freiherr von Leuven*

Garrison
Pilsen in Bohemia (1755); Olmütz (1765)

Campaigns[113]
War of Austrian Succession: Present at Mollwitz (10 Apr 1741). In 1742 it fought at Chotusitz and the siege of Prague. In 1743-44, the regiment was on the Rhine then Bohemia. In 1745 it fought at Hohenfriedberg (4 June) and Soor.

Seven Years War Fought at Lobositz (1 Oct 1756), Prague (6 May 1757), and two companies participated in the siege and storm of Schweidnitz. The regiment suffered heavy losses at Breslau (22 Nov 1757) and Leuthen. In 1758 at Hochkirch, its commander, Leopold Freiherr von Lagelberg was killed. Detachments were present at the defence of Olmütz (28 May-2 July 1758) and the whole regiment at Hochkirch (14 Oct 1758). In 1760, the regiment was distinguished in the sorties from Dresden. This regiment was almost wiped out at Torgau (3 Nov) by the Bayreuth Dragoons and in July 1761 it was described as being almost entirely made up of recruits.[114]

1762 Albertini

IR1

---

[113] Thürheim (1880) I: 2, Wrede I-120

IR7 Neipperg

The regiment was raised in 1691. The regiment was generally considered unfortunate in combat.[115] In 1918, IR8 Graf Kevenhuller.

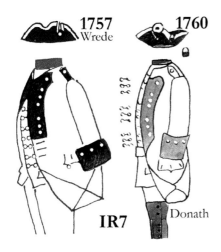

1757 Wrede

1760

IR7 Donath

POM-POMS: None.
COAT: Blue cuffs and lapels. White turnbacks.
WAISTCOAT: White.
BUTTONS: White then brass by 1762.
SHOULDER STRAP: Blue then white in 1760.

Inhaber
1691 *Wilhelm Notger Graf von Oettingen-Baldern*
1692 *Johann Ferdinand Frhr. Pfeffershofen*
1700 *Eberhard Frhr. Neipperg*
1740 *Wilhelm Reinhard Freiherr von Neipperg* (Vice-President of the *Hofkriegsrat*) – d. 1774)
1774 *Franz Xavier Graf Harrach* (d. 1781)

Commander
1750 *Heinrich Voith von Salzburg*
1757 *Adolph Frhr. von Pfuhl*
1760 *Wilhelm Frhr. von Schröder*

Garrison
1754 Troppau; 1763 Leipnik (Lipník nad Bečvou)

Campaigns[116]
War of Austrian Succession. In 1741-42, part of *Corps Khevenhüller* in the winter expedition to Upper Austria and Bavaria then the siege of Prague. In 1744 it was on the Rhine and Bohemia. In 1745 it fought at Habelschwert (1 Feb), Hohenfriedberg (4 June) and Trautenau (30 Sept). In 1747, in the Netherlands at Lawfeld (2 July).

Seven Years War In 1757, fought at Kolin (18 June), Breslau (22 Nov) (I-III Bns) and Leuthen (5 Dec) where it took heavy casualties. In 1758, only the Grenadiers were present at Hochkirch. In 1760, the regiment was ridden down by the Bayreuth Dragoons at Torgau (3 Nov) where it suffered the third highest infantry losses. Re-raised as a result in Moravia in 1761 and later fought at Burkersdorf (20-21 July 1762).

1762 Albertini

IR7

[114] Duffy (2008) 428
[115] Duffy (2008) 429
[116] Thürheim (1880) I: 29

IR8 Hildburghausen

The regiment was raised in 1647. A consistently good infantry regiment.[117] In 1918, IR8 Erzherzog Carl Stephan.

POM-POMS: Red rosettes.
COAT: Scarlet cuffs, lapels and turnbacks from 1732. The turnbacks became white in 1760.
WAISTCOAT: Scarlet the white in 1760.
BUTTONS: Brass.
SHOULDER STRAP: White.

1757 Wrede

1760

Donath

IR8

Inhaber
1647 *Johann Reichardt Graf Starhemberg* (d. 1661)
1661 *Hubert Marchese Pio di Savoya*
1676 *Prosper Graf Arco* (d. 1679)
1679 *Max Laurenz Graf Starhemberg*
1689 *Philipp Frhr. von Chizzola* 1691 *Leonhard Alexander Frhr. von Lapaczek* (d. 1700)
1700 *Nikolaus Graf Pálffy* (d. 1732)
1732 *Joseph Friedrich Prinz von Sachsen-Hildburghausen*
1787 *Carl Graf Pallavicini* (d. 1789)

Commanders
1752 *Friedrich Freiherr von Bülow*
1758 *Caspar Freiherr von Treys*

Garrison
1755 Prague in Bohemia; 1763 Gross-Meseritsch (Velké Meziříčí)

Campaign[118]
War of Austrian Succession. In 1742, part of Khevenhüller's winter expedition to Upper Austria and Bavaria. In 1743, at Simbach (9 March). In 1744 it was on the Rhine. In 1745 it was at Pfaffenhofen. In 1746 transferred to Italy where it participated in Graf *Corps Browne* invasion of Provence. In 1747 it was at the siege of Genoa.

Seven Years War Fought at Lobositz (1 Oct 1756). In 1757 it fought at Prague (6 May), Breslau (22 Nov) and received heavy casualties at Leuthen (5 Dec). Good record at Hochkirch (1758). In 1759, transferred to the *Reichsarmee* where it fought at Meissen (21 Sept) and Maxen (20 Nov) and the defence of Dresden. In 1760 it counterattacked together with IR2 Erzherzog Carl at Torgau (3 Nov). In 1761, the three Bns were at the siege of Glatz. In 1762, the regiment was part of the *Reichsarmee* in Saxony and present at Freiberg (29 Oct).

1762 Albertini

IR8

[117] Duffy (2008) 429
[118] Thürheim (1880) I: 37

IR12 Botta

The regiment was formed as the *Wolfenbüttel Regiment* in 1702 and entered Austrian service in 1712. In 1918, IR12 Parmann.

1757 Wrede **1760**

Donath

IR12

POM-POM: White
COAT: Blue cuffs, lapels and turnbacks. White turnbacks with blue turnback tab in 1757.
WAISTCOAT: Blue then white c1762.
BUTTONS: Brass.
SHOULDER STRAP: Bright blue.

Inhaber
1702 *Duke Adolf August von Holstein-Plön*
1704 *Dominik Frhr. D'Arnant Hubert, Graf de Sain*
1728 *Christof Bernhard Frhr. von Kettler* (d. 1734)
1734 *Franz Ignaz Graf Rumpf* (d. 1745)
1736 *Gottfried Ernst Frhr. von Wuttgenau* (d. 1739)
1739 *Anton Otto Marquis Botta d'Adorno* (d. 1775)
1775 *Johann Josef Graf Khevenhüller-Metsch* (d. 1792)

Commander
1755 *Karl Ulrich Fürst Kinsky*
1757 *Friedrich Freiherr von Elmendorf*
1760 *Franz von Lattermann*

Garrison
Prossnitz (Prostějov), Moravia (1755); Kaurim (1765).

Campaigns[119]
War of Austrian Succession. In 1741, there were 10 coys in Neisse Fortress. The Regiment fought at Mollwitz (10 Apr). The III Bn and Grenadiers garrisoned Brieg that capitulated on 4 May. In 1742 it was present at the siege of Prague. In 1743 it campaigned on the Rhine. In 1745, the regiment fought at Hohenfriedberg (4 June) and Trautenau (30 Sept) before transferring to the Netherlands. The regiment took part in battles of Rocoux (11 Oct 1746) and Lawfeld (2 July 1747). One Bn was at the siege of Maastricht.

1762 Albertini

IR12

Seven Years War In 1757, at Kolin (18 June) held the line against the Prussian breakthrough. The grenadiers were present at the storm of Gabel (14-15 July) and Koischwitz (26 Sept). Four companies were at the siege of Schweidnitz. The regiment fought at Breslau (22 Nov) and Leuthen (5 Dec). The regiment lost 20 officers and 600 men as prisoners on the surrender of Breslau. In 1758, at Hochkirch (14 Oct) and Dresden (29 Oct). In 1759, large detachments were captured at Pretzch (29 Oct). The grenadiers were present at Maxen (20 Nov). In 1760, the regiment was present at Torgau (3 Nov). In 1761, one Bn was at the storm of Schweidnitz (1 Oct) and participated in its defence the next year. In 1762, the regiment fought at Fischerberg (18 Aug).

---

[119] Thürheim (1880) I: 66-67

IR20 Alt-Colloredo

1743-56   **1757**

Brauer

The regiment was raised in 1681. It was known as Alt-Colloredo after 1754 to distinguish it from IR40. In 1918, IR20 Heinrich Prinz von Preussen.

POM-POM: White-blue
COAT: 1740 blue, In 1743 red, 1757 blue cuffs and lapels. White turnbacks with blue tab.
WAISTCOAT: White.
BUTTONS: Brass.
SHOULDER STRAP: Blue

Inhaber
1682 *Prinz Johann Ludwig Anton von Pfalz-Neuburg*
1694 *Hans Carl Graf von Thüngen* (d. 1709)
1710 *Friedrich Wilhelm Prinz von Holstein-Beck*
1719 *Johann Friedrich Graf Diesbach*
1744 *Anton Graf Colloredo zu Waldsee*
1785 *Franz Wenzel Graf Kaunitz-Reitberg*

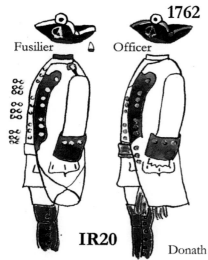

1762

Fusilier   Officer

IR20

Donath

Commander[120]
1754 *Franz Graf Lacy*
1757 *August Anton Fürst Lobkowitz*
1762 *Blasius Columbanus von Bender*
1769 *Anton Gazzinelli*

Garrison
1752 Mons; 1763 Loeben

1762
Albertini

IR20

[120] Wrede I: 257

Campaigns[121]

War of Austrian Succession: In 1742, part of the Winter Expedition in Upper Austria and Bavaria. In 1743, transferred to Italy and fought at Campo Santo. On 8 Feb 1744 it was part of the invasion of Naples. In 1746, the regiment fought at Rottofreddo, the expedition to Genoa and the invasion of Provence. In 1747 it was present at the siege of Genoa and action at Exilés.

Seven Years War In 1756, fought at Lobositz (1 Oct). In 1757 at Moys, Prague (6 May), Görlitz, and Breslau (22 Nov). The whole regiment was lost at the surrender of Breslau (Dec 1757). In 1758 it was raised anew and was distinguished at Hochkirch (14 Oct). Took part in Lacy's raid on Berlin, present at Torgau (3 Nov 1760) and Reichenbach. In 1762 a battalion was distinguished in the siege of Dresden and a detachment was at the siege of Schweidnitz.

Inf.-Regt. Alt-Colloredo

Grenadier   Trommler   Füsilier

IR20 Alt-Colloredo, c1760

---

[121] Thürheim (1880) I: 125

IR22 Lacy

Formed in 1709. In 1918, IR22 Graf von Lacy.

POM-POM: Yellow-red-white pom-pom.
COAT: Red collar, cuffs and turnbacks then white turnbacks with red tab in 1760.
WAISTCOAT: Blue then white in 1760.
BUTTONS: Brass.
SHOULDER STRAP: Red

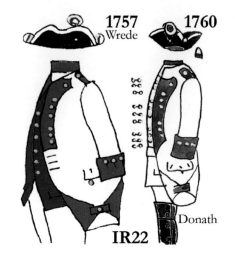

1757 Wrede 1760

IR22 Donath

Inhaber
1709 *Engelhart von Plischau* (d. 1717)
1717 *Franz Carl Laimpruch Frhr. zu Eppurg*
1723 *Albrecht Wolfgang Markgraf zu Brandenburg-Culmbach* (k. at Parma (29 June 1734))
1734 *Heinrich Jakob Frhr. von Suckow* (d. 1740)
1741 *Wilhelm Moriz Frhr. von Roth* (d. 1747)
1748 *Jacob Ignato Freiherr von Hagenbach* (d. 1756)
1757 *Salamon* (or *Simon*) *Sprecher von Bernegg*
1758 *Franz Moritz Graf von Lacy* (*Lascy* or *Lacey*)
1802 *Friedrich Josias Prinz zu Sachsen-Coburg-Saalfeld*
Commander
1750 *Valentin Freiherr von Browne*
1757 *Carl Freiherr von Elrichshausen*
1759 *Joseph Graf Colleredo-Waldsee*

Garrison:
1750 Cremona; 1756 Lombardy; 1763 Znayn

Campaign[122]
War of Austrian Succession: From 1740-43 in Italy. In 1744 it was involved in the enterprise to Naples. In 1746 it fought at Rottofreddo and the siege of Genoa then the expedition to Provence. In 1747, the regiment was at the siege of Genoa.

Seven Years War In 1757, one Bn participated in the raid on Hirschfeld (20 Feb), fought at Prague (6 May), Moys (7 Sept) and Breslau (22 Nov). Captured at the fall of Breslau (Dec 1757). In 1758, the regiment was raised anew and one Bn took part in the siege of Neisse. In 1759, at Dommitzch (25 Oct). In 1760, at Liegnitz, participated in Lacy's raid on Berlin and Torgau (3 Nov). In 1761 it campaigned in Saxony. In 1762, present at Burkersdorf (20-21 July). A detachment was part of the defence of Schweidnitz.

1762 Albertini

IR22

---

[122] Thürheim (1880) I: 140

IR29 Alt-Wolfenbüttel

Raised in 1709 from five companies of IR11 Hasslinger and the disbanded Wirich-Daun IR.[123] Should not be confused with the Loudon Green Grenadiers when Loudon became its Inhaber.

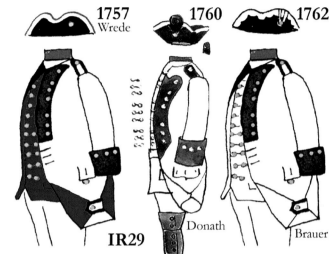

HEADWEAR: No pom-pom. In 1760, blue with red centre pom-pom. By 1762, the tricorn had white scalloped lace.
COAT: Blue cuffs, lapels and turnbacks. In 1760 white turnbacks.
SHOULDER STRAP: Blue
TURNBACKS: White with white turnback tab edged blue
BUTTONS: Yellow

Inhaber
1704 *Johann Adam Graf De Wend*
1709 *Ferdinand Albert Herzog von Braunschweig-Wolfenbüttel-Bevern*
1736 *Carl Herzog von Braunschweig-Wolfenbüttel*
1760 *Gideon Ernst Graf von Loudon* (d. 1790)
1791 *Olivier Remigius Graf Wallis* (d. 1799)

Commander
1752 *Friedrich Freiherr von Müffling*
1758 *Johann Marchese Botta d'Adorno*
1761 *Patrick Olivier Graf Wallis*

Garrison
1755 Brüx; 1763 Tschaslau in central Bohemia

Campaigns[124]
War of Austrian Succession: In 1742, at the siege of Prague. In 1743, the regiment was in Bavaria. In 1745 it was part of Traun's Army on the Main before transferring to Italy.

Seven Years War In 1756, present at Lobositz (1 Oct). In 1757, the regiment was at Reichenberg (21 Apr), Prague (6 May), at Breslau (22 Nov) in the attack on the redoubts of Schmiedefeld and Leuthen (5 Dec) where it suffered heavy losses. In 1758 it fought at Gundersdorf and Domstadtl (28-30 June) where it played a prominent role capturing 2 guns and at Hochkirch (14 Oct). A detachment was captured at the capitulation of Schweidnitz (16 Apr). In 1759, present at Meissen (2-3 Dec). In 1760, at Landeshut (23 June), Liegnitz (15 Aug). In 1761, a Bn was at the storm of Schweidnitz (1 Oct). In 1762 it was present at Burkersdorf (21 July) and Leutmannsdorf. A detachment was lost of Schweidnitz.

---
[123] Thürheim (1880) I: 187
[124] Thürheim (1880) I: 188

IR40 Jung (Karl) Colloredo

The regiment was raised in 1733. On 9 July 1761, *FM Daun* reported that the regiment was in a poor state being made up of mainly new recruits.[125]

POM-POM:
White with light blue centre
COAT: Blue cuffs and lapels. White turnbacks with blue badge.
WAISTCOAT: White.
BUTTONS: Brass.
SHOULDER STRAP: White

1757 Wrede

1760 Fusilier

1760 Drummer

1762 Drummer

IR40

Donath

Inhaber
1733 *Wolfgang Sigmund Frhr. von Damnitz*
1754 *Carl Borromaus Graf Colloredo-Waldsee*
1786 *Josef Graf Mitrowsky* (d. 1808)

Commander
1754 *Franz Fürst Sulkowski*
1758 *Carl Freiherr von Stein*
1763 *Friedrich Freiherr Haller von Hallerstein*

Garrison
1752 *Mons*; 1763 *Loeben*

Campaigns[126]
War of Austrian Succession: In 1742, siege of Freiburg. In 1745, the regiment was at Trautenau (30 Sept) where it was shattered by the Prussian CR9 Bornstadt Cuirassier Regiment.

Seven Years War In 1756, most distinguished at Lobositz under Franz Moritz Lacy. In 1757 it fought at Prague (6 May), Moys (7 Sept), a detachment with Hadik's raid on Berlin. In 1758 it was assigned to the *Reichsarmee*. In 1759 it fought at Pretzch and Maxen (20 Nov). In 1760 it was distinguished at Torgau (3 Nov). In 1761 it was with the main Army. In 1762, the regiment fought at Freiberg.

1762 Albertini

IR40

[125] Duffy (2008) 435
[126] Thürheim (1880) I: 268-9

IR56 Mercy

In 1684, formed 10 companies with a total of 1500 men in Breslau. Also known as Merci-Argenteau.

POM-POM: Blue
COAT: Blue cuffs and lapels. White with dark blue tab.
WAISTCOAT: White.
BUTTONS: Brass
SHOULDER STRAP: Blue

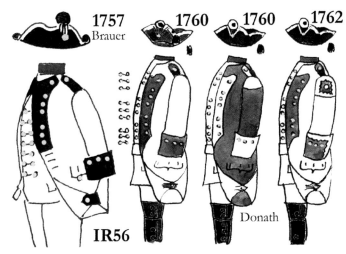

1757 Brauer

1760

1760

1762

Donath

IR56

Inhaber
1684 *Paul Anton Frhr. von Houchin* (d. 1699)
1690 *Philipp Wirch Graf von Daun* (d. 1771)
1741 *Antoine Graf Merci-Argenteau* (d. 1767)
1767 *Jakob Graf Nugent* (d. 1784)

Commander
1750 *Johann Jakob Graf Herberstein*
1758 *Leopold Freiherr von Stain*
1763 *Joseph Freiherr von Dreschel*

Garrison
1748 Milan and Lodi; 1763 Peterwardein (Petrovaradin)

Campaigns[127]
War of Austrian Succession: In 1741, at Mollwitz (10 Apr). In 1742, the regiment was at Sahay (25 May) and siege of Prague. In 1743 it was in Bavaria and in 1744 in Bohemia. In 1745 it was at Pfaffenhofen (15 Apr). In 1746, in Italy at siege of Genoa and in December part of the invasion of Provence.

Seven Years War In 1757, fought at Reichenberg (21 Apr), I-II Bn & grenadiers at Prague (6 May), III Bn at Kolin (18 June), Moys (7 Sept), storm of Schweidnitz (11 Nov), Breslau (22 Nov) and Leuthen (5 Dec) where it stood outside the village before it ran away. In 1758 it was present at the siege of Neisse and Hochkirch (I-III Bn). In 1759 it was with the main army. In 1760, the regiment was distinguished at Torgau (3 Nov) where it received heavy losses. In 1761, one battalion was present at the Loudon's storm of Schweidnitz. In 1762 it was at Leutmannsdorf and Burkersdorf (20-21 July). The whole regiment was at Reichenbach. A detachment of 200 men was at the defence of Schweidnitz.

1762 Albertini

IR56

---

[127] Thürheim (1880) I: 382-3

Chapter 11
Italian Infantry

Italy was administered through Italian viceroys. It included the Duchy of Lombardy, Duchy of Mantua and Tuscany.

**Map 9:
Lombardy and
Tuscany**
Stephen Summerfield,
2014

OOB 9: Infantry Regiments in Italy, June 1756.

LOMBARDY
Infantry Regiments (I-II, Grenadiers and Garrison Bn)

IR15 Pallavicini	2,000	
IR16 Königsegg	2,000	
IR22 Hagenbach	2,000	
IR24 Starhemberg	2,000	
IR56 Mercy	2,000	
IR57 Andlau	2,000	12,000

Infantry Regiments (I-II, Grenadiers)

IR19 Leopold Pálffy	1,570	
IR32 Forgách	1,581	
IR34 Batthyány	1,550	
IR51 Gyulai	1,463	

Dragoon Regiments (6+1 depot squadrons)

DR5 Jung-Modena Dragoons	600	600

FRIULI

IR52 Bethlen 1,548	1,548	
		14,148

Duchy of Lombardy became Austrian territory in 1713 with its capital being *Milan*. Napoleon conquered Lombardy in 1796 which became the *Cisalpine Republic* and in 1806, the *Kingdom of Italy*. The Congress of Vienna returned Lombardy to Austria in 1815.

Kingdom of Tuscany was acquired in exchange for Lorraine in 1736 just three months after *Francis Stephen of Lorraine* married *Maria Theresa*.

IR48 c1760

In summer of 1756, the two national-Italian regiments stationed in Italy had fusilier companies of only 3 officers and only 113 men due to lack of recruits. This gave battalion strength of 18 officers and 678 men.

IR48 c1756

IR44 Clerici

The regiment was raised in 1744 by Antonio Marquis Clerici at his own cost. It had a dashing reputation from the outset. Interestingly, this regiment in 1859, proved the most loyal of the Milanese regiments with many re-engaged by the Austrians after Milan was lost.[128]

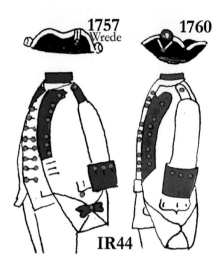

1757 Wrede

1760

IR44

POM-POM: None then red with yellow centre in 1760.

COAT: Red cuffs and lapels. White with red turnback badge.

BUTTONS: Brass

SHOULDER STRAP: Red then white.

Inhaber
1744 *Anton Georg Marquis Clerici* (d. 1768)
1769 *Rudolf Carl Graf Gaisrück* (d. 1778)

Commander
1745 *Ascano Graf Cocogna*
1752 *Franz Frbr. von Valentini*
1758 *Francesco de Feretti*
1771 *Antonio Lombardi*

Garrison:
1756 *Hungary* and *Banat*.

Campaigns[129]

War of Austrian Succession: In 1744 it was at Coni (30 Sept). In 1745 it was stationed in Bassignana, Piedmont, Italy. In 1746-47 it was stationed in Mantua.

Seven Years War In 1757, fought at Schweidnitz, Breslau (22 Nov), Leuthen (5 Dec). In 1758 it was at Hochkirch (14 Oct) where it received the heaviest losses of any regiment during its unsuccessful attacks upon the churchyard. Its brutal commander, Obrist Valentini was mortally wounded. In 1759, the regiment was surprised at Hoyerswerda (29 Sept 1759). Fought at Pretzch (29 Oct) and Maxen (20 Nov). In 1761-62, the regiment suffered heavy desertion.

---

[128] Duffy (2008) 436
[129] Thürheim (1880) I: 294-5

IR48 Luzan

Italian national regiment recruited in Austrian Lombardy, Görz (Gorizia) and Gradisca. During the Seven Years War it suffered the sixth highest desertion at 1078 men with a large number of raw recruits 1761-62.[130] Disbanded in 1795 after France had taken Lombardy.

POM-POM: None
COAT: Green cuffs, lapels and turnbacks. In 1760, white turnbacks.
WAISTCOAT: Green then white in 1760.
BUTTONS: Brass.
SHOULDER STRAP: Green then white in 1760.

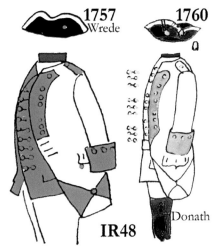

IR48

1757 Wrede   1760   Donath

Inhaber
1721 *Anton Graf Alcaudete, Marchese di Portugalo*
1734 Johann Jakob *Vasquez de Pinas*
1755 *Emanuel Graf Luzan*
1765 *Joseph Heinrich Frhr. Ried*

Commanders
1722 *Bartgolomäus Valparaiso, Marchese d'Andia*
1727 *Graf Scotti*
1739 *Obrist Bulvarini*
1744 *Emanuel Graf Luzan*
1748 *Anton Marchese Velasco*
1754 *Heinrich Frhr. von Uracca*
1757 *Guido von Bagno*
1758 *Carl Marchese Gaggi*
1770 *Christoph Graf Migazzi zu Wall-Sonnenthurm*

Garrison:
Banat (1721-36), Hermannstadt (1739), Peterwardein (1746), Esseg (1748), Temesvar (1750), Essegg (1753), Temesvár (1755) and Cremona (1763).

Campaigns
War of Austrian Succession: In 1743, I-II Bn and Grenadiers were with the army in Bavaria and III Bn was in Italy. In 1744 it participated in the invasion of Naples.

Seven Years War In 1757, I-II Bn and Grenadiers were in Bohemia where it was present at Schweidnitz, Breslau (22 Nov 1757) and Leuthen. In 1758, at Hochkirch (14 Oct). In 1759, the regiment was with the Main Army. In 1760, one Bn participated in the defence of Dresden (1760). In 1761 it was with the main army. In 1762, the regiment was in Saxony fighting at Döbeln and Pretzschendorf.

1762 Albertini

IR48

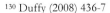

[130] Duffy (2008) 436-7

Chapter 12
Netherlands Infantry

Immediately following the French defeat at Ramillies in 1706, many from Belgium loyal to Philip V of Bourbon went over to Spain. Others, sickened by the greed and taxation of Louis XIV in the Low Countries to support his grandson's forces, formed seven infantry (Sart, Claude de Ligne, Los Rios, Hartog, Maldeghem, Lannoy and Pancarlier), two dragoon (Ligne and Holstein-Norburg) and one heavy cavalry regiments (Westerloo) in the national army of Charles of Habsburg in opposition to Philip V of Spain.

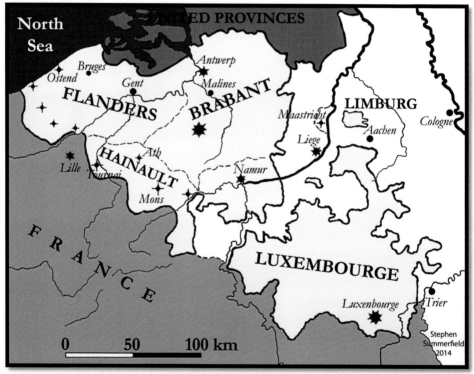

Map 10: Austrian Netherlands and Luxembourg
Stephen Summerfield, 2014

The Treaty of Utrecht (1713) that ended the War of Spanish Succession ceded the Spanish Netherlands to Austria. It was only after negotiation with the Dutch Republic was completed with the Barrier Treaty of 15 November 1715 that the greatly reduced **Austrian Netherlands** was handed over that comprised of 11 provinces.[131] The principle goal of Habsburg rulers was to exchange the Austrian Netherlands for Bavaria that would consolidate the Habsburg possessions in southern Germany. In 1725, the Netherlands National Regiments were incorporated into the Austrian army in the Low Countries.

---

[131] Hochedlinger (2003) 222-4

By the 1757 Treaty of Versailles, Austria agreed to the creation of an independent state in the Southern Netherlands ruled by Duke Philip of Parma and garrisoned by French troops in exchange for French help in recovering Silesia. The four Walloon infantry battalions attached to the French army in 1757 were from IR9, 30, 38, and 58. These took to the field with only 5 companies each of 2 officers and 112 men plus a single grenadier company of 90 grenadiers. This agreement was revoked by the Third Treaty of Versailles just a year later. The Walloon Infantry Regiments had 3 battalions of 4 companies each throughout most of the Seven Years War. During the course of the war, their garrison battalions were disbanded due to insufficient replacements. It is interesting that the Walloon Infantry suffered among the lowest desertion rates of the infantry.

OOB 10: Regiments in the Netherlands, June 1756.

Walloon Infantry Regiments (I-II, Grenadiers and Garrison Bn)

IR9 Los Rios	2,000	
IR30 Sachsen-Gotha	2,000	
IR38 de Ligne	2,000	
IR55 d'Arberg	2,000	8,000

German Infantry Regiments (I-II, Grenadiers and Garrison Bn)

IR3 Lothringen	2,000	
IR14 Salm	2,000	
IR28 Wied	2,000	
IR40 Jung-(Karl) Colloredo,	2,000	
IR41 Bayreuth	2,000	
IR43 Platz	2,000	12,000

Cavalry Regiments (6+1 depot squadrons)

KR11 Anhalt-Zerbst	800	
DR9 de Ligne 1,000	1,800	
		21,800

1760

Fusilier   Feldwebel   Officer   Grenadier   Drummer

IR38

Donath

IR9 Los Rios

This Walloon regiment first served in the Dutch service at Oudenaarde (1708) and Malplaquet (1709). In May 1725, transferred into Austrian service and recruited in the Netherlands and Liege. During the Seven Years War, it suffered the lowest infantry desertion rate of only 224 men.[132]

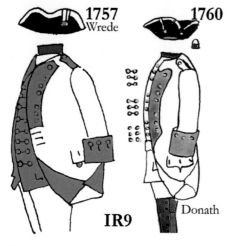

1757 Wrede

1760 Donath

IR9

POM-POM: None
COAT: Apple green cuffs, lapels and turnbacks. In 1760, the turnbacks were white.
WAISTCOAT: Apple green waistcoat and in 1760 white.
BUTTONS: Brass.
SHOULDER STRAP: Apple green

Inhaber
1725 *Francesco Gutierrez, Marquis Los Rios*
1775 *Carl Graf Clerfait* (d. 1798)

Commanders
1756 *Franz Marquis Los Rios de Gutierrez*
1757 *Joseph Murray de Melgum*
1761 *Franz Fürst Gavre d'Aiseau*

Garrison
1748-56 Brussels and Bruges; 1763 Mons.

Campaigns[133]
War of Austrian Succession: In 1743, at Dettingen (27 June). In 1744 it was part of Arenberg Corps. In 1745, the regiment was in Traun's Army. In 1746, campaigned along the Main Valley at Rocoux (11 Oct) and Lawfeld (2 July 1747).

Seven Years War In 1757, the III (garrison) Bn was part of the Austrian Contingent sent to the assistance the French for the invasion of Hanover. It occupied Wesel before participating in the blockade of Guelders and was present at Hastenbeck (1757). In 1758, the III Bn was recalled to reinforce the Austrian army in Bohemia. The I-II Bns fought at Prague where it received heavy losses during the counterattack. In 1757 it performed well at Kolin (18 June), Moys (7 Sept), Breslau (22 Nov) and Leuthen (5 Dec). In 1758 it was at Hochkirch. In 1759, after Kunersdorf (12 Aug) reduced to only one Bn for the rest of the war due to the cumulative losses and problems of obtaining recruits from the Netherlands. Fought at Czenstochowa (1759), Landshut, Liegnitz (1760), Reichenbach (16 Aug 1762) and the defence of Schweidnitz (8 Aug-9 Oct 1762).

1762 Albertini

IR9

---

[132] Duffy (2000) 446
[133] Thürheim (1880) I: 43-44

IR30 Sachsen-Gotha

The regiment was raised on 1 May 1725 from the Netherlands National Regiments of Pancarlier, Lannoy and Maldeghem.[134] During the Seven Years War it suffered the lowest desertion rate of only 268 men.[135]

1757 **1758**

IR30 Sachsen-Gotha

POM-POM: Red.
COAT: Red cuffs, lapels and turnbacks until 1757 then blue cuffs, lapels and turnbacks in 1758 and by 1762 blue cuffs and lapels with white turnbacks.
WAISTCOAT: Red then blue (1758) and by 1762, white waistcoat.
BUTTONS: Brass.
SHOULDER STRAP: White with red stripes.

Inhaber

1725 *Johann Anton Prie-Turinetti, Marquis de Pancarlier* (d. 1753)
1753 *Wilhelm Prinz von Sachsen-Gotha*
1771 *Prince Charles Joseph de Ligne* (d. 1814)

Commander

1752 *Franz Baxeras*
1758 *Joseph von Navarro*
1762 *Peter von Langlois*

Garrison

1749 Ostend and Bruges; 1763 Luxemburg.

Campaigns[136]

War of Austrian Succession. In 1742, in the Netherlands. In 1743, at Dettingen (27 June). In 1744 it garrisoned the Netherlands. In 1745, the regiment was at the siege of Dendermonde and Ostend. In 1747 it occupied Luxembourg castle.

Seven Years War In 1757, a Bn took part in Domstasle's contingent with the French Army at Hastenbeck (26 July). Another Bn was at Kolin, Moys (7 Sept), Breslau (22 Nov) and Leuthen. In 1759, at Hochkirch (14 Oct). In 1760, a Bn and the Grenadiers were at the siege of Dresden then at Strehlen (24 Aug), Torgau (27 Sept) and Wittenberg (2 Oct). In 1761, the grenadiers were distinguished at Loudon's storm of Schweidnitz. In 1762, the grenadiers lost 2 officers and 200 men when the magazine exploded which caused the capitulation of Schweidnitz.

1762
Albertini

IR30

---

[134] Thürheim (1880) I: 194
[135] Duffy (2000) 446
[136] Thürheim (1880) I: 194-5

IR38 de Ligne

The regiment was raised in 1725 from the Netherlands national Regiment. Disbanded in 1809.

1757

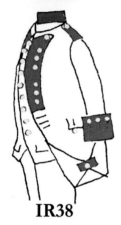

IR38

POM-POM: None
COAT: Pink cuffs and lapels.
TURNBACKS: White with pink turnback tab.
BUTTONS: White
SHOULDER STRAP: Pink.

Inhaber
1725 *Claude Lamoral Fürst de Ligne*
1766 *Carl Merode Marquis d'Ayne*

Commander
1725 *Leves Graf de Chanclos*
1730 *Jakob Graf Rumigny-Peyssant*
1748 *Herzog D'Ursel*
1752 *Max Graf Bournonville*
1760 *Carl Prinz de Ligne*
1764 *Nikolaus Graf D'Arberg*

Garrison
1733-35 Luxembourg; 1754 Bruges; 1763 Brussels

Campaigns[137]
War of Austrian Succession: In 1743, the I Bn was present at Dettingen. In 1744-5 it was stationed in Luxembourg. In 1746, one Bn and the grenadiers were at the siege of Mons. In 1747, I-II Bn was at Lawfeld.

Seven Years War
In 1756, I Bn and the grenadiers were in Bohemia. In 1757, one Bn was in Dombasle's contingent at Hastenbeck. In 1757, the rest of the regiment fought at Kolin (18 June) and Moys near Görlitz (7 Sept). In 1758, transferred to the Reichsarmee and was distinguished at Hochkirch (14 Oct). In 1759, Pretzch, Maxen (20 Nov). The III Bn was in Luxembourg. In 1760 it participated in Lacy's raid on Berlin. In 1761 it was with the main army. In 1762 it fought at Burkersdorf (20-21 July) and a detachment under Obrist-Lt Hörger in Schweidnitz.

1762
Albertini

IR38

[137] Wrede II: 237

IR55 D'Arberg

The regiment was raised in 9 May 1742 by Obrist Graf d'Arberg from the 1st Netherlands National Regiment. In 1747-48 it absorbed the Heister and Jung-Arenberg Regiments. In 1769 it received the regimental number 55. Disbanded in 1809.

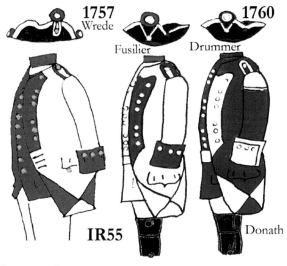

1757 Wrede

Fusilier

1760 Drummer

IR55

Donath

POM-POM: Red with white centre.
COAT: Red cuffs, lapels and turnbacks then white turnbacks in 1760.
WAISTCOAT: Red then white in 1760.
BUTTONS: White then Brass in 1760.
SHOULDER STRAP: White edged red.

Inhaber
1746 *Carl Anton Graf d'Arberg*
1768 *Joseph Graf Murray de Melgum*

Commander
1742 *Carl Graf D'Arberg*
1745 *Carl Herzog D'Ursel*
1748 *Gustav Prinz Stollberg-Geldern*
1755 *Graf Clarincini*
1757 *Philipp Graf Merode*
1759 *Hyppolit Chevalier Orlandini*
1760 *Carl Graf Vinchant de Gontreuil*
1769 *Nikolaus Graf D'Arberg*

Garrisons
1748 Netherlands, 1753 Bruges, 1764 Gent.

War Austrian Succession. In 1743, fought at Dettingen. In 1744 it was in the Netherlands. In 1745 it was at the siege of Nieuport.

Seven Years War I-II Bns arrived in Bohemia from the Netherlands in 1757 and fought at Prague, Moys, Breslau and Leuthen. III Bn was in Corps Dombasle at Hastenbeck. In 1759 it was with the main army in Saxony, fighting at Landeshut, Liegnitz, Adelsbach and Burkersdorf.

IR58 – Formed in 1756 and was transferred from French service in 1763.

1762 Albertini

IR55

Chapter 13
Kingdom of Hungary

In 1515, Ferdinand (brother to Charles who became Holy Roman Emperor in 1519) married the heir of the Kingdom of Hungary. In 1726, Ferdinand became the first Habsburg King of Hungary upon the death of King Louis II who was killed at Mohacs (29 Aug 1526) when the Hungarian Royal Army was destroyed by Sultan Suleiman I of Turkey (1494-1566). The Kingdom of Hungary was reduced to western and northern Hungary before this was conquered by the Turks in 1541.[138] The Kingdom of Hungary included Hungary, Transylvania (*Siebenbürgen*), Banat, Croatia and Slavonia.

1702   Officer, 1748   1756
Hungarian Infantry

---

[138] Rickett (1983) 23-33

The Habsburg Kings of Hungary ruled from Vienna through the *Hofrat* (Royal Council). The *Hofkammer* (Ministry of Finance) in Vienna remained the policy-making body for the government of Hungary through the Hungarian Chancellery. Its executive council in Buda was nominated by the king and had no connection with the diet that was responsible only for the voting of war taxes. The administration of the taxes and all other financial questions were in the hands of the *Kammer* (Treasury) that was answerable only to the Viennese *Hofkammer*.

Hungary suffered from being the main area of contention between the Christians and Turks for centuries. Only in 1699 were the Turks finally driven out of Hungary and Transylvania.

In 1703, the Hungarian rebels under Francis II Rákóczi (1676-1735) refused to recognize the Habsburg hereditary claim to the throne of Hungary or the separation of Transylvania from Hungary that was now directly ruled from Vienna. The Treaty of Szatmár (1711) did little to remove the grievances. The Hungarian Diet between 1715 and 1722 established a common Austro-Hungarian standing army to replace the poorly trained and disciplined Hungarian

Soldat   Offizier   Offizier u. Soldat   Offizier
v. Rgt. Kökényesdi   v. Rgt Ujváry   v. Trenk'schen Panduren-Corps   v. Rgt. Josef Esterházy
(heute No. 34).   (heute No. 2).   (heute No 53).   (heute No. 37).
1742.   1742.   1742.   1745.   1758.
Ungarische Infanterie.

Insurrectio. The population had fallen, the government was in chaos and the refused to pay Imperial taxes. Only nobles and the church owned land. The Esterhazy family held 7 million acres (2.83 million hectares) of land.[139]

Maria Theresa appealed for support from Hungary. In September 1741, the Hungarian *Landtag* voted to raise 13 infantry regiments in addition to the original three Hungarian regiments. However, there were only enough to raise five regiments and a sixth was raised in 1756.

---

[139] Durant (1965) IX: 431

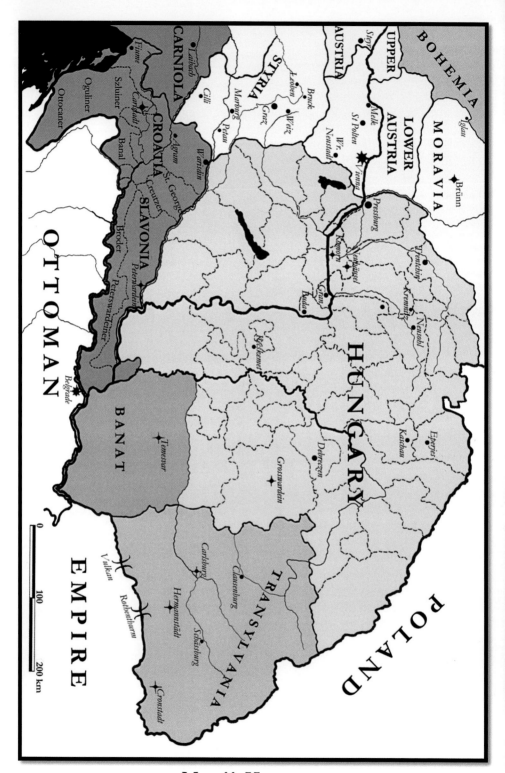

Map 11: Hungary
Stephen Summerfield, 2014

OOB 11: Regiments in Kingdom of Hungary, June 1756.

HUNGARY

Infantry Regiments (I-II, Grenadiers and Garrison Bn)

IR4 Deutschmeister	2355	
IR44 Clerici (in Hungary and Banat)	1918	4,272

Garrison Battalions

IR2 Erzherzog Karl	430	
IR19 Pálffy, Leopold	431	
IR31 Haller	460	
IR32 Forgách	419	
IR33 Nicolaus Esterhazy	430	
IR34 Batthyány	450	
IR37 Esterhazy, Joseph	430	
IR52 Bethlen	430	3,480

Cuirassier Regiments (6 + 1 depot squadrons)

KR3 Pálffy 771		
KR4 Birkenfeld	806	
KR5 Serbelloni	809	
KR6 Cordova	793	
KR7 Schmerzing	815	
KR8 Trautmansdorff	799	
KR9 Kalckreuth	795	
KR10 Birkenfeld	780	
KR13 Radicati	791	
KR14 Brettlach	780	
KR16 Gelhay	749	
KR17 Lucchesi	782	9,470

Dragoon Regiments (6 + 1 depot squadrons)

DR2 Liechtenstein	809	
DR4 Savoyen	807	
DR7 Hessen-Darmstadt	806	
DR8 Sachsen-Gotha	801	
DR10 Kollowrat	806	
DR12 Porporati	783	4,812

SLAVONIA AND BANAT

Infantry Regiments (I-II, Grenadiers and Garrison Bn)

IR23 Baden-Baden	2,350	
IR48 Luzan (Banat and Slavonia)	1,940	4,290

Cavalry Regiments

KR12 Emanuel Infant von Portugal (in Banat)	782	
DR13 Koharn	759	1,541

TRANSYLVANIA

Infantry Regiments

IR26 Puebla	2,388	
IR45 Heinrich Daun	2,263	4,651

Garrison Battalion

IR51 Gyulai	537	537

Cavalry Regiments

KR18 Herzog (Alt-) Modena	822	
DR11 Württemberg Dragoons	809	1,631

Hungarian Fusilier Uniform (1740-55)

Hungarian Fusilier and Officer, 1741-55
Courtesty of Dr. J. Sissak

Table 14: Hungarian Infantry Uniforms 1741-55

	Est.	Coat,	Facings	Waistcoat	Trousers
IR2	1741	Blue (1741)	Green	Blue	Blue
IR19	1734	White	Blue	Light blue	Light blue
IR31	1741	Dark blue	Dark blue	Light blue	Light blue
IR32	1741	Blue	Red	Light blue	Light blue
IR33	1741	Blue (1743)	Yellow	Blue	Blue
		White (1748)	Yellow	Blue	Blue
IR34	1733	Blue (1738)	Yellow	Blue	Blue
		White (1748)	Yellow	Blue	Blue
IR37	1741	White	Red	Red	Red
IR39	1756	Blue (1756)	Red	White	Red
IR51	1702	Blue (1738)	White	Blue	Blue
IR52	1741	White (1748)	Green	Green	White
IR53[140]	1741	Green (1744-46)	Red	Red	Red

---

[140] *Panduran-Corps* in 1741, renamed the *Trenck Panduren Regiment* in 1745 and reduced to a single battalion as the *Slavonisches Panduren Bn* in 1748 before finally being raised to a full regiment in 1757. In 1769, it received the Regimental Number of IR53.

Hungarian Fusilier Uniform (1755-65)

1762
Brauer

IR37

HEADGEAR: Black tricorn laced white and black cockade on the left. At the rear corners were bobs that often followed the facing colour. Some regiments had pom-poms. The sprig of green leaves was normally worn on campaign as the field sign. Simple cloth forage cap made from old coats was worn for manual work.

HAIR: Unpowdered queue at the rear, braids at the temple and moustaches for the rank and file.

STOCK: A red and a black fabric stock. For parades the regimental commanders agreed before on the colour of the neck-stocks.

COAT: White woollen collarless coat without lapels. The large square cuffs, turnbacks and button lace (Litzen) were in the facing colour. The shoulder strap was on the left shoulder only. The buttons were arranged one, two and three from the top of the coat, each had lace in the facing colour.

WAISTCOAT: Long skirted single or double breasted Hussar style waistcoat in the facing colour.

SASH: A barrel sash.

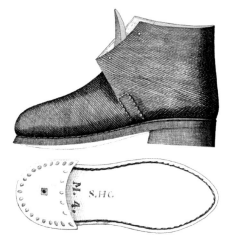

LEGWEAR: Breeches with Hungarian knots. Short black "Hungarian" boots instead of gaiters.

Hungarian infantryman's shoe
Contemporary drawing courtesy of Dr J. Sissak

Hungarian Trousers
Courtesy of Dr. J. Sissak

Table 15: Hungarian Infantry Uniforms in 1757 and 1762

		Coat	Cuffs	Turnbacks	Waistcoat	Trousers	Buttons
IR2	1757	Yellow	Yellow	Yellow	Dark blue	Brass
	1762						
IR19	1757	Blue	Blue	Blue	Light blue	Brass
	1762	Light blue	White	Light blue		
IR31	1757	Blue	Blue	Blue	Light blue	Brass
	1762	Light blue	Light blue	Light blue		
IR32	1757	Blue	Blue	Blue	Light blue	Brass
	1762	Light blue	Light blue	Light blue		
IR33	1757	Blue	Blue	Blue	Dark blue	Brass
	1762	Dark blue	Dark blue	Dark blue		
IR34	1757	Yellow	Blue	Yellow	Dark blue	Brass
	1762	Dark blue	Dark blue	Dark blue		
IR37	1757	Red	Red	Red	Red	Brass
	1762					
IR39	1756	Red	None	White	Red	White
	1758	Red	White	Red		
	1762	Red	Red	Red		
IR51	1757	Blue	Blue	Blue	Dark blue	Brass
	1762	Dark blue	Dark blue	Dark blue		
IR52	1756	Light green	Light green	Light green	Light blue	Brass
	1759	Light blue	Light Blue	Light blue		
IR53	1757	Red	Red	Red	Red	Brass
	1762					

EQUIPMENT: White leather belt over the left shoulder carrying a black cartridge box with a small brass plate carrying the initials "MT" was worn on the right hip. A white waist belt carrying the bayonet and sabre was worn under the coat. A narrow white belt for the calfskin knapsack was worn over the right shoulder. The drum or egg shaped canteen had a brown leather strap.

SIDEARMS: The M1745 musket for fusiliers with bayonet until they were replaced by the M1754 musket. Black bayonet scabbard and grenadier sabre.

Hungarian Fusilier and Grenadier, c1756
Courtesy of Dr. J. Sissak

Hungarian Fusilier NCO Uniform

HEADWEAR: Sergeants had gold hat lace and corporals had white hat lace to their black tricorns.

UNIFORM: As Fusiliers.

SIDEARMS: Sergeants carried a halberd (or half pike) until 1759, a wooden cane suspended from a coat button and grenadier sabre. Corporals had silver hat lace, a halberd until 1759 and a grenadier sabre.

Hungarian Fusilier Officer Uniform

HEADWEAR Tricorn laced gold or silver hat lace depending upon button colour.

STOCK: White cloth neck stock.

COAT: Similar cut to the other ranks but with finer cloth and no turnbacks. No shoulder strap.

SASH: Yellow and black silk sash.

FOOTWEAR: Short Hungarian boots in black leather.

SWAGGER STICKS: As German Fusiliers.

| IR2 Erzherzog Karl Officer | IR32 Forgach Officer | IR52 Bethlen Officer | IR53 Simbschen Officer |

Hungarian Infantry Officers
After Donath (1970) and Pengel (1982)

IR2 Erzherzog Karl

The regiment was raised in Western Hungary and Transylvania in 1741. An excellent regiment with a remarkable officer corps including the commentator *Jacob Cogniazzo* and *Lieutenant Waldhütter* who was an unlikely hero of Schweidnitz (8 Aug - 9 Oct 1762).[141]

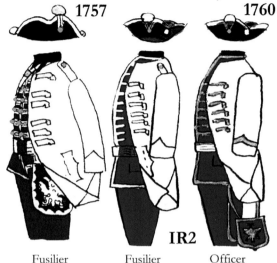

1757

1760

IR2

Fusilier   Fusilier   Officer

POM-POM: Yellow pom-pom
COAT: Yellow cuffs, buttonhole lace and turnbacks.
WAISTCOAT: Dark blue with yellow lace
BUTTONS: Brass
SASH: Yellow and dark blue barrel sash.
SHOULDER STRAP: One white.
GRENADIER CAP: Yellow bad with yellow piping and tassel.

Inhaber
1741 *Ladislaus Frhr. Ujvaryi* (d. 1749)
1749 *Erzherzog Karl Joseph* (d. 1761)
1762 *Erzherzog Ferdinand* (d. 24 Dec 1806)

Commander
1752 *Joseph Freiherr von Siskovics*
1757 *Joseph Freiherr von Kokenyesdy de Vettes* (killed at Breslau (22 Nov 1757))
1757 *Ignaz Szallaghi*
1760 *Joseph Freiherr Orosz von Csicser*

Garrison
1752 Olmütz in Moravia; 1763 Netherlands

Campaigns[142]
War of Austrian Succession. In 1743, at the siege of Ingolstadt. In 1744 it was present at the battle of Prague. In 1746 it transferred to the Netherlands and fought at Rocoux (11 Oct) and Lawfeld (2 July).

Seven Years War Distinguished at Kolin (18 June 1757) under Obrist Graf Siskowitz, Meuselwitz (8 Oct), siege of Schweidnitz, Breslau (22 Nov 1757), Leuthen (5 Dec 1757). In 1758 it was present at Domstadtl and Hochkirch. In 1760, suffered the heaviest losses at Torgau (3 Nov) resulting from its numerous counterattacks. The regiment was reformed in Bohemia before participating in the storming of Schweidnitz 1761). In 1762, a detachment was part of its defence before fighting at Burkersdorf.

1762
Albertini

IR2

---

[141] Duffy (2008) 429
[142] Thürheim (1880) I: 6-7

IR19 Pálffy

The regiment was formed in 1734 at the cost of the first *Inhaber*.

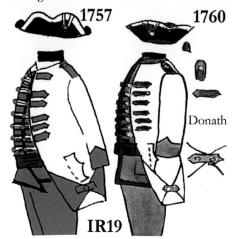

1757   1760

Donath

IR19

COAT: Medium blue cuffs, buttonhole lace and turnbacks. By 1760, the turnbacks were white.
WAISTCOAT: Medium blue with red lace.
BUTTONS: Brass and white metal by 1762 (Donath)
SHOULDER STRAP: Medium blue
SASH: Red barrel sash.
GRENADIER CAP: Medium blue bag with white piping and tassel

Inhaber
1734 *Leopold Graf Pálffy ab Erdöd*
1773 *Richard Graf d'Alton*

Commanders[143]
1736 *Leopold Frhr. von Andrassy*
1739 *Jakob Frhr. von Preysach*
1752 *Joseph Ziggan von Cserma*
1758 *Wolfgang Frhr. von Faber du Faur*
1767 *Leopold Schuller de Raad*

Garrison
1756 *Lombardy* with Garrison Bn in *Hungary*.

Campaigns[144]
War of Austrian Succession: In 1742, participated in the Winter Expedition in Upper Austria and Bavaria before transferring to Bohemia to fight at Chotusitz (17 May) and at the siege of Prague. In 1743 it was in Bavaria. In 1746 it was in Italy fighting at Rottofreddo and the siege of Genoa. III Bn was part of the invasion of Provence. In 1747, the regiment was at the siege of Genoa.

Seven Years War: In 1757, fought at Hirschfeld, Prague (6 May), Moys (7 Sept), distinguished at the siege of Schweidnitz, Breslau (22 Nov) and Leuthen (5 Dec). In 1758, at Hochkirch (14 Oct). In 1759 at Kunersdorf (12 Aug) and Troppau (18 Nov). In 1760 at Landshut and Liegnitz (15 Aug). In 1761, present at the storm of Schweidnitz and suffered heavy losses at Torgau.

---

[143] Wrede I: 249
[144] Thürheim (1880) I: 6-7

IR31 Haller

The regiment was raised on 1 November 1741 in Transylvania with strength of 1500 men in two battalions.[145]

POM-POM: White with blue centre.
COAT: Light blue cuffs, shoulder strap, buttonholes lace and turnbacks.
WAISTCOAT: Light blue with red lace. By 1762, light blue with yellow lace.
BUTTONS: Brass.
SASH: Red and light blue. By 1762, red and yellow.
GRENADIER CAP: Medium blue bag with white piping and tassel.

Inhaber
1741 *Samuel Frhr. Haller von Hallerstein*
1777 *Anton Graf Esterhazy de Galantha*

Commanders
1754 *Franz Deseö*
1758 Johann Graf Rhedey
1760 *Sigmund von Kerekes*
1769 *Joseph Georg Browne.*

Garrison
1756 Moravia with Garrison Bn in Hungary.

Campaign[146]
War of Austrian Succession. In 1742, campaigned in Bohemia and was present at the siege of Prague. In 1744, in Bohemia. In 1745, transferred to the Netherlands being present at Rocoux (1746), Lawfeld (1747) and the siege of Maastricht (1748).

Seven Years War In 1757, the grenadiers showed great bravery at Reichenberg (21 Apr). The regiment was distinguished at Kolin (18 June) losing 689 dead and Obrist Deszö, Major Kerekes, 27 Officers and 906 men wounded. Present at Gabel, Zittau (5 Sept) and Moys (7 Sept). A detachment was part of the defence of Schweidnitz, Breslau (22 Nov). The regiment fought at Breslau and Leuthen (5 Dec). In 1758, participated in the ambush at Gundersdorf and Domstadtl, fought at Hochkirch (14 Oct) where it stormed a redoubt and lost 500 men, and at Maxen (20 Nov 1759). In 1760, part of the expedition to Berlin and fought at Torgau (3 Nov). In 1762, the Regiment was at Burkersdorf (21 July) and a detachment at the defence of Schweidnitz.

---

[145] Thürheim (1880) I: 201
[146] Thürheim (1880) I: 201-2

IR32 Forgách

Raised in 1741 in Hungary.

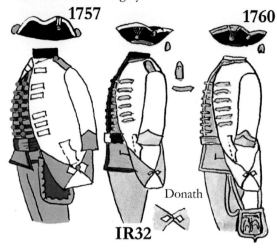

1757   **1760**

Donath

IR32

POM-POM: None thee by 1762 light blue.
COAT: Light blue cuffs, shoulder strap and turnbacks with white diamond badge. White buttonhole lace.
WAISTCOAT: Bright blue with red lace
BUTTONS: Brass
SASH: Red and bright blue barrel sash.
GRENADIER CAP: Medium blue bag with yellow piping and tassel

Inhaber
1741 *Ignaz Graf Forgách de Ghymies*
1773 *Samuel Graf Gyulai* (d. 1802)

Commanders
1754 *Friedrich Frhr. von Altkirchen*
1768 *Anton Graf Grisoni*

Garrison
Lombardy with Garrison Bn in *Hungary* (1756).

Campaigns[147]
War of Austrian Succession: In 1743, at the siege of Ingolstadt. In 1744, at Lautenberg (4 July) and Weissenberg (5 July). In 1745 it was on the Main before transferring to Italy. In 1746 it was at Piacenza, the siege of Genoa and participated in the invasion of Provence. In 1747, at Exilles it captured the French General Chevalier Belle Isle.

Seven Years War In 1757, present at Prague (7 July), Moys (7 Sept), a battalion surrendered at Schweidnitz, Breslau (22 Nov) and Leuthen (5 Dec). In 1758, the regiment fought at Hochkirch and Maxen. It suffered heavy losses at Torgau and Liegnitz (15 Aug 1760). In 1761, one battalion was distinguished at Loudon's storm of Schweidnitz (1 Oct). In 1762, at Fischerberg (16 Aug).

1762
Albertini

IR32

---

[147] Thürheim (1880) I: 209

IR33 Nicolaus Esterhazy

The regiment was raised in 1741. A hard fighting regiment.[148]

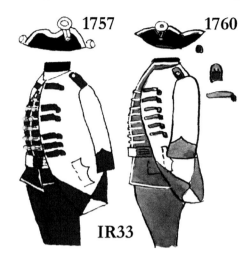

1757   1760

IR33

COAT: Blue collar, buttonhole lace, shoulder straps and turnbacks.
WAISTCOAT: Dark blue with yellow lace.
BUTTONS: Brass.
CUFFS: Yellow with white centre
SASH: Yellow and blue barrel sash.
GRENADIER CAP: Dark blue bag with white piping and tassel

Inhaber
1741 *Johann Adam Frhr. von Andrassy* (d. 1753)
1753 *Nicolaus Joseph Graf Esterhazy de Galantha* (d. 1790)
1791 *Anton Graf Sztaray* (d. 1808)

Commander
1756 *Johann von Gueber*
1757 *Carl Frhr. von Amadei*
1761 *Johann Joseph Khevenhüller-Metsch*

Garrison:
In Bohemia with Garrison Bn in Hungary (1756).

Campaign[149]
War of Austrian Succession. In 1742-3, campaigned in Bavaria before transferring to Italy for the invasion of Naples (1744). In 1746, the regiment fought at Rottofreddo and present at the siege of Genoa. One Bn was part of the expedition to Provence.

Seven Years War In 1756, at Lobositz (1 Oct). In 1757, at Prague (6 May), Schweidnitz, Breslau (22 Nov) and at Leuthen (5 Dec) lost heavily with many taken prisoner. In 1758, distinguished at Hochkirch where it had the second highest regimental losses. Present at the defence of Dresden. In 1761, the regiment was at Loudon's storm of Schweidnitz and at the battle of Dommitzch. In 1762 it was with the *Reichsarmee* in Saxony. One Bn was distinguished at Teplitz.

1762
Albertini

IR33

---

[148] Duffy (2008) 434
[149] Thürheim (1880) I: 215-6

IR34 Batthyány

The regiment was raised on 13 November 1733 with 2300 men from Pest and Debreczin at the Inhaber's expense.[150]

CUFFS: Yellow with black centre. By 1762 white with red centre.
COAT: Yellow cuffs, buttonhole lace and turnbacks in 1757. Dark blue collar, cuffs and turnbacks with yellow buttonhole lace in 1760. White cuffs and turnbacks with red buttonhole lace by 1762.

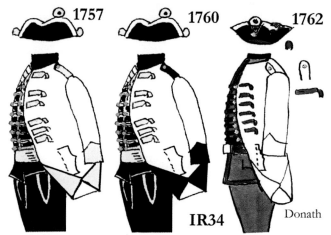

WAISTCOAT: Dark blue with yellow lace. By 1762, blue with red lace.
BUTTONS: Brass
SHOULDER STRAP: Dark blue
SASH: Yellow barrel sash. By 1762, red and white barrel sash.
GRENADIER CAP: Dark blue bag with white piping and tassel

Inhaber
1734 *Ladislaus Frhr. von Kökenyesdi de Vettes* (d. 1754)
1756 *Adam Wenzel Graf Batthyány* (*Batthyányi*) (d. 1787)
1780 *Anton Fürst Esterhazy de Galantha* (d. 1794)

Garrison
From 1748-56 in Lombardy with Garrison Bn in Hungary.

Campaigns[151]
War of Austrian Succession: In 1742, part of the winter expedition to Upper Austria and Bavaria. Fought at Czaslau (17 May) where it was attacked by two Prussian regiments losing 7 officers and 491 men. It participated in the siege of Prague. In 1743 it was at the siege of Straubing and Ingolstadt. In 1744 it campaigned in Bohemia. In 1745, at Hohenfriedberg (4 June) and Trautenau (30 Sept). In 1746, in Italy at Piacenza (16 June), Rottofreddo and occupied Genoa. In 1748 it was at the siege of Genoa.

Seven Years War In 1757, one Bn and the grenadiers were present at Reichenberg, Moys (7 Sept), Breslau (22 Nov), Leuthen (5 Dec). In 1758 it was at Hochkirch (14 Oct) where it suffered heavy casualties of 400 men while capturing 4 guns and 4 flags. In 1759, Czenstochowa (21 Nov). In 1760 it was at Landeshut (23 June), storm of Glatz (26 July) and Liegnitz (15 Aug) where it received heavy casualties of 928 men. In 1761 it participated in Loudon's storm of Schweidnitz. In 1762, the regiment was at Reichenbach (16 Aug).

---

[150] Thürheim (1880) I: 223
[151] Thürheim (1880) I: 224

IR37 Joseph Esterházy

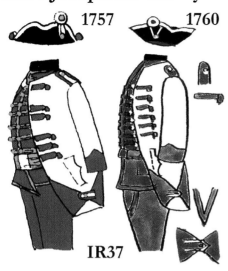

1757 **1760**

IR37

Commanders
1752 *Ladislaus von Szent-Ivany*
1756 *Franz Anton Graf Karolyi*
1759 *Joseph von Weiss*
1760 *Nikolaus Lumaga*
1768 *Carl Frhr. von Haugwitz*

Garrison:
Bohemia with Garrison Bn in Hungary.

Campaign[152]
War of Austrian Succession: In 1742, at the siege of Prague. In 1743 it was part of the blockade of Eger and then the siege of Ingolstadt. In 1744 it fought at Lautenberg. In 1745, a Bn with Trenk's Pandours at the storming of Kosel in Silesia before the regiment transferred to Italy. In 1746, the regiment was at siege of Genoa and the invasion of Provence. In 1747 it was at siege of Genoa.

Seven Years War Present at Lobositz (1 Oct 1756) and part of Browne's relief expedition to relieve the Saxons surrounded at Pirna. Fought at Prague (6 May 1757), Breslau (22 Nov 1757), Leuthen (5 Dec 1757), Gundersdorf and Domstadtl. The regiment ran away at Hochkirch (14 Oct 1758). Present at Maxen, Meissen (2-3 Dec 1759), Landeshut and covered the retreat from Liegnitz (15 Aug 1760).

Raised in 1741

POM-POM: Yellow with red centre
COAT: Red cuffs and buttonhole lace. Red turnbacks with white turnback tab edged red. White edged red shoulder straps
WAISTCOAT: Red with green lace
BUTTONS: Yellow
SASH: Red and green.
GRENADIER CAP: Red bag with yellow trim and tassel

Inhaber
1741 *Thomas von Szirmay* (d. 1743)
1744 *Joseph Graf Esterhazy de Galantha* (d. 1762)
1762 *Joseph Graf Siskovics* (d. 1783)
1784 *Josef Nikolaus Frhr. De Vins* (d. 1798)

1762
Albertini

IR37

[152] Thürheim (1880) I: 248-9

IR39 John Pálffy

The regiment was raised by John Pálffy ab Erdöd in 1756 in Hungary. An impressive campaign record.[153]

1757   1758

IR39

COAT: Hungarian national costume of blue dolman with red cuffs and lace in 1756 then as with other Hungarian Regiments had white red cuffs and white buttonhole lace in 1758. By 1762, the turnbacks were red instead of white.
WAISTCOAT: White with white lace then in 1758 red with white lace.
BUTTONS: White
SHOULDER STRAP: White then white edged red.
SASH: Red and white barrel sash.
GRENADIER CAP: Red bag with white piping and tassel

Inhaber
1756 *Johann Leopold Pálffy ab Erdöd*
1758 *Jacob Frhr. von Preysach* (d. 1787)
1787 *Thomas Graf Nádasdy* (d. 1800)

Commanders
1756 The *Inhaber*
1758 *Joseph Frhr. Formentini*
1760 *Johann von Komka*
1768 *Gabriel Anton Frhr. Splényi von Miháldy*

Garrison in *Hungary* (1756).

Campaigns[154]
Seven Years War In 1757, present at Prague (6 May), Moys (7 Sept), Schweidnitz (11 Nov), Breslau (22 Nov) and Leuthen (5 Dec).

In 1758 it was in Moravia at the defence of Olmütz (28 May-2 July), siege of Neisse, Troppau and Hochkirch. In 1759 it participated in numerous actions in Bohemia and Saxony. In 1760 it was distinguished at Landeshut (23 June), Loudon's storm of Glatz (26 July), then Liegnitz (15 Aug). In 1762 it fought at Burkersdorf (20-21 July). A detachment was present at the defence of Schweidnitz.

1762
Albertini

IR39

---

[153] Duffy (2008) 435
[154] Thürheim (1880) I: 258-9

IR51 Gyulai

In 1702, Adam Frhr. von Baboczay raised 2,000 men and this regiment was the oldest Hungarian Infantry Regiment. Also known as the Transylvanian National Regiment (*Siebenbürgisches National-Regiment*)

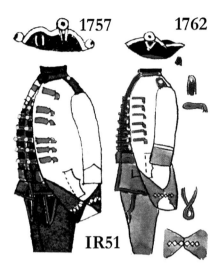

COAT: White cuffs, red buttonhole lace.
TURNBACKS: Blue.
BUTTONS: Yellow.
SHOULDER STRAP: Blue.
CUFFS: Yellow with black centre.
SASH: Red and blue barrel sash.
GRENADIER CAP: Dark blue bag with yellow piping

Inhaber
1702 *Adam Frhr. von Baboczay* (d. 1707)
1707 *Franz Graf Gyulai* (d. 1729)
1729 *Franz Graf Pálffy von Erdöd* (d. 1734)
1735 *Stephan Graf Gyulai* (d. 1759)
1759 *Franz Graf Gyulai* (d. 1788)
1788 *Gabriel Frhr. Splényi von Miháldy* (d. 1818)

Commanders
1752 *Thomas Graf Kálnoky*
1757 *Adolph von Gernert*
1760 *Samuel Graf Gyulai*
1767 *Joseph Frhr. Orosz von Csicser*

Garrison
Lombardy with Garrison Bn in Transylvania (1756).

Campaigns[155]
War of Austrian Succession: In Dec 1741, in Italy with Khevenhüller Corps. In 1742 it was part of the winter expedition to Upper Austria and Bavaria. In 1744 it campaigned on the Rhine and in Bohemia. In 1745 it was at Habelschwert, Hohenfriedberg and Trautenau before transferring to Italy. In 1746 it was part of the siege of Genoa and the invasion of Provence. In 1747 it participated in the siege of Genoa.

Seven Years War In 1757, present at Reichenberg (21 April), Prague (6 May). A detachment was present in Lacy's raid on Berlin. Fought at Moys (30 June), Pretzch. In 1759, Maxen (20 Nov) and Torgau. In 1761 it participated in Loudon's storm of Schweidnitz. In 1762, its outstanding performance decided the battle of Teplitz in the Austrian favour.

1762
Albertini

IR51

---

[155] Thürheim (1880) I: 338

IR52 Bethlen

Formed in 1741. One of the best Hungarian regiments but difficult to handle.[156]

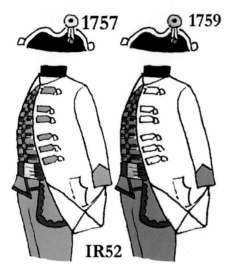

POM-POM: Yellow with black centre.
COAT: Light green cuffs and buttonhole lace in 1757. Light blue cuffs and white buttonhople lace.
WAISTCOAT: Light green with red lace in 1757. Light blue with red lace in 1759 and by 1762, the lace was yellow.
BUTTONS: Brass buttons.
SHOULDER STRAP: None
SASH: Red and yellow barrel sash.
GRENADIER CAP: Medium blue bag with white piping

Inhaber
1741 *Wolfgang Graf Bethlen* (d. 1763)
1763 *Franz Anton Graf Károly* (d. 1791)
1791 *Erzherzog Anton Victor*

Commanders
1741 *Wolfgang Graf Bethlen*
1745 *Joseph Graf Nádasdy*
1749 *Gabriel Frhr. von Balassa*
1752 *Franz von Reinhardt*
1758 *Joseph Maximilian Frhr. von Tillier*
1771 *Paul Orosz de Balasfalva.*

Garrison: in Friaul (*Friuli*) in north-eastern Italy with Garrison Bn in Hungary.

Campaigns[157]
War of Austrian Succession: In 1742, siege of Prague. In 1743 it blockaded Eger. In 1744 it was in Bohemia. In 1745it was at Kesseldorf before transferring to the Netherlands. In 1746, at Rocoux (11 Oct). In 1747, at Lawfeld (2 July).

Seven Years War In 1757, present at Prague (6 May), Schweidnitz, distinguished at Breslau (22 Nov), and Leuthen (5 Dec). In 1758, Hochkirch (14 Oct). In 1759 it was part of Corps Loudon at Kunersdorf (12 Aug). In 1760, Liegnitz (15 Aug) and Torgau (3 Nov). In 1762 it was distinguished at Adelsbach (6 July), Leutmannsdorf (21 July) and a detachment in the defence of Schweidnitz.

---

[156] Duffy (2008) 437
[157] Thürheim (1880) I: 345-6

Panduren-Corps (1741-1756)

On 27 February 1741, Major Franz Frhr. von der Trenck raised *Panduren-Corps* in Slavonia. On 17 March 1745 it was renamed the *Trenck Panduren Regiment* with 20 coys and 2 grenadier coys. In 1748 it was reduced to a single battalion and renamed the *Slavonisches Panduren Bn* and in 1756 became IR56.

Inhaber *Panduren-Corps (Regiment)*
1741 *Franz Frhr. von der Trenk* (d. 1749)

Commander *Panduren-Corps (- Regiment)*
1741 *Franz Frhr. von der Trenck*
1747 ad Interim *Obrist-Lt D'Olne*
then *Major Graf Madrenas*

Commander *Slavonisches Panduren-Bn*
1748 *Christian von Mainstein*
1750 *Adam von Buday*
1753 *Joseph Carl Frhr. von Simbschen*

Campaign History
War of Austrian Succession: In 1741, the Pandour Corps was in Silesia. Near Neisse captured 34 wagons and 300 horses before transferring to Khevenhüller Corps. In 1742, part of the winter expedition to upper Austria and Bavaria. In 1743 it campaigned on the Rhine. In 1744, at Lautenberg (4 July) and attack on Kolin (14 Nov). In 1745, in Silesia at Radaun (11 Feb), Habelschwert (14 Feb), Loslau (29 Mar), Ratibor (20 Apr), the storm of Cosel (26 May) and Trautenau (30 Sept). In 1746, at Rocoux (1746). In 1747, a Bn was present at Lawfeld (2 July) before transferring to Italy.

After Morier (1748)

Pandur Trenck

IR53 Simbschen

This on 8 September 1756, the *Slavonisches Panduren-Bn* became a regular infantry battalion and by early 1757 it had been augmented to 16 Füsilier and 2 Grenadier Coys. It was recruited mainly in Croatia and Slavonia so not strictly a Hungarian regiment. In 1769 it received infantry number 53.

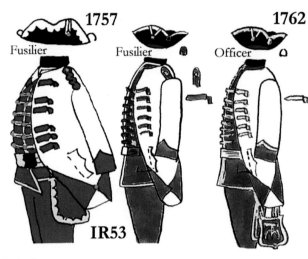

1757 Fusilier Fusilier Officer **1762**

IR53

Cuffs & turnbacks: Red
Piping & buttons: Yellow (*Brauer*) or white (*Donath*)
COAT LACE: Lilac (Brauer)
SASH: Yellow and black barrel sash.
SHOULDER STRAP: Lilac
CUFFS: None
GRENADIER CAP: Red bag with white piping and tassel

Inhaber
1756 *Joseph Carl Frhr. von Simbschen* (d. 1763)
1763 *Levin Philipp Frhr. von Beck* (d. 1768)
1768 *Johann Leopold Graf Pálffy von Erdöd* (d. 1791)

Commander
1756 *Joseph Carl Frhr. von Simbschen*
1758 *Robert Freiherr von Amelungen*
1764 *Lorenz Frhr. von Rasp*

Garrison:
Peterwardein (1749), Philipsburg (1750), Freiberg in Moravia (1751), Fulnek (1755), Troppau (1756 and 1763).

Campaigns
Seven Years War In 1756, in Silesia at Reinerz (4 Nov). In 1757, the regiment was present at the storming of Gabel (14-15 July), Moys (7 Sept), Schweidnitz, Breslau (22 Nov). In 1758 it was distinguished in the defence of Olmütz. In 1760, at Landeshut (23 June), distinguished at Liegnitz (15 Aug) and Leutmannsdorf.

Chapter 14
Grenadiers

The first Austrian grenadiers were raised in 1670 specifically to throw the grenade. In 1700, each *Regimenter zu Fuss* ad a grenadier company. In 1701, grenadiers received the M1701 sabre and the rank of Oberleutnant Grenadier introduced. In 1711, the number of grenadiers companies were increased to two. Only in 1727, did the Hungarian Infantry (*Hayduckenregimenter*) receive two Grenadier Companies.

1720	1748	1760

Grenadiers of German Infantry Regiments
J. Bermann & Sohn

These soon evolved into elite companies attached to Infantry Regiments and in time of war were combined. From 1757, the grenadiers were normally formed into battalions of 4 to 8 companies. These in turn were usually concentrated into the elite "Grenadier Corps." That varied throughout the campaign. Grenadiers deployed in 3 ranks. The grenadier company was divided into 4 platoons (pelotons). When the grenadiers were present with their regiment, the artillery piece was placed within the 6 paces interval separating the battalion and the flanking grenadiers.

Table 16: Grenadier Company organisation in 1748

(3 officers, 6 NCOs, 4 Musicians 1 Pioneer, and 99 Grenadiers)

	Austrian Rank	Notes
Officers (3 officers)		
1	*Hauptmann*	Captain /2nd Captain
1	*Oberlieutenant*	1st Lieutenant
1	*Fähnrich / Unterlieutenant*	Ensign/2nd Lieutenants
NCOs (6 NCOs)		
1	*Feldwäbel*	Company Sergeant-major
4	*Corporal*	Corporal
1	*Fourier*	Company clerk (civilian)
Men (97 men)		
83	*Grenadiere*	Grenadier
2	*Zimmerleute*	Pioneer/Sapper
1	*Fourierschützen*	Officer's servants (batmen)
2	*Tambour*	Drummers
2	*Pfeifer*	Fifers
1	*Fourier*	Civilian clerk

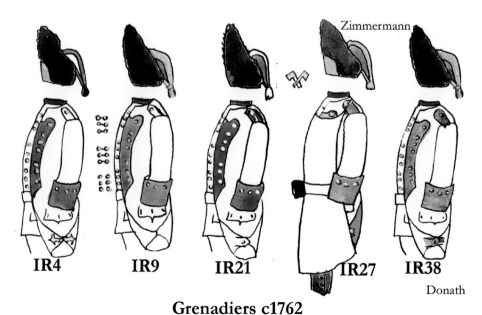

IR4   IR9   IR21   IR27   IR38

Zimmermann

Donath

Grenadiers c1762

~ 132 ~

Grenadier Uniform

HEADWEAR: Conical black or dark brown bearskin and a hanging bag in facing colour piped with button colour.

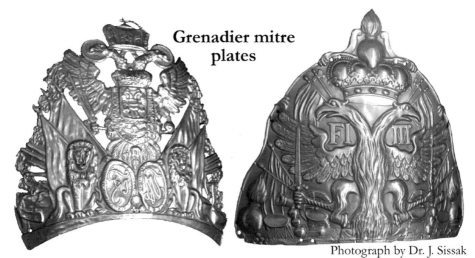

Grenadier mitre plates

Photograph by Dr. J. Sissak

Some had the metal plate or grenade badge in brass or white metal normally depending on button colour was introduced. Some know examples below.

IR4: silver plated mitre plate.

IR2, IR12 and IR21: Brass single flaming grenade

IR17: Brass plate with the Württemberg coat of arms surmounted by a crown. Also depicted is a star surrounded by supporters.

IR26: Brass plate with a grenade in the centre.

IR27: Silver plated mitre plate with the Hessen Kassel Coat of Arms.

IR31, IR35 and IR36: Brass mitre plate.

HAIR: Unpowdered queue at the rear and no rolls at the temple because these would not fit under the cap. Moustaches were worn by the rank and file.

Fusilier covering a Grenadier with grenade, c1750
By von Zinburg, Courtesy of Dr. J. Sissak

UNIFORM: As parent regiment.

EQUIPMENT: Grenadiers carried a small black cartridge box at the front and a brass match case on the front of the cartridge belt. This was a relic from the time when they carried hand grenades. Otherwise the uniform was as for Fusiliers.

SIDEARMS: Model 1754 musket for grenadiers. Grenadiers carried a sabre and bayonet.

No.35   No.36   No.50

German Grenadiers of IR35, IR36 and IR50.

After Morier (1748)

It is interesting that they are wearing black Prussian style gaiters in 1748 rather than the regulation white. It was not until 1754 that black gaiters were stipulated for field use. The sack on the grenadier caps are in facing colour and trimmed in button colour. The match case is clearly depicted on the cross belt.

- The Grenadier of IR35 has red lapels, cuffs and turnbacks.
- The Grenadier of IR36 has red collar and cuffs, no lapels and white turnbacks.
- The Grenadier of IR50 has red collar, cuffs, lapels and turnbacks.

Hungarian Grenadiers of IR2, IR31 and IR52[158]

After Morier (1748)

All the grenade sacks were in the facing colour with yellow or white lacing according to the button colour.

- The Grenadier of IR2 has bearskin hat with single brass flaming grenade, yellow pointed cuffs, turnbacks, blue waistcoat, blue & yellow barrel sash and dark blue Hungarian breeches with yellow Hungarian knot.
- The Grenadier of IR31 had a blue background to the grenadier plate with white border and single flaming grenade, blue pointed cuffs, turnback and *Litzen*, blue waistcoat, blue & white barrel sash and blue trousers with buff shorts.
- The Grenadier of IR52 had green pointed cuffs, turnbacks and *Litzen*, green waistcoat, green & white barrel sash and white Hungarian trousers with yellow lace knots.

---

[158] These are assigned according to Bleckwenn. Pengle & Hurt confused IR2 and IR52.

Grenadier NCOs

HEADWEAR: Conical black or dark brown bearskin and a hanging bag in facing colour battens in gold or silver lace for sergeants and yellow or white lace according to the button colour.

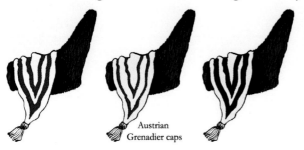

Austrian
Grenadier caps

UNIFORM: As Fusiliers.
SIDEARMS: Carried muskets, a wooden cane suspended from a coat button and a grenadier sabre. Corporals had silver hat lace, a musket and a grenadier sabre.

Grenadier Drummer

They wore the same uniform as the drummers of the parent regiment but a bearskin hat.

IR56 Merci-Argenteau

Grenadier Officers

HAIR: Unpowdered queue at the rear and no rolls at the temple because these would not fit under the cap. Officers were normally clean shaven.
COAT: Similar cut to the other ranks but with finer cloth and no turnbacks. No shoulder strap.
SIDEARMS: Silver mounted black wooden canes, straight bladed sword and were armed with a musket instead of the Partizan.

Grenadier Officers
1749 Drill Book courtesy of Dr. J. Sissak

~ 136 ~

Grenades

Grenadier throwing a grenade

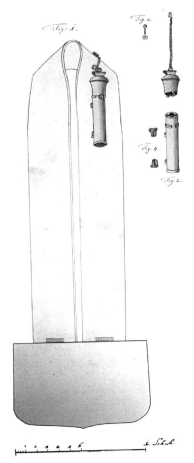

Grenades were cumbersome, difficult to ignite and were marginally less perilous to the thrower. By the War of Austrian Succession, they had become exclusively used in siege warfare. The Grenadiers retained the brass match case worn on the leather crossbelt.

Grenadier match case

Grenadier in tricorn training to throw a grenade
1749 Drill Book courtesy of Dr. J. Sissak

Pioneers

Each infantry company had two *Zimmerleuthe* (singular *Zimmermann*) or pioneers who were expert with the axe to clear paths and other obstructions, repaired wheels, and made gabions, fascines and ladders.

Each infantry company had two Zimmerleuthe (pioneers)
1749 Drill Book courtesy of Dr. J. Sissak

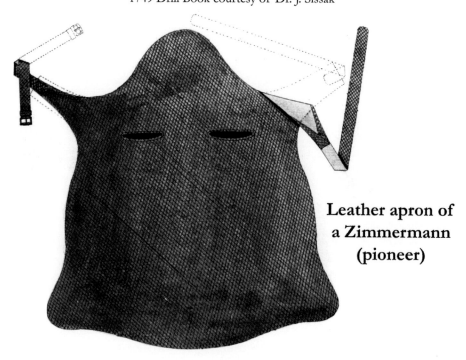

Leather apron of a Zimmermann (pioneer)

Chapter 15
Infantry Weapons

Austria had widely separated firearms factories located in Vienna, Wiener-Neustadt, Hainfeld and Steyr in Upper Austria, and Carlsbad (*Karlovy Vary*), Pressnitz (*Přísečnice*) and Weipert (*Vejprty*) in Bohemia. In 1656, the state owned arms factory at Wiener-Neustadt just 50km south of Vienna was established with 100 armourers and gunsmiths from Liege and the Spanish Netherlands. This produced about 2,000 muskets per year. With the introduction of the flintlock musket, production in Steyr declined from 1700. In the 1720s, Anton Penzendener took over the arms factories in Steyr as well as controlled the production facilities in and around Vienna including Hainfeld after obtaining a guaranteed order from the government.[159]

On 12 May 1757 it was decreed that all gunsmiths and swordsmiths in the Hereditary Lands would work only for the Imperial Army for the duration of the war and their weapons would be delivered to the Vienna Arsenal in return for payment.

Muskets

In 1702, the regulations stated that the infantry were armed with flintlock muskets and that the old matchlock muskets would be handed in and scraped or modified. It was not until spring 1722 that a standardised musket was introduced with a socket bayonet.[160]

At the beginning of 1758, the Austrians had a reserve of 45,000 muskets mostly in poor condition. The Austrians were faced with another shortfall at the end of 1762 when they were threatened by a Turkish invasion. The largest contractor was Anton Penzeneter who had factories in Vienna, Steyr and Hainfeld that could produce 20,000 muskets per year.

Further muskets were obtained from Malines in the Austrian Netherlands, the Bishopric of Liege and from north-west Europe, in particular Thuringia. On 10 January 1758, Major Franz de Piza of the Wied IR who had been wounded at Moys on 7 September 1757 arrived in Brussels with the task to obtain 10,000 firearms and 6,000kg of gunpowder.[161]

The stock of the musket was stained black or brown for fusiliers and polished walnut for grenadiers. The sling and lock covers were white. Austrian muskets suffered from wooden ramrods and the poor quality of coarse musket powder that was reluctant to ignite compared to the Prussian musket powder. In 1744, iron ramrods were introduced.[162]

---

[159] Hochedlinger (2003) 128-9
[160] Hochedlinger (2003) 127
[161] Duffy (2000) 320
[162] Duffy (2000) 247

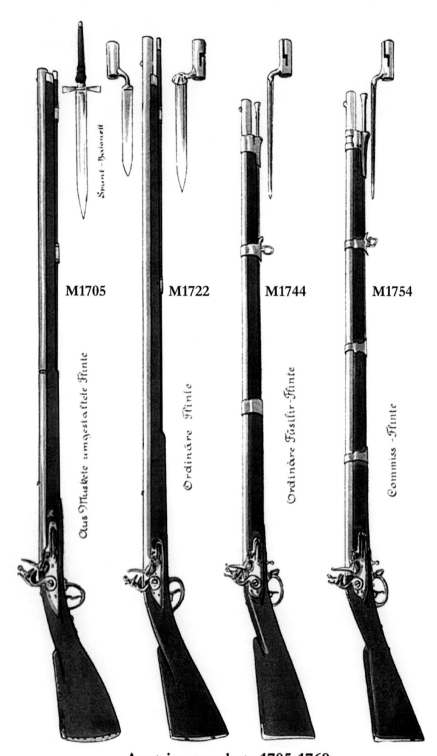

Austrian muskets 1705-1769

After Ottenfeld (1895)) – Courtesy of Ken Trotman publishing

M1722 *Ordinäre Flinte* (Musket) was the first standardised flintlock musket used by the Austrian Army and was based upon the musket produced by Suhl in Thuringia that had been supplied during the Spanish War of Succession.[163] It had a curved lock plate and the barrel secured by pins. The bayonet was a triangular pointed knife. The wooden ramrod was found to be a disadvantage in the Silesian War when the Prussians had replaced theirs with iron. From 1744, the wooden ramrod was replaced with iron.

M1744 Musket had a curved lock plate and the barrel was secured with steel bands instead of pins through the stock as in the previous pattern muskets. An iron ramrod was issued for the first time. The knife bayonet was retained.

M1748 Musket: The lock plate was now flat rather than curved and the bayonet was replaced by a triangular-section bayonet that had far superior penetrating power.

M1754 *Commissflinte* (Musket) was designed by a committee presided over by General-Artillerie-Director Prince Liechtenstein and incorporated the design features from the designs of Johann Schmeid and Anton Penzeneter. It had four bands that secured the barrel to the stock with a barrel of high grade iron bored in a single controlled operation. The trigger guard and butt plate was of iron rather than brass as in Prussian weapons. In October 1755, all infantry regiments in Bohemia were equipped with this new musket except KR1 Kaiser that had captured French muskets with their own pattern bayonet.[164] From 1759, officers were armed with M1754 *Commissflinte* with brass instead of steel fittings.

Table 17: Infantry small-arms[165]

	Calibre	Length	Weight	Rifling
Muskets				
M1722 Musket	18.3mm	157cm	4.8kg	None
M1744 Musket	18.3mm	151cm	5.0kg	None
M1745 Musket	18.3mm	150cm	4.86kg	None
M1748 Musket	18.3mm	150cm	5.0kg	None
M1754 Musket	18.3mm	151cm	4.9kg	None
Rifles				
M1759 Penzeneter Jäger Rifle	14.8mm	112cm	3kg	6 grooves
M1769 Jäger Rifle	14.5mm	105½cm	4.2kg	7 grooves
Grenade Pistol				
M1761 Grenade Pistol	74mm	32½cm	1.60kg	None

M1759 Penzeneter Rifle: The first Austrian Jäger was armed with forester rifles. These were replaced in 1759 by the M1759 Penzeneter Jäger Rifle of 14.8mm had a 79cm barrel and six rifle groves.

---

[163] Hochedlinger (2003) 127
[164] Duffy (2000) 246-7
[165] Ottenfeld (1898 rp 2003) II: 850-3

Bayonet

Fusilier fixing the bayonet to the musket
1749 Drill Book courtesy of Dr. J. Sissak

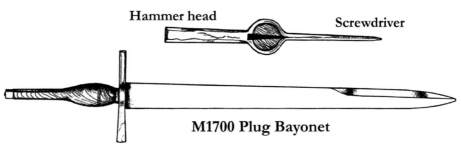

M1700 Plug Bayonet

M1700 Plug Bayonet had a single edged straight blade without fullers. The 18.5cm long wooden grip was painted. The straight cross-guard ended in screwdriver and hammer head.

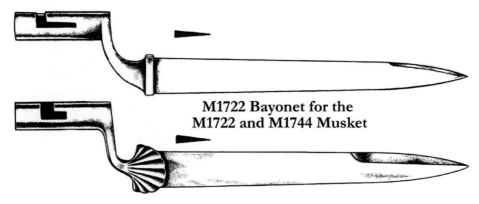

**M1722 Bayonet for the
M1722 and M1744 Musket**

M1722 Socket Bayonet had a 32cm straight blade without fullers. It was used for the M1722 and M1744 Musket.

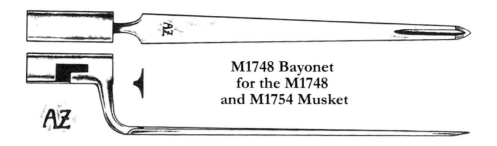

M1748 Bayonet
for the M1748
and M1754 Musket

M1748 Socket Bayonet had a 33cm straight blade of triangular section. It was used for the M1748 and M1754 Musket.

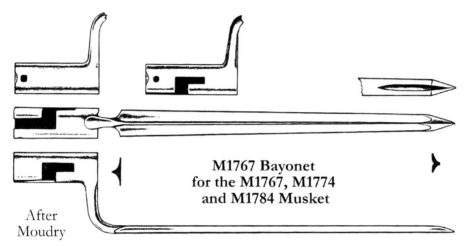

M1767 Bayonet
for the M1767, M1774
and M1784 Musket

After
Moudry

M1767 Socket Bayonet had a 37cm straight blade of triangular section and safety catch. It was used for the M1767, 1774 and M1784 Musket

Table 18: Austrian bayonets[166]

	Blade length	Muzzle ring diameter	Total length
M1700 Plug Bayonet	43cm	-	61.5cm
M1722 Socket Bayonet	32cm	24mm	43cm
M1744 Socket Bayonet	33.1cm	24mm	41xm
M1767 Socket Bayonet	36.8cm	24mm	45cm

[166] Ottenfeld (1898 rp 2003) II: 835

NCO Halberds

NCOs wore the same uniform as the ordinary soldier were equipped with a polearm and a stick. The latter was used to denote their rank and to beat their inferiors. The *Kurzgewehr* (halberd) was used by company NCOs until 1759 when they were exchanged for muskets.[167]

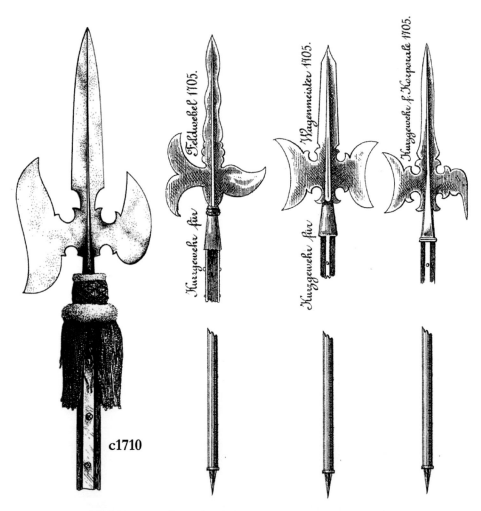

M1705 Halberds (Kurzgewehr) for NCOs
After Moudry and Ottenfeld

The Feldwebel (Senior NCO) Halberd (left) has two curved axe blades and a central flat blade with a rib screwed into a conical socket that is strengthened by two steel plates alonge the wooden cylindrical shaft. The red tassel was attached.

---

[167] Duffy (2000) 229

Table 19: NCO pole-weapons[168]

	Blade length	Blade width	Wooden shaft length	Total length	Weight
M1705 NCO halberd (*Feldwebel Kurzgewehr*)	45cm		155cm	200cm	2.2kg
M1705 Corporal halberd (*Kurzgewehr*)	45cm		155cm	200cm	2.0kg
NCO halberd (*Feldwebel Kurzgewehr*) c1710	36cm	7cm		204cm	1.1kg
M1705 half-pike (*Springstock des Fähnrich*)	15cm		190cm	205cm	1.0kg
Half-pike	29cm		200cm	229cm	1.6kg

Feldwebel   Fähnrich   Corporal

1   *2*   *3*

NCOs with Kurzgewehr (half pikes)
1749 Drill Book courtesy of Dr. J. Sissak

[168] Ottenfeld (1898 rp 2003) II: 835

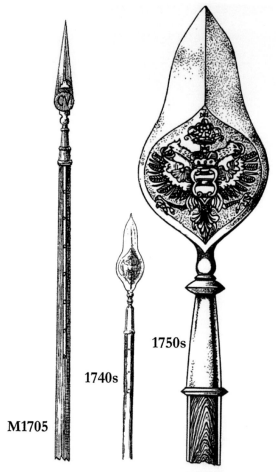

Springstock des Fähnrich (ensign half-pike) [left] was used by the *Fähnrich* (Ensign / 2nd Lieutenant) from 1748 when the colour (*Fahnen*) was permanently carried by the *Fuhrer* (a senior NCO).

1750s

1740s

M1705

M1705 Springstock (half-pike) and NCO spontoons.
Moudry and Ottenfeld

Table 20: NCO and Fähnrich half pike.[169]

	Blade length	Blade width	Wooden shaft length	Total length	Weight
M1705 Ensign half-pike (*Springstock des Fähnrich*)	15cm		190cm	205cm	1.0kg
NCO spontoon	28.7cm	11.1cm		195.5cm	0.81kg

---

[169] Ottenfeld (1898 rp 2003) II: 835

Infantry Swords

Grenadiers and Hungarian infantry carried swords. German Fusiliers did not receive swords until 1765. The scabbards were constructed of wood and leather except the M1705 Grenadier Sabre had a leather scabbard.[170]

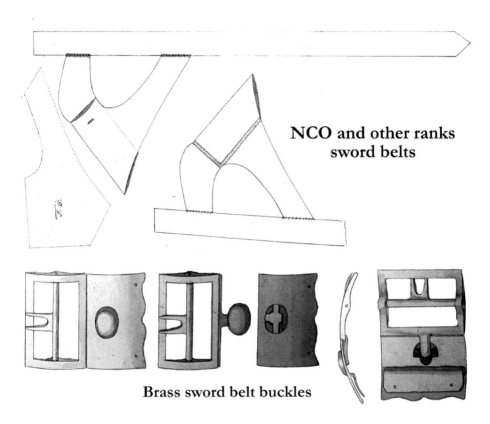

NCO and other ranks sword belts

Brass sword belt buckles

Table 21: Grenadier sabres

	Blade length (cm)	Blade width (mm)	Weight (kg)
M1705 Grenadier Sabre	75cm	40mm	1.3kg
M1765 Grenadier Sabre	58cm	40mm	0.8kg

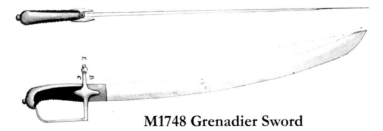

M1748 Grenadier Sword

---

[170] Ottenfeld (1898 rp 2003) II: 827

Table 22: German NCO sabres

	Blade length (cm)	Blade width (mm)	Weight (kg)
M1748 Sabre for Senior NCOs	70cm	42mm	1.6kg
M1748 Sabre for NCOs	66cm	42mm	1.5kg

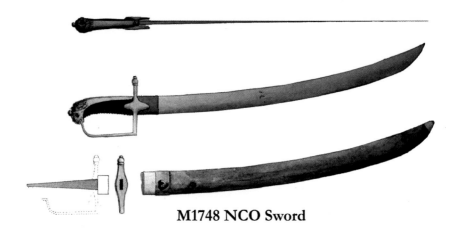

M1748 NCO Sword

Table 23: Hungarian Fusilier and NCO sabres

	Blade length (cm)	Blade width (mm)	Weight (kg)
M1748 Hungarian NCO sabre	66cm	42mm	1.5kg
M1748 Hungarian sabre	66cm	42mm	1.1kg

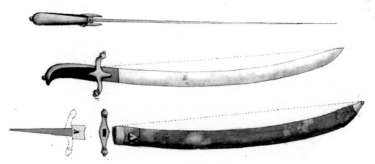

Hungarian Fusilier Sword

Table 24: Light infantry and sapper sabres

	Blade length (cm)	Blade width (mm)	Weight (kg)
M1754 Jäger sabre	53cm	45mm	1.0kg
M1748 Büchsenmeister-Hirschfänger	58cm	40mm	0.9kg

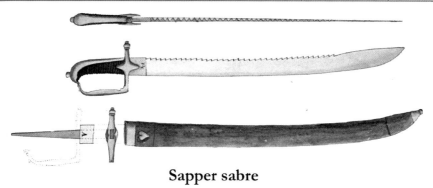

Sapper sabre

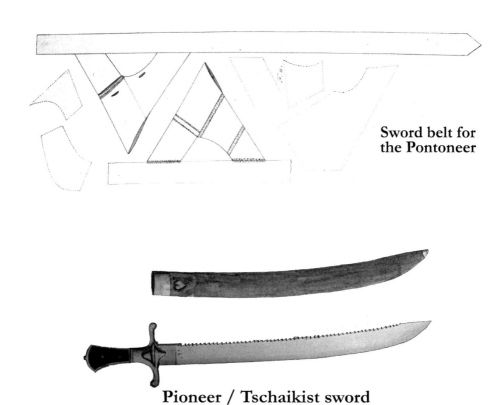

Sword belt for the Pontoneer

Pioneer / Tschaikist sword

Officer Polearms and Sidearms

By 1759, officers were only armed with swords instead of Spontoons. The partisans (or spontoons) had engraved heads and fringed depending upon rank.

Table 25: Obrist partizan

	Blade length	Blade width	Wooden shaft length	Total length	Weight
Obrist Partizan c1730	28.7cm	11.1cm	181.3cm	210cm	1.1kg
Obrist Partizan c1750	30.3cm	11cm	184.2cm	214.5cm	1.1kg

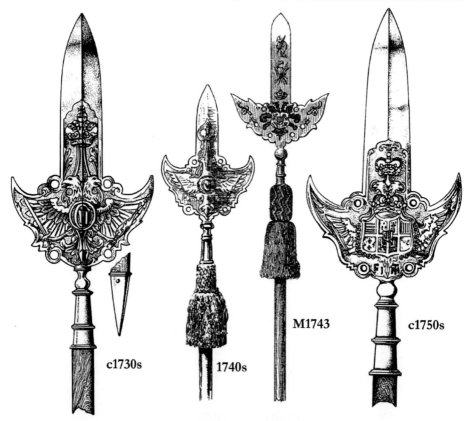

c1730s

1740s

M1743

c1750s

Obrist (Oberst) Partizans
After Moudry and Ottenfeld

Obrist – The blade was gold-plated and the tassel (fringe) was gold or silver depending upon button colour of the regiment.

Obristlieutenat - Tassel (fringe) was gold and black. The blade was partially gold-plated.

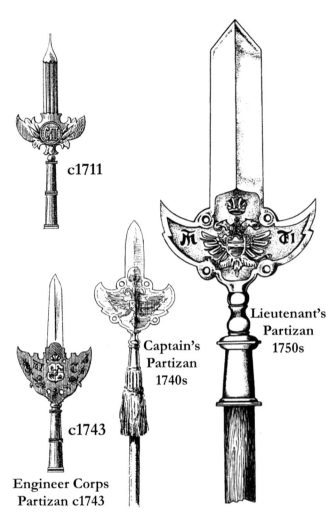

c1711

Engineer Corps
Partizan c1743

c1743

Captain's
Partizan
1740s

Lieutenant's
Partizan
1750s

Junior officer Partizans
After Moudry and Ottenfeld

The Junior Officer's Partizan used by the Lieutenant and Captain had a blade that widened into two crescents. It was mounted on a cylindrical wooden shaft.

Lieutenant carried a partizan without tassel (fringe), bare iron.

Hauptmann carried a partizan with a tassel (fringe) silk, yellow, black and silver, engraved iron.

Obristwachmeister (Major from 1756) did not carry the partisan.

The Partizan c1750 (right) has the Austrian Coat of Arms with the FI (Francis I) and MT (Maria Theresa) upon a grainy background.

Table 26: Officer Partizans[171]

	Blade length	Blade width	Wooden shaft length	Total length	Weight
M1711 Officer partisan (*Partizan*)	30cm	10cm	160cm	1190cm	1.4kg
Junior Officer Partizan c17l50	32cm	11cm	180xm	212cm	1.2kg

171 Ottenfeld (1898 rp 2003) II: 835

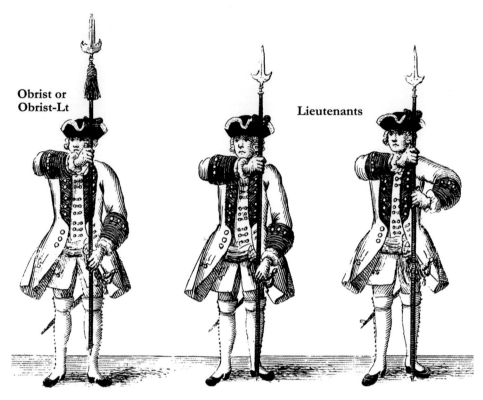

Obrist or Obrist-Lt

Lieutenants

Officers with polearms from the 1749 Drill Book
Courtesy of Dr. J. Sissak

M1740 Infantry Officer's Sword

Table 27: Ceremonial pole-weapons[172]

	Blade length	Hilt length	Total length	Weight
M1711 Hayduk guard axe (*Leibhajdukenbeil*)	24cm	120cm	144cm	1.6cm
M1666 Trebant halbard (*Trebanten-Hellebarde*)	60cm	190cm	250cm	3.0kg
M1690 Fortress halberd (*Festungshellebarde*)	100cm	160cm	260cm	2.2kg
M1740 Glaive (*Couse der Hartschiere*)	56cm	140cm	196cm	2.5kg

---

172 Ottenfeld (1898 rp 2003) II: 835

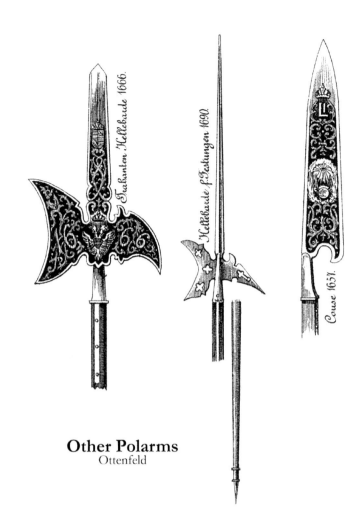

Couse der Hartschiere (Glaive) was a ceremonial pike with a flat engraved blade. By Maria Theresa's reign, the blade had been reduced to 56cm.

The *Copia* was a 3-6m long light lance used by Hussars.

The *Pikenierpike* was the standard issue long pike for pikemen.

Other Polarms
Ottenfeld

Table 28: Obsolete pole-weapons[173]

	Blade length (cm)	Hilt length (cm)	Total length (cm)	Weight (kg)
Boarding axe (*Enterbeil*)	12cm	45cm	57cm	0.9kg
Half-pike (*Enterpike*)	29cm	200cm	229cm	1.6kg
Pike (*Pikenierpike*)	10cm	5-600cm	610cm	2.8kg

173 Ottenfeld (1898 rp 2003) II: 835

Chapter 16
Infantry Flags

On October 21 1740, when Maria Theresa inherited but unlike previous monarchs were unable to issue new colours due to the poor state of finances during the War of the Austrian Succession hence earlier models of flags are also discussed. Each infantry regiment had 1 *Leibfahne* and 15 *Ordinairefahnen*. The *Leibfahne* was carried by the *Leib* company of the first battalion.

During the 30 Years War, Emperor Ferdinand III (r. 1737-57) declared that the Virgin Mary, Mother of God as the patroness of the army. Hence, from then on many of the infantry flags had her depicted especially the *Leibfahne*. Some were even used at the start of the Seven Years War. Traditionally the *Leibfahne* had a white field and the *Ordinairefahne* (battalion flag) had a coloured field often yellow. The flagpoles had a brass finial. The streamers were gold or silver depending upon the regimental button colour. The flags were carried by NCOs known as *Führers*.

In 1741, the new regiments raised in the Austrian Netherlands and Hungary were issued with only two flags per battalion.

From 1748, the number of flags was halved to 8 from 16. Each infantry regiment now consisted of 2 grenadier companies and 16 fusilier companies in four battalions. Each battalion carried two flags. The I Bn carried a *Leibfahne* and an *Ordinairefahne* while II-IV Bns carried two *Ordinairefahnen*. In peacetime, each of the four battalions of had one colour with the I Bn carrying the *Leibfahne*.

In 1756, after the reorganisation of the line infantry, each regiment consisted of 2 grenadier companies, two field Bns of six fusilier companies each and one garrison (depot) Bn of 4 companies. The distribution of two flags per battalion was retained. The I

Standard Bearers from the 1749 Drill Book
Courtesy of Dr. J. Sissak

Bn carried a *Leibfahne* and an *Ordinairefahne*. The II Bn carried two *Ordinairefahnen*. It is unclear whether the garrison (depot) Bn carried any flags. The spare flags were returned to the Arsenal and were probably used to replace any loses.

Flags of Leopold I and Charles VI (1680-1740)

The 174-221 (5 *Fuss* 6 *Zoll* - 7 *Fuss*) square flag was nailed on a 316-379 cm (10-12 *Fuss*) pike with three to four rows of gilt-headed nails. The finials of the pikes were decorated with gilt spear-points pierced with the double eagle, the Imperial cipher, a patron saint, the *Inhaber's* crest, or a provincial badge. The flag borders had stripes or flames of red-white-blue, black-white-red-yellow, black-yellow-black-white, black-white-red, blue-red etc...

Leibfahne

IR4 (c1700)

Ordinairefahne

The *Leibfahne* had a white field the Blessed Virgin on one side and the Imperial double headed eagle on the other. The borders differed between regiments.

The *Ordinairefahnen* had either a yellow, green, red or red-white-red fields and normally on both sides was the Imperial double headed eagle with the Emperor's cypher in the centre or an orb. LI for Leopold I (

Ordinairefahne of IR28 (Est. 1698)

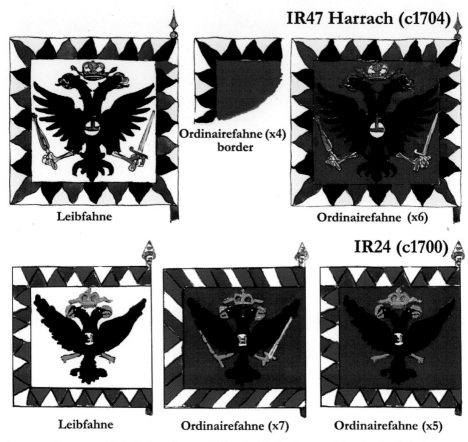

IR47 Harrach (c1704)

Leibfahne

Ordinairefahne (x4)
border

Ordinairefahne (x6)

IR24 (c1700)

Leibfahne

Ordinairefahne (x7)

Ordinairefahne (x5)

Some regiments with Inhaber from within the Holy Roman Empire had their coat of arms instead of the Virgin Mary on their Leibfahne. For example IR23 Baden-Baden.

IR23 (c1700)

Leibfahne

Ordinairefahne

Flags of Hungarian regiments differed with the Hungarian coat of arms in the centre of the Imperial double headed eagle.

IR51 (Est. 1702)

Hungarian
Infantry
Regiment

Leibfahne

Ordinairefahne

Ordinairfahne
of an
unidentified
Regiment c1712

Charles VI
(1711-40)

After the death of Charles VI in 1740, the old flags were still used and the new issued flags were of the same pattern but with changed ciphers. In 1741-42, new infantry regiments were raised in the Austrian Netherlands and Hungary. The *Hofkriegsrat* stipulated that these new regiment should carry only 2 flags per battalion; the *Leibfahne* had a white field and the *Ordinairefahnen* had a red field. The *Hofkriegsrat* did not specify the flag design. Dr. Sissak's research at the HGM, *Kriegsarchive* and University of Wien (Vienna) suggests that the M1741 pattern did not exist.

An example of a *Leibfahne* made in 1741 for a new regiment.

> The white field had the Madonna and Child within an oval of golden rays and standing on a crescent moon and a red cartouche below bearing the white rampant Bohemian lion, holding the Hungarian cross in its right claw, its left claw placed on the oval Austrian badge, surmounted by a grand duke's crown (the cipher "MT" on the central white bar of this shield). The flag was edged in black-red-black-white flames. The finial represented the Madonna with Child over the Hungarian crest on the one side and on the other is the lion with the cross and Austrian shield with the date "1741" beneath it.

**IR27 Fahnen-Lieutenant carrying a M1743
"Hungarian" Ordinairefahne, c1756**
By F Würbel. Courtesy of Dr. J. Sissak.

M1743 "Hungarian" Infantry Flags

After the election of Charles Albert Wittelsbach of Bavaria as Holy Roman Emperor as Charles VII on 24 January 1742, Austria had to remove Imperial insignia (including all black and gold colours) from their flags.

On 19 October 1743, Maria Theresa ordered that German and Hungarian Infantry Regiments would have a white field for the *Leibfahne* and a green field for the *Ordinairefahne*. All the M1743 "Hungarian" flags had a flame border with alternating green, white and red flames of the Hungarian flag. The 316 - 348 cm (10-11 *Fuss*) pike was painted in green and red spirals (sometimes plain black) with a gilt finial. A short red-green cravat with golden fringes at each end was knotted around the pike. Each infantry regiment had 16 1 *Leibfahne* and 15 *Ordinairefahnen* / *Compagniefahnen* (16 flags in total).

M1743 "Hungarian" Ordinairefahne

It should be emphasised that these flags were carried by German and Hungarian infantry regiments and were approximately 174-192 cm (5 *Fuss* 6 *Zoll* to 6 *Fuss*).

The M1743 white **Leibfahne**

> White with either had the Madonna and Child within an oval of golden rays on both sides or on one side with the coat of arms of Hungary and Bohemia on the other side. At the feet of the Madonna were coat of arms of Hungary and Bohemia and combined "Austrian" shield with the initials "MT." The flag had an alternating green, white and red flame border.

The M1743 green **Ordinairefahne**

> Grass green field bordered with red-white-green flames; the centre device consisted of Maria Theresa's small crest under an arched crown. The badge bore the crests of new Hungary, Bohemia, old Burgundy and Tyrol with the red-white-red Austrian heart shield topped by an archducal crown. On each side of the centre device stood Maria Theresa's cipher (MT) and Francis' cipher (FC) of *Franciscus Corregens*.

However, as long as colours were considered as serviceable, they were not replaced by this new pattern. Furthermore, the new rules concerning the designs of colours were widely ignored.

Leibfahne

Ordinairefahne

Variant 2

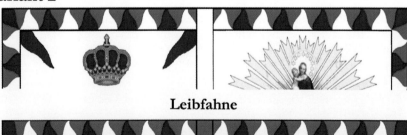

Leibfahne

Ordinairefahne

There were at least three were at least four different border variants.

- Green-white-red-white flame border
- Green-red-white flame border (Variant 1)
- Green-red-green-white flame border (Variant 2)
- Green-white-red flame border (Variant 3)

M1743 "Hungarian" Infantry Flag, Variant 3   Issued 1743-45

Leibfahne

Ordinairefahne

Due to financial reasons, it was ordered in 1745 that the old flags would be used if they were still good repair. The *Hoffkriegsrath* dated 20 January 1754 that, the coats of arms of the regiments in the standard are not the same and the old flags were still carried by some regiments. This suggests that these old flags included those of Leopold I and Charles VI that were retired to garrison as well as newer M1743 "Hungarian" flags. It is likely that they were still carried by a number of the German and Hungarian Infantry Regiments were carried into the early years of the Seven Years War.

M1745 Flags

Maria-Theresa Finial

On 13 Sep 1745, Maria Theresa's consort, Franz (Francis I), was elected *Kaiser* of the Holy Roman Empire upon the death of Charles Albert Wittelsbach of Bavaria (Charles VII). All the imperial insignia could once again be borne on the colours and standards once again. On 22 December 1745, Maria Theresa introduced a new white *Leibfahne* and yellow *Ordinairefahne*. Each regiment had a flag for each company (1 *Leibfahne*, 15 *Ordinairefahnen* / *Compagniefahnen*). The regulation of 1743 was rescinded. Only regimental Chefs who were closely related to Empress Maria Theresa or her husband Francis I (1708-65) were permitted to deviate from this norm.

Each infantry regiment had an additional flag for their regimental baggage train including the wives, children and other civilians according to the 1749 Drill Regulations[174], It was a plain 179 x 127cm ((5 *Fuss* 8 *Zoll* by 4 *Fuss*) flag in the facing colour and did not have borders. An example, the regimental baggage flag for IR4 Deutschmeister was blue with Deutschmeister in black writing.

The borders were about 16 cm (6 Zoll) wide. The hand painted silk flags were 178cm by 127 cm on a 261 cm (8 *Fuss* 3 *Zoll*) flag pole. The brass finial on top of the pole - brass had the "MT" on one side and "FCIM" (*Corregens Franciscus Imperator Magnus*) on the reverse. The wooden pole was painted stripes for the *Leibfahne* was painted in black, yellow, red, white.

1745-68

M1745 Infantry Leibfahne

Stephen Summerfield 2014

---

[174] *Regulament und Ordnung für IR 1749,* Part II, p 55.

The **M1745 *Leibfahne*** had a white field bordered with alternating white-yellow outer wavy triangles pointing inwards, and alternating red-black inner wavy triangles pointing outwards. The order of these often varied between regiments. The flag measured 179 cm by 127cm (5 *Fuss* 8 *Zoll* by 4 *Fuss*).[175]

> **REVERSE** (left): The black Imperial double-eagle has a silver sword in his right hand and a golden orb in his left hand. The "*Lothringen-Toscanian*" arms on a halved shield and surmounted by a gold crown. The left has a red diagonal with three flying eagles in white on a yellow field. The right has five red circles and a blue circle with three white lilies. The initials of the "CF" (*Franciscus Corregans*) on the left wing and "IM" (*Imperator = Emperor*) on the right.

> **OBVERSE** (right): The Madonna in a white dress on a pale blue or white cloud, crushing a snake under her foot and surrounded by golden rays of light. Her cloak was royal blue with red lining. Emperor Ferdinand III declared her as the patroness of the army.

Some regiments had the Madonna on both sides.

1745-68

M1745 Infantry Leibfahne

Stephen Summerfield 2014

The **M1745 *Ordinairefahne*** had a yellow field with a border of alternating white and yellow outer waved triangles pointing inwards, red and black inner waved triangles pointing outwards. The order of these often varied between regiments. The flag measured 179cm by 127cm (5 *Fuss* 8 *Zoll* by 4 *Fuss*).[176]

> **REVERSE** (left): The black Imperial double headed eagle did not have a sword or orb. On the outstretched wings, there is an "M" (left) and "T" (right) standing for "Maria Theresa." On the chest of the eagle was the coat of arms of Hungary and Bohemia. The first quarter had four horizontal white lines on red field. The second quarter had a white cross of Lorraine surmounted by a golden crown on a red field. The right half had an upright lion with a crown on its head.

---

[175] Dr J. Sissak (2014) *Private Communication.*
[176] Dr J. Sissak (2014) *Private Communication.*

OBVERSE (right): The black Imperial double-eagle had a silver sword in his right hand and a golden orb in his left hand. The *"Lothringen-Toscanian"* (Lorraine-Tuscan) arms on a halved shield were surmounted by a gold crown. The left has a red diagonal with three flying eagles in white on a yellow field. The right has five red circles and a blue circle with three white lilies. The initials of the "CF" (*Franciscus Corregans*) on the left wing and "IM" (*Imperator = Emperor*) on the right.

1745-68

M1745 Infantry Ordinairefahne

Stephen Summerfield, 2014

M1745 Ordinairefahne of IR4 Deutschmeister, c 1757
Reconstruction from an original flag in the HGM, Courtesy of Dr. J. Sissak

M1765 Flags

In September 1765, Franz Moritz Graf von Lacy introduced new flags that were silk painted in oils rather than appliqués and embroidery. These new flags replaced only issued when the old flags were worn out so this was a very gradual process.

Chapter 17
Grenz Regiments

In 1538, Emperor Ferdinand I established the *Militärgrenze* along the Austro-Ottoman border that gave sanctuary and permanent settlement to the displaced Serbs escaping from Turkish rule. This chain of fortified villages, blockhouses and watch towers were garrisoned by settled military colonists. This placed them under Austrian military administration in exchange for freedom of religion and tax exemption in return for military service in the Austrian army. This also gave them license to raid and pillage Turkish settlements across the border.

The three Serb captaincies of Koprivnica in northern Croatia, Kreutz (*Križevci*) in central Croatia and Ivanic near Zagreb eventually formed the Warasdin (*Varaždin*) Command. The victory at Zenta (11 Sept 1697) by Prince Eugene of Savoy marked the turning point in the Austrian struggle against the Turks. Following the Treaty of Karlowitz (26 Jan 1699), the Carlstädt (*Karlovac*), Warasdin (*Varaždin*), and Banat Grenz Commands were created. In 1702, the Slavonian border was established along the Save, Theiss and Maros Rivers, which were largely incorporated into Hungary in 1747. After the Seven Years War, the Székely (1764) and Wallachian (1766) Command were formed.

A new administration presided over the Grenz and replaced the tribal structure in 1744. Prince Joseph Saxe-Hildburghausen reorganised the Grenz into regiments according to their districts.
- Carlstädt (1746) – Likaner, Ottochaner, Oguliner and Szluiner GIR from Croat Roman Catholics.
- Warasdin (1745) – Creutzer and St. Georg GIR from Croat Roman Catholics.
- Slavonian (1747) – Broder, Grasdiscaner and Peterwardeiner Grenz Infantry Regiments were formed from Greek Orthodox and Serbians. The Czarkisten Battalion was also from this area.
- Banal (1750) – 1st and 2nd Banal Grenz Infantry Regiments.

Regimentsstab (regimental staff)
1st Battalion
      Bataillonsstab (battalion staff),
      1. *Grenadier* Company,
      1.-6 *Füsilier* Companies,
      1. *Schützen* Company (Rifle Company)
2nd Battalion
      Bataillonsstab (battalion staff),
      2. *Grenadier* Company,
      7.-12. *Füsilier* Companies,
      2. *Schützen* Company (Rifle Company)
3rd Battalion (Depot)
      Bataillonsstab (battalion staff),
      13.-16. Füsilier Companies

In 1748, Grenz-Infantry Regiments were re-organized into 16 fusilier companies, 2 grenadier and 2 rifle companies which formed two field battalions and a depot battalion. The company strength was 100 men. Each field battalion also had a squadron of 130 Grenz hussars attached and a detachment of gunners manning 1-pdr Mountain Guns that were used during the early part of the Seven Years War. In times of war, the grenadier companies were detached from their parent regiments to serve in the Grenadier Corps.

Map 12: Croatia and Slavonia.

Kingdom of Croatia following the Battle of Mohács in 1527, the nobles chose *Ferdinand of Habsburg* as their new king.

Kingdom of Slavonia was taken from the Ottoman Turks in 1745. The main contribution was the Slavonian Grenz.

The *"Kleine Krieg"* (Small or Petty War) was an important part of the Seven Years War. The Austrians had an inherent advantage over the Prussians in their ability to call upon large forces of skilled light infantry- the *Grenz-Infanterie* (Border Infantry), generally referred to as Croats, from the Military Border.

At Kolin (18 June 1757), Prussian infantry were unnerved by the unusual sound of 1-pdr battalion guns employed by the Austrian Grenz opposing them. The Grenz through their constant practice against the Turks were among the most experienced soldiers of the Austrian army. They fought primarily in open order, taking advantage of difficult terrain which favoured skirmishes. They played an important part in raids against enemy supply lines and outposts.

General Adolf Buccow and, following his death in 1764, András Reichsgraf Hadik von Futak established the Transylvanian border, consisting of the Székely (1764) and Wallachian borders (1766). By 1770-87, the cordon sanitaire was complete and a system of permanent cantonments was installed.

After the Seven Years War further Grenz Regiments were formed.

- Transylvania (*Siebenbürgen*)
  - *1ˢᵗ & 2ⁿᵈ Székely* GIR were formed in 1764 from Hungarians
  - *1ˢᵗ & 2ⁿᵈ Wallach* GIR were formed from Greek Orthodox Wallachians in 1766.
- Banat of Temesvár (formed 1765-6)
  - *Deutsch-Banater* GIR formed from German colonists in 1765. Also known as *Tremescar Ansiedlungs Regiment* (Tremescar Colony Regiment). In 1769, became IR71.
  - Renamed *Illyrisches-Banater* in 1766 and in 1769 became IR72. In 1775 amalgamated with the *Walakische* GIR to become IR72 *Walachisch-Illyrisches* GIR

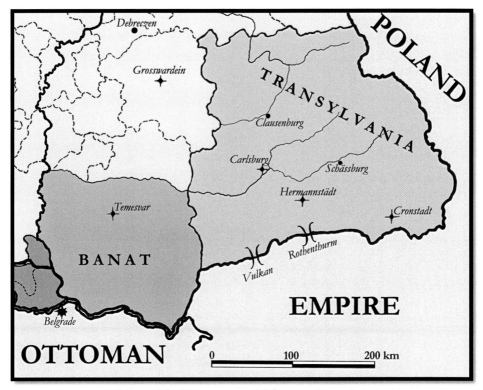

Map 13: Banat and Transylvania.

Banat of Temesvár was a territory north of the Danube in south east Hungary captured from the Turks by Eugene of Savoy in 1716 and ceded to Austria in the Peace of Passarowitz (1718). It remained under military administration until 1751 and only became part of Hungary in 1779.

Transylvania (*Siebenbürgen*) was lost to Austria in 1809 and regained in 1814.

Grenz Uniform

The Grenz-Regiments initially wore a variety of regional costume or folk dress that was regularised by the introduction of Hungarian style military uniforms after 1750. This was generally unpopular among the independent minded Croats. The regulations required the Grenz to uniform and equip themselves at their own expense.

In December 1754, the Warasdiners were ordered to purchase new uniforms and equipment despite there only having been four years of peacetime wear. This caused unrest. On 29 June 1755, it was decided that the uniforms and swords would be purchased by the men at controlled priced and the muskets provided by the state.[177]

In 1757, FM Neipperg, as Vice-President of the *Hofkriegrath*, reported that the prickly Croats should retain their favourite colours for their uniforms.

- Carlstädt – red and blue (Catholic)
- Slavonian Broder and Gradiscaner – dark blue (Greek Orthodox).
- Warisdiner regimets – green dolmans. (Catholic)

In August 1760, the Warisdiners and the Slavonians were issued free clothing to alleviate the burden on the ordinary soldier.[178]

In 1767, the Grenz adopted the *Casket* and the single breasted coat

The uniforms depicted were issued at different dates and as the men were rotated from border guards to the main army, it is little wonder the uniforms varied considerably within the same regiment.

HEADWEAR: Brimless tubular felt or fur caps. In 1749, FML Johann Sigismund Maguire introduced German style tricorns among the newly raised Warasdiner Regiments although none of the illustrations from the 1760s show them. Grenadiers wore the regulation bearskin. These were often lost being unsuitable for the Grenz style of fighting.
HAIR: Plaits or pigtails and normally with a moustache.
TUNIC: The Carlstädt (Croat) and Banal Grenz Infantry Regiments wore Hungarian style short coats with pairs of *Litzen* down the front pointed cuffs. Warasdin (Serb) and

---

[177] Diffy (2000) 304
[178] Diffy (2000) 312.

Slavonian Grenz-Regiments were distinguished by their open fronted jacket that was longer than the Hungarian pelisse and round cuffs. The Slavonians also often wore a simple brown home-made coat (called a *Hausmontur*).

WAISTCOAT: Most Grenz Regiments wore a Hungarian style dolman.

CLOAKS: Red cloaks instead of greatcoats were worn. They were rolled up and tied to the knapsack when they were not worn. The Banal regiments wore a large cavalry style *Mantel* that was often worn rolled up across the chest.

LEGWEAR: Tight-fitting Hungarian breeches with elaborate decorations down the front.

FOOTWEAR: The Warasdiner Regiments wore regular army shoes. Others wore short Hungarian boots. Most of the Croats wore the comfortable waterproof laced Opanken sandals done up with elaborate leather bindings.

SIDEARMS: They were issued with regulation muskets and the 58cm long brass hilted cavalry sabres. These replaced the diverse Balkan weapons. The cartridge box had 36 musket balls and 6 shrapnel bullets. Additional ammunition was carried in the company wagons.

1746
Officer uniforms
HEADWEAR: Black tricorn laced gold with a green and white cockade.
COAT: The western style coat of the same colour as those of the soldiers had vertical pockets, square cuffs.
DOLMAN: Same colour as the soldiers.
SASH: Black and gold sash worn over the dolman and under the coat.
LEGWEAR: Coloured breeches. Black cavalry boots.

Szluiner Grenz Infantry Regiment
Ottenfeld, 1895

CROATIAN GENERAL COMMAND
- Carlstädt District

The Carlstädt (*Karlstädt*) Command was largely Croat in nationality and Roman Catholic. Ceded to France in 1809 and provided Napoleon's Croatian Léger.

GIR1 Likaner Grenz Infantry Regiment[179]

The regiment was raised in 1746 around Lika and Korbavja in the south-east of the Carlstädt General Command with its staff stationed in Gospic. In 1754, it had six Bns. In 1769, IR60 Carlstädter Likaner.

1762
Albertini

Inhaber
1746 *Graf Guicciardi:*
1754 *Benvenuto Graf Pestazzi*

Commander
1753 *Franz Friedrich von Vela;*
1758 *Max Pelican*

Albertina (1762)
HEADWEAR: Black felt peak-less shako with dark blue with red centre tuft.
COAT: Red with green cuffs piped yellow.
BREECHES: Red piped yellow.
LACE: Yellow.
SHOULDER STRAP: None.
WAISTCOAT: Green with yellow lace.
SASH: Red and green barrel sash.

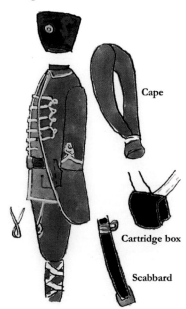

Cape

Cartridge box

Scabbard

Donath (1970)
HEADWEAR: Black felt peak-less shako with dark blue with brass button.
COAT: Red with green cuffs piped yellow.
BREECHES: Red piped yellow.
WAISTCOAT: Green with yellow lace
SASH: Red and green barrel sash.
LEGWEAR: Red Hungarian trousers and sandals.

GIR1 Likaner Grenz IR
Donath (1970)

---

[179] Also spelt *Liccaner* (now *Lica*).

Raspe (1762)
HEADWEAR: Yellow (or brass) cockade on the shako.
SASH: Green barrel sash with 2 rows of oval-shaped red barrels.

Bautzener Bilderhandschrift (1762)

Officer Uniform
HEADWEAR: Black tricorn lace with gold braid and black cockade.
COAT: White coat collarless with gold braid. Green cuffs.
BUTTONS: Gilt.
WAISTCOAT: Green with gold braid.
LEGWEAR: Green Hungarian trousers with gold braid trim and yellow Hungarian boots.
SASH: White sash belt.

Soldier's Uniforms
HEADWEAR: Black felt shako without cockade.
COAT: White coat edged green with green collar, turnbacks, buttonholes laced with green tassels, green square cuffs and brass buttons.
DOLMAN: Green dolman with white edging and braids and brass buttons.
SASH: White barrel-sash.
LEGWEAR: White Hungarian trousers decorated without any decorative lace.

It is probably that the red and white uniforms were used by different battalions in the same regiment.

Likaner GIR
Bautzener (1762)

Campaigns
Seven Years War
In 1757, at Prague (6 May), Moys (7 Sept). In 1759 at Kunersdorf (12 Aug). In 1760 at Landeshut (23 June), storm of Glatz (26 July) and Liegnitz (15 Aug). In 1761, distinguished in Loudon's storm of Schweidnitz. In 1762 in Saxony and the defence of Schweidnitz.

GIR2 Ottochaner Grenz Infantry Regiment

The regiment was raised in 1746 in the southern mountainous region of *Carlstädt General Command*. Also spelt Ottocaner (now *Otocac*). In 1769, IR61 Carlstädter Ottochaner.

1762
Albertini

Inhaber:
1746 *Graf Herbenstein*

Commander
1753 *Joseph Dietrich von Adelsfels*
1762 *Peter Vukassovich*

HEADWEAR: Black peak-less shako with dark blue with red centre tuft.
COAT: Red coat with yellow lace and light blue cuffs piped yellow.
SHOULDER STRAP: None.
WAISTCOAT: Light blue with yellow lace.
SASH: Red and blue barrel sash.
LEGWEAR: Red piped yellow breeches.

Raspe (1762)
LEGWEAR: Red Hungarian trousers without decoration.

Donath (1970)
HEADWEAR: Black peak-less shako with dark blue with red centre tuft.
COAT: Red with light blue cuffs piped yellow.
WAISTCOAT: Light blue with yellow lace.
SASH: Red and yellow barrel sash.
LEGWEAR: White Hungarian trousers without decoration and short boots.

Richard Knötel
SASH: Red and yellow barrel sash.
LEGWEAR: Light blue Hungarian trousers without lace decoration.

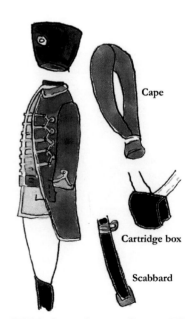

Cape

Cartridge box

Scabbard

GIR2 Ottochaner Grenz IR
Donath (1970)

Bautzener Bilderhandschrift (1762)

Officer

Officer Uniform
HEADWEAR: Black tricorn lace with gold braid and green & white cockade.
COAT: Red coat lined deep sky blue. Blue collar and cuffs. Gold braid.
BUTTONS: Gilt.
WAISTCOAT: Deep sky blue edged with gold braid.
LEGWEAR: Deep sky blue Hungarian trousers with gold braid and black cavalry boots.
SASH: White black sash belt.

Soldier

Soldier
HEADWEAR: Black felt shako without cockade.
COAT: Red Hungarian style coat with light blue pointed cuffs edged yellow.
WAISTCOAT: This is not shown but probably deep sky blue Hungarian dolman style.
SASH: Light blue barrel-sash.
CLOAK: Red cloak.
LEGWEAR: Red Hungarian breeches with yellow knots and sandals.

Ottochaner Grenz IR
Bautzener Bilderhandschrift (1762)

Campaigns
Seven Years War
In 1757, at Prague. In 1758 it captured a Prussian Bn at Liebau in Bohemia. In 1759, a detachment was distinguished at Kunersdorf and Meissen (2-3 Dec). In 1760, at Landeshut (23 June), the storm of Glatz (26 July) and Liegnitz. In 1761. one Bn was at Loudon's storm of Schweidnitz. In 1762, with the *Reichsarmee*.

GIR3 Oguliner Grenz Infantry Regiment

The regiment was raised in 1746 in the Oguliner (now *Ogulin*) district of the Carlstädt General Command. In 1769, IR62 Carlstädter Oguliner.

1762
Albertini

Inhaber
1746 *von Dillis*

Commanders
1746 *Von Adelsfels*
1762 *Peter Vukassovich*

Albertini (1762)
HEADWEAR: Black felt peak-less shako without tuft.
COAT: Dark blue with light blue cuffs and yellow lace.
WAISTCOAT: Dark blue with yellow lace.
SASH: Red and yellow barrel sash.
LEGWEAR: Red piped yellow and sandals.

Reichsarmee (1756)
HEADWEAR: Black felt peak-less shako without tuft.
COAT: Dark blue with yellow cuffs and yellow lace.
WAISTCOAT: Dark blue with yellow lace.
SASH: Red and white barrel sash.
LEGWEAR: Red Hungarian breeches piped white with yellow knee patches and sandals.

GIR3 Oguliner Grenz IR
Reichsarmee 1756

Donath (1970)
HEADWEAR: Black felt peak-less shako.
COAT: Blue with yellow cuffs and lace.
WAISTCOAT: Blue with yellow lace.
SASH: Red and yellow barrel sash.
LEGWEAR: Red Hungarian breeches.
CAPE: Red

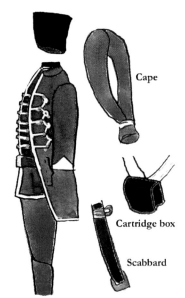

Cape

Cartridge box

Scabbard

Officer

GIR3 Oguliner Grenz IR
Donath (1970)

Bautzener Bilderhandschrift (1761)
Officer Uniform
HEADWEAR: Tricorn with gold braid edging and white-green cockade.
COAT: Blue coat with red collar and cuffs.
WAISTCOAT: Red waistcoat.
SASH: White sash belt.
LEGWEAR: Red and black cavalry boots.

Soldier's Uniform
HEADWEAR: Black peak-less shako.
COAT: Blue coat with red pointed cuffs edged white, white braids and brass buttons.
SASH: Red barrel-sash.
LEGWEAR: Red Hungarian trousers decorated with a white lace.
CLOAK: Red.

Campaigns
Seven Years War
In 1756, at Lobositz (1 Oct). In 1757, at Prague (6 May) and some were lost at Breslau. In 1759, at Kunersdorf (12 Aug) and Meissen (2-3 Dec). In 1760, one Bn was at Landeshut (23 June), the storm of Glatz (26 July) and Liegnitz (15 Aug). It suffered heavy losses at Troppau. In 1762, one Bn was involved in the defence of Schweidnitz.

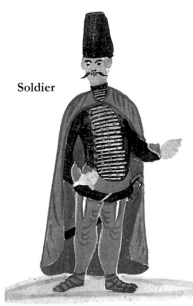

Soldier

Oguliner GIR
Bautzener (1762)

GIR4 Szluiner Grenz Infantry Regiment

Raised in 1746 in the north east of Carlstädt General Command. In 1769, IR63 Carlstädter Szluiner.

1762
Albertini

Inhaber
1746 *Graf Petazzi*

Commanders
1746 *von Kleefeld*
1758 *Peter Vukassovich*
1761 *Johann Kallinic*
1762 *Frhr. von Lezzeny*

Albertini (1762)
HEADWEAR: Black felt peak-less shako with brass plate and red top.
COAT: Blue with red cuffs piped yellow.
WAISTCOAT: Red with yellow lace
BREECHES: Blue piped yellow.
SHOULDER STRAP: None.
SASH: Blue and yellow barrel sash.

Donath (1970)
HEADWEAR: Black felt peak-less shako with brass plate and red top.
COAT: Medium Blue coat with red cuffs edged yellow and blue collar.
WAISTCOAT: Red with yellow lace and edging.
LEGWEAR: Blue Hungarian trousers without lace decoration.
SASH: Blue and yellow barrel sash.
CLOAK: Red.
SABRETASCHE: Red leather

top of shako

Cape

Barrel sash

Catridge box

Coat details

Sabretasche

GIR4 Szluiner Grenz IR
Donath (1970)

Richard Knötel
SASH: a light blue and yellow barrel sash.

Bautzener Bilderhandschrift (1761)
A very different uniform.

Officer Uniform
HEADWEAR: Tricorn with gold braid edging and white-green cockade.
COAT: Blue coat with red collar and cuffs.
WAISTCOAT: Red waistcoat.
SASH: White sash belt.
LEGWEAR: Red and black cavalry boots.

Soldier's uniform
HEADWEAR: Black felt shako without cockade.
COAT: Dark brown coat with red pointed cuffs and white lace.
WAISTCOAT: Red waistcoat with white lace.
LEGWEAR: Red Hungarian trousers with white knots and sandals.
SASH: Red and white barrel-sash.

Szluiner GIR
Bautzener (1762)

Campaigns
Seven Years War
In 1757, small detachments were involved in numerous small actions in Silesia and Bohemia. It fought at Kaltenberg. In 1759, the regiment was part of Hadik's raid on Berlin, at Maxen, Meissen and other small actions in Saxony. In 1760, once again in Saxony. Also present at Dresden, Torgau, and Strehla. In 1762, Wartenleben's Bn was distinguished at Pretzschendorf.

CROATIAN GENERAL COMMAND
– Warasdin District

GIR5 Kreutz Grenz Infantry Regiment
Raised in 1749 from the west of Warasdin Military Command.

Commander
1749 *Michael Frhr Mikassinovich Schlangenfeld.*

1762
Albertini

Albertini (1762)
HEADWEAR: Black felt peak-less shako with yellow tuft.
COAT: White with light green cuffs.
COAT LACE: Light green.
SHOULDER STRAP: Green.
WAISTCOAT: Light green with white lace.
SASH: White and yellow barrel sash.
CLOAK: Red cloak.
BREECHES: White with no piping.

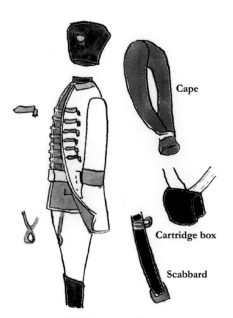

Cape

Cartridge box

Scabbard

Donath (1970)
COAT: yellow edging and yellow braids on the dolman.
WAISTCOAT: Light green with white lace.
SASH: White and yellow barrel sash.
LEGWEAR: green decorations (Schoitasch) on the trousers.
CLOAK: Red.

GIR5 Kreutz Grenz IR
Donath (1970)

Bautzener Bilderhandschrift (1761)

Officer

Officer uniform
HEADWEAR: Black tricorn lace with gold braid and white-green cockade.
COAT: White coat with green collar and cuffs. Gold braid.
BUTTONS: Gilt.
WAISTCOAT: Green with gold lace braid.
GLOVES: Yellow leather gloves.
LEGWEAR: Green Hungarian breeches with gold braid laces and yellow leather Hungarian boots edged with gold braid.
SASH: White sash belt.

Soldier

Soldier's Uniform
HEADWEAR: Black felt shako without cockade.
STOCK: Black stock.
COAT: White with green cuffs and green buttonhole lace.
WAISTCOAT: Dark green with white lace.
BUTTONS: Brass.
SASH: White barrel sash.
LEGWEAR: Green Hungarian trousers with white decorations.

Kreutz GIR
Bautzener (1761)

Campaigns
Seven Years War
In 1757, one Bn was at Prague (6 May) and another was at Kolin (18 June). The whole regiment surrendered at Breslau. In 1758-59, the regiment was reconstituted as detachments in Saxony. It was present at Meissen (2-3 Dec 1759). In 1760, *Major Eder's* Bn participated in Lacy's raid on Berlin, at Landeshut (23 June), Sebastiansberg, Leutmannsdorf and Peilau. In 1762 it was distinguished at Adelsbach, Burkersdorf and Reichenbach.

GIR6 St. George Grenz Infantry Regiment

1762
Albertini

Raised in 1749 in the east of the Warasdin Military District. In 1769, IR65 Warasdiner St. George.

Commander
1749 *Joseph Brentano-Cimarolli*
1758 *Franz Frhr. Reise*

Albertini (1762)
HEADWEAR: Black felt peak-less shako with no tuft.
COAT: White with green cuffs and green buttonhole lace.
SHOULDER STRAP: Dark green.
WAISTCOAT: Dark green with white lace.
SASH: White and yellow barrel sash.
LEGWEAR: White with no piping.

Donath (1970)
HEADWEAR: Black shako without cockade.
STOCK: Black neck stock.
COAT: Green edged white with white lace and white pointed cuffs.
WAISTCOAT: Green with white lace.
SASH: Yellow and white.
LEGWEAR: White breeches and black leather boots.
CLOAK: White cloak.

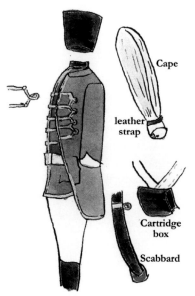

GIR6 St. George Grenz IR
Donath (1970)

Bautzener Bilderhandschrift (1761)

A different uniform:

Officer

Officer uniform

HEADWEAR: Black tricorn lace with gold braid and white-green cockade.
COAT: White coat with green collar and cuffs. Gold braid.
BUTTONS: Gilt.
WAISTCOAT: Green with gold lace braid.
GLOVES: Yellow leather gloves.
LEGWEAR: Green Hungarian breeches with gold braid laces and yellow leather Hungarian boots edged with gold braid.
SASH: White sash belt.

Soldier

Soldier's Uniform

HEADWEAR: Black felt shako without cockade.
STOCK: Red stock.
COAT: White with green cuffs and green buttonhole lace.
WAISTCOAT: Dark green with white lace.
BUTTONS: Brass.
SASH: White barrel sash.
LEGWEAR: Green Hungarian trousers with white decorations.
EQUIPMENT: Plain white waistbelt.

St. George GIR
Bautzener (1761)

Campaigns
Seven Years War

In 1756 it was stationed in Bohemia. In 1757 it was present at Prague (6 May), Moys and one Bn was lost at the surrender of Breslau. In 1758 it operated in Bohemia and Saxony. In 1759, at Maxen (20 Nov) and Meissen (2-3 Dec). In 1760, part of Lacy's raid on Berlin, at Landeshut (23 June) and Stolpen. In 1761, part of *Loudon's* storm of Schweidnitz. In 1762, at Adelsbach (6 July), Burkersdorf (20 July) and Reichenbach.

SLAVONIAN DISTRICT
GIR7. Broder Grenz Infantry Regiment

Recruited along the lower Sau (Sava) River in the Slovonian General Command in 1747. In 1769, IR Slavonisch Broder.

1762
Albertini

Inhaber
1747 *Antoine Graf Mercy d'Argenteau.*

Commander
1747 *Michael Prodanovich von Ussicka.*
1761 *Friedrich Graf Dönhoff*

Albertini (1762)
HEADWEAR: Black felt peak-less shako with yellow and light blue centre to the tuft.
COAT: Dark brown coat with yellow cuffs.
SHOULDER STRAP: Yellow.
WAISTCOAT: Dark brown with yellow lace.
SASH: Yellow and dark brown.
LEGWEAR: Dark blue with yellow piping Hungarian breeches and short black leather boots.

Richard Knötel
As above but does not a shoulder strap.

Donath (1970)
COAT: Light brown coat with light yellow collar and cuffs
WAISTCOAT: Medium blue waistcoat with yellow lace.
SASH: Medium blue and yellow barrel sash.
LEGWEAR: Short black Hungarian or short boots edged yellow.

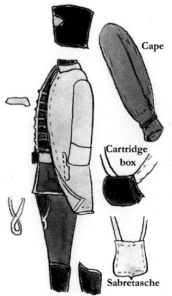

Cape

Cartridge box

Sabretasche

GIR7. Broder Grenz IR
Donath (1970)

Officer

Bautzener Bilderhandschrift (1761)
A very different uniform is depicted.

Officer uniform
HEADWEAR: Black tricorn lace with gold braid and black cockade.
COAT: Red coat lined green and edged. Yellow collar and cuffs. Gold braid.
BUTTONS: Gilt.
WAISTCOAT: Blue with gold lace braid.
LEGWEAR: Dark blue Hungarian breeches with yellow laces and yellow leather Hungarian boots.
SASH: Yellow sash belt.

Soldier

Soldier's Uniform
HEADWEAR: Black felt shako without cockade.
COAT: dark blue coat lined yellow with 19 yellow braids and 3 rows of yellow buttons; yellow pointed cuffs; golden collar.
WAISTCOAT: Dark blue dolman with 19 yellow braids and 3 rows of yellow buttons.
LEGWEAR: Dark blue Hungarian trousers decorated with golden laces.
SASH: Dark blue and golden barrel-sash.

Broder Grenz IR
Bautzener Bilderhandschrift (1762)

Campaigns
Seven Years War
In 1756, one Bn was distinguished at Brandeis. In 1757, at Kolin (18 June), Moys (7 Sept) and one Bn lost at the surrender of Breslau. In 1760, at Landeshut (23 June) and the 2nd Bn was at Torgau (3 Nov).

GIR8. Grasdiscaner Grenz Infantry Regiment

Raised in 1747 in the Slavonian General Command. In 1769, IR67 Slavonisch Gradiscaner.

Inhaber
1747 *Frederic Daniel Frhr. von Saint Andre*

Commanders
1747 *Joseph Frhr. von Reid.*
1758 *Hieronymus Liubibratich von Trebinya*

Uniform 1750-57
According to Khedel (1937)

Officer uniform
HEADWEAR: Black tricorn lace with scalloped gold braid.
COAT: Dark blue collarless coat lined red and red lapels. Red cuffs.
BUTTONS: Gilt.
WAISTCOAT: Red waistcoat.
LEGWEAR: Red Hungarian trousers with yellow knot lace and short boots.

HEADWEAR: Black felt peak-less casket with brass shako plate.
COAT: Sky blue collarless coat with red round cuffs and red lapels.
WAISTCOAT: Sky blue.
LEGWEAR: Sky blue Hungarian breeches with yellow piping.

Officer   **NCO**

Gradiscaner GIR 1750-57
F. Khedel, 1937

Donath (1970)
HEADWEAR: Black felt peak-less shako with brass plate.
COAT: Dark blue with white round cuffs.
SHOULDER STRAP: White.
WAISTCOAT: Dark blue with white lace.
SASH: White and yellow barrel sash.
LEGWEAR: Medium blue breeches with white piping.

Officer

Bautzener Bilderhandschrift (1761)

Officer Uniform
HEADWEAR: Black tricorn lace with gold braid and black cockade.
COAT: Red coat lined blue and gold braid. Blue collar and cuffs.
BUTTONS: Gilt.
WAISTCOAT: Blue with yellow lace braid.
LEGWEAR: Red Hungarian trousers with yellow laces and yellow leather Hungarian boots.
SASH: White sash belt.

Soldier

Grenz Uniform
HEADWEAR: Black felt shako with a red and light blue cockade.
STOCK: Black.
COAT: Red edged yellow with 3 rows of small brass buttons and yellow braid. Dark blue collar and dark blue pointed cuffs edged yellow without button. No shoulder strap.
WAISTCOAT: Medium blue dolman edged yellow with 3 rows of brass buttons and yellow braids.
SASH: Dark blue and yellow barrel sash.
CAPE: Red cape.
LEGWEAR: Red Hungarian trousers without lace and short black boots.
EQUIPMENT: White belts.

Grasdiscaner GIR
Bautzener Bilderhandschrift (1762)

Campaigns
Seven Years War
Fought at Kolin (18 June 1757). Distinguished at Passberg (1759) and Loudon's storm of Schweidnitz (1761).

GIR9. Peterwardeiner Grenz Infantry Regiment

Raised in 1747

1762
Albertini

Inhaber
1747 *Christian Frhr. von Helfreich*
1757 *Friedrich Frhr. von Lietzen*
1762 *Christian Frhr. Wulffen*

Commander
1747 *Franz Joseph Eberstädt*
1758 *Carl Graf Lanjus von Wellenburg*

Albertini (1762)
HEADWEAR: Plain black felt peak-less shako.
COAT: Plain dark brown with red collar and cuffs. Coat and turnbacks edged red.
WAISTCOAT: Light blue with red lace.
LEGWEAR: Light blue breeches with red piping.
SHOULDER STRAP: Red.
SASH: Red and yellow barrel sash.

Raspe (1762)
HEADWEAR: Plain black felt peak-less shako
COAT: Light blue coat edged red, red collar; red cuffs, 6 rows of red braids with red tassels on the chest.
BUTTONS: White metal buttons.
TURNBACKS: red turnbacks.

Officer

Bautzener Bilderhandschrift (1761)
Officer uniform
HEADWEAR: Black tricorn lace with gold braid and black cockade.
COAT: Red coat lined green and edged in gold braid. Green collar and cuffs.
BUTTONS: Gilt.
WAISTCOAT: Green with yellow lace.
LEGWEAR: Red Hungarian trousers with yellow knot lace and Hungarian boots.
SASH: White and green sash belt.

Soldier

Grenz Uniform
HEADWEAR: Black felt shako without cockade.
COAT: Red coat lined green and edged yellow with 3 rows of yellow buttons and yellow braids.
DOLMAN: green dolman edged yellow with 3 rows of brass buttons and yellow braids.
COLLAR and CUFFS: Green collar and green pointed cuffs edged yellow.
LEGWEAR: Red Hungarian trousers with yellow lace and sandals.
SASH: Green and orange barrel-sash.

Peterwardeiner GIR
Bautzener Bilderhandschrift (1762)

Campaigns
Seven Years War
In 1757 it was distinguished at the storm of Schweidnitz. In early summer 1758, the regiment operated around Olmütz. In 1759, one Bn was at Kunersdorf and another at Maxen (20 Nov). The regiment was present at Landeshut (23 June 1760) and Loudon's storm of Schweidnitz. In 1762, distinguished at Saubsdorf in Silesia.

BANAL DISTRICT

Ceded to France in 1809 and provided Napoleon's Croatian Légere.

GIR10. 1st Banal Grenz Infantry Regiment

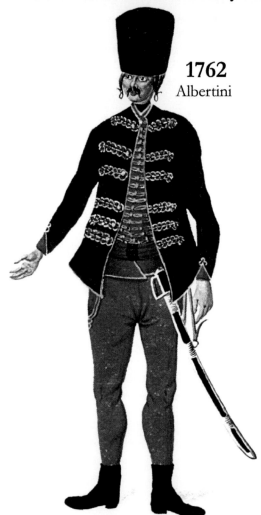

1762
Albertini

Raised in 1750 by *Franz Leopold Graf Nádasdy* in his capacity as Ban of Croatia from the south-western part of the *Banal Military Command*. In 1769, IR69 1st Banal Regiment.

Inhaber
1750 *Franz Leopold Graf Nádasdy*

Commanders
1750 *Johann Frhr. von Zedtwitz*
1762 *Friedrich Göhlichich*

HEADWEAR: Black felt peak-less shako with white and black centre to the tuft.
COAT: Dark blue with yellow lace and yellow cuffs.
WAISTCOAT: Dark blue with yellow lace.
SHOULDER STRAP: None.
SASH: Dark blue and red.
LEGWEAR: Red Hungarian breeches with yellow piping.

Raspe (1762):
COAT: Dark blue coat edged and braided pink with pink pointed cuffs.
WAISTCOAT: Red dolman with pink braids.
SASH: Dark blue and red barrel sash.
LEGWEAR: Dark blue trousers with pink lace.

Bautzener Bilderhandschrift (1761)

Officer uniform
HEADWEAR: Black tricorn lace with gold braid and black cockade.
COAT: Red collarless coat lined yellow and gold braid. Yellow collar and cuffs.
BUTTONS: Gilt.
WAISTCOAT: Red with gold lace braid.
LEGWEAR: Red Hungarian breeches with gold braid and yellow leather Hungarian boots.
SASH: Yellow sash belt.

Grenz Uniform
HEADWEAR: Black peak-less shako.
STOCK: Black stock.
COAT: Red coat with gold edging, gold braid lacing and yellow pointed cuffs.
WAISTCOAT: Red dolman with gold braid lacing.
SASH: Yellow barrel-sash.
LEGWEAR: Red Hungarian breeches decorated with golden edging and braids. Sandals.

1st Banal GIR
Bautzener (1762)

Campaigns
Seven Years War
In 1757, at Prague (6 May), Kolin (18 June), Moys (7 Sept) and the storm of Schweidnitz. In 1758, at the siege of Neisse and at Gruenberg. In 1759, at Meissen (2-3 Dec 1759). The regiment was heavily engaged in Saxony. In 1761-2, in Saxony and Silesia.

GIR11. 2ⁿᵈ Banal Grenz Infantry Regiment

Raised in 1750 by *Franz Leopold Graf Nádasdy* in his capacity as Ban of Croatia from the south-western part of the *Banal Military Command*. In 1769, IR69 2ⁿᵈ Banal Regiment.

1762
Albertini

Inhaber
1750 *Franz Leopold Graf Nádasdy*

Commanders
1750 *Christoph Frhr. von Orssich*
1761 *Peter Graf Sermage.*

HEADWEAR: Black felt peak-less shako with no tuft.
COAT: Dark blue coat with yellow lace and red cuffs edged yellow.
WAISTCOAT: Red with yellow lace.
LEGWEAR: Red with yellow piping.
SHOULDER STRAP: None.
SASH: Red and dark blue barrel sash.

Raspe (1762):
HEADWEAR: Black felt peak-less shako with no tuft.
COAT: Dark blue coat with yellow lace and yellow pointed cuffs.
WAISTCOAT: Dark blue dolman with yellow lace.
SASH: Red and blue barrel sash.
LEGWEAR: Dark blue Hungarian trousers and short black boots.

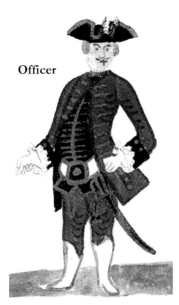

Officer

Bautzener Bilderhandschrift (1761)

Officer uniform
HEADWEAR: Black tricorn lace with gold braid and black cockade.
COAT: Red collarless coat lined yellow and gold braid. Yellow collar and cuffs.
BUTTONS: Gilt.
WAISTCOAT: Red with gold lace braid.
LEGWEAR: Red Hungarian breeches with gold braid and yellow leather Hungarian boots.
SASH: Yellow sash belt.

Soldier

Grenz Uniform
HEADWEAR: Black peak-less shako.
COAT: Red coat decorated with white edging and braid lacing.
WAISTCOAT: Dark blue dolman with white edging and braid lacing.
CUFFS: Dark blue pointed cuffs.
SASH: Red and white barrel sash.
LEGWEAR: Red Hungarian breeches with white lace and sandals.

2nd Banal Grenz IR
Bautzener Bilderhandschrift (1762)

Campaigns
Seven Years War
In 1756, at Lobositz (1 Oct). In 1757, at Prague, and Kolin (18 June). In 1758-59 it participated in Welmina (Reschni-Auje), Nollendorf and Gottleuba. In 1759, at Meissen, Buchau and Strehla. In 1760 it was heavily engaged in Saxony and fought at Torgau (3 Nov). In 1761-2 it was involved in numerous small engagements.

Chaplains

Each battalion had a pope (chaplain).

HEADWEAR: Black tricorn.
STOCK: Black neck stock.
COAT: Black coat edged blue with white braids and blue cuffs.
LEGWEAR: Blue trousers.
GLOVES: black gloves decorated in white.
EQUIPMENT: Brown staff, green cross edged gold worn around the neck on a black ribbon

HEADWEAR: Black tricorn.
STOCK: Black neck stock.
COAT: Dark blue long coat edged blue with white braids and blue cuffs.
LEGWEAR: Blue trousers.
EQUIPMENT: Brown staff.

Pope of the Likaner Grenz IR
Reichsarmee 1756

Tschaikist Bn

It was raised in 1740 as a naval river protection force operating along the river borders of Slavonia and Syrmia against smuggling and the spread of the bubonic plague. In 1763 it was redeployed to Titl between the Danube and Theiss Rivers. In 1764, the battalion establishment was increased from two to four companies. The Tschaikist battalion operated small oared and sail gunboats (Imperial *Freikriegsschiffe*) armed with one heavy and several smaller guns. Tschaika gunboats (Slavic for "lapwing") were similar in construction to the Nassadist flat-bottomed gunboats built in Hungary. *Komárom* (*Komorn*) Fortress in Hungary became the key strongpoint, naval shipyard and repair facility. It was renamed the *Titler Grenz-bataillon* in 1769

Pope of the Oguliner Grenz IR
Reichsarmee 1756

Chapter 18
Freikorps

The Austrians had a long tradition of raising Freikorps. During the Seven Years War, the Freikorps unlike the Prussians was not widely used by the Austrians due to large number of inexpensive light troops from the Grenz.

Green-Loudon Freikorps

In 1757, Obrist Gideon Ernst Freiherr von Loudon led light troops with great effect against the Prussians in Bohemia. Loudon had first considered setting up grenadier units to support the Croats in the autumn of 1757 when he was actively engaged in small war operations, and he noted that the Croats' general inability to fight in formed bodies was a great disadvantage, as it prevented the successful conclusion of numerous promising situations.

In April 1758, Loudon formed a force of grenadiers that was officially called *Freiwilligen-bataillon Loudon*. Unofficially they became known as the *Loudon-Grenadiere* or *Grün Loudon*. These were raised mostly from foreigners and Prussian deserters.

The letter of GFWM Loudon dated 11 May 1758 is interesting as he mentions in passing that he had already once before attempted to set up a corps of 1,500 grenadiers from the Croats without success. He also stated that he chose green instead of white uniforms because this would relieve the regular task of cleaning them.

Commander
1758 *Major Richard Chevalier d'Alton*
1763 Disbanded

The Staff (11 men) consisted of:
   1 *Obrist-Lt*, 2 *Obristwachtmeister*,
   1 *Regimentsquartiermeister*, 1 *Auditor*, 1 *Caplan*,
   1 *Regiments Feldscher*, 1 *Proviantmeister*,
   1 *Wagenmeister*, 1 *Bataillon Feldscher*,
   1 *Profos cum suis*
The battalion had six companies of 154 men.
   1 *Hauptmann*, 1 *Ober-Lt*, 2 *Unter-Lts*, 2 *Feldwäbel*, 1 *Fourier*, 1 *Feldscher*, 6 *Corporals*, 3 *Tambours*, 1 *Pfeiffer*, 12 *Gefreiten*, 2 *Fourierschützen*, 2 *Zimmerleute*, 120 men.

1762
Bautzener

1762
Bautzener

Green-Loudon Freikorps

1762
Albertini

Green-
Loudon
Freikorps

In early March 1759, Loudon in his Pro-Memoria (Memorandum) to Empress Maria-Theresa, he requested permission to form a second battalion and describes the use of the battalions in detail, together with sources of manpower etc. The report dated 13 March 1759 of FM Graf Harrach (President of the *Hofkriegsrat*) and Graf Neipperg (Vice-President of the *Hofkriegsrat*) to the Queen-Empress supported the establishment of a second battalion. On 16 March 1759, Loudon was directed by Graf Harrach to set up the second battalion.

POM-POM: None.
COAT: Light green coat and waistcoat.
LAPELS & CUFFS: Red.
TURNBACKS: Light green or red.
BUTTONS: Yellow.
SHOULDER STRAP: Light green.
LEGWEAR: Light green with black gaiters and shoes.

Campaigns
Seven Years War
These fought throughout their existence under Loudon. In 1758, they were distinguished at Arnsdorf. In 1759 they fought well at Kunersdorf. In 1760 they were distinguished at Landeshut and were then involved in covering the retreat after Liegnitz. In 1761, they participated it manoeuvred in Silesia, and in 1762, they took part in the defence of the redoubts at Leutmannsdorf. They were disbanded in 1763.

**Green Loudon
Freikorps**

Von Böck Freikorps

GFWM Philipp Levin Beck raised in Silesia a battalion from Prussian deserters who were mainly native Silesians in March 1760. They were better disciplined than *Loudon's Green Grenadiers*. Disbanded in 1763. Also known as the *Voluntaires Silesiens* or *Voluntaires Beck*. During the Seven Years War, the battalion lost to desertion 871 men and 253 killed.[180]

1762
Bautzener

COAT: Dark green with light green waistcoat.
LAPELS & CUFFS: Buff or straw yellow.
TURNBACKS: Light green.
BUTTONS: White.
SHOULDER STRAP: None or green shoulder strap.
LEGWEAR: White breeches and black gaiters.
SIDEARMS: Grenadier sabre.

Commander
1759 *Major Rochus Montagutti*

Campaigns
Seven Years War
Fought in numerous small actions. Then in Corps Beck at Reichenberg.

1762
Albertini

Von Böck Freikorps

1762
Bautzener

Von Böck Freikorps

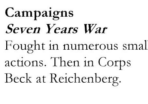

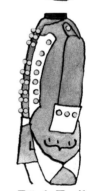

von Böck Freikorps
c1760

[180] Duffy (2008) 439

1762
Albertini

Company
de Lacy

Company de Lacy

Formed by Lacy in 1758.

Inhaber
1758 *Lacy*
1763 Disbanded

HEADWEAR: Casket with brass front plate bearing a black doubled headed eagle and black tipped red plume.
LAPELS & CUFFS: Yellow with white Litzen.
TURNBACKS: White with yellow tab.
BUTTONS: White.
SHOULDER STRAP: Yellow.

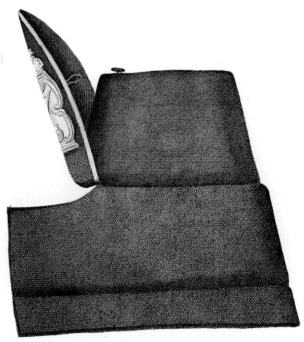

Construction of a Casket

Seven Years War Netherland Freikorps

These were intended for the local defence of the Netherlands.

Frei-Corps Baron Drais 1757.

Freikorps Bethune

In 1757, Oberstlieutenant Jacques de Bethune raised a Freikorps of three companies (Bethune, Le Clerque and du Beyne de Bruleanter) of Netherlands infantry. As a captain he had raised a Freikorps in 1744 during the War of Austrian Succession.

In 1760, Bethune was succeeded by Oberstlieutenant Baron Drai who increased the Freikorps to eight foot companies (936 men) and seven horse companies (445 troopers) of hussars and mounted Jäger. Each of these weak companies had 117 men and 63 troopers respectively. The corps were dissolved on the 15 February 1763.

Inhaber
1757 *Obrist-Lt Jacques de Bethüne*;
1760 *Obrist-Lt Frhr. Drais*

Infantry uniform,
HEADWEAR: Tricorn hats.
COATS: Pale straw-yellow coats with red cuffs and lapels. White waistcoat.
LEGWEAR: breeches and gaiters.

The cavalry uniform is not known.

Freikorps Le Bon

Raised 1762 with 3 foot Jäger coys (563 men) and 1 squadron each of hussars and *Jäger zu Pferde* (223 mounted men).[181]

Freikorps Kühlwein

Raised 1762 with foot Jäger companies and two grenadier companies (1,038 men) and two hussar squadrons (224 troopers).[182]

Korps Wurmser

Raised in 1763 with an infantry regiment of two grenadier and six fusilier companies totalling 808 men) commanded by Obrist Kirchheim, a hussar regiment of two battalions (952 troopers) and an artillery detachment of six guns.[183]

---

[181] Ottenfeld and Teuber (1895 rp 2003) II: 597
[182] Ottenfeld and Teuber (1895 rp 2003) II: 597

Chapter 19
Jäger

The Jäger were professional gamekeepers employed by the great estates to provide game for their master's table. The rifle was their classic weapon. It was slow to load but had a longer effective range and accuracy than the musket.

1762
Bautzener

Deutsches Feld-Jäger Korps

Raised in 1756 from 50 game keepers (*Jäger*) volunteered by the nobility. They worked closely with the Pioneers and at the immediate call of the General Staff. In 1758, it was increased to 2 coys then and 10 coys in 1760. In 1761, the Jäger became independent of the Pionier-Korps.

This very successful unit paid the price of the close association with Lacy who fell out of favour with Kaunitz. It suffered a low desertion of only 374 men and only 24 men killed in action. Disbanded in 1763.[184]

HEADWEAR:
Black leather helmet with upright front.
COAT: Light blue grey (*Hechtgrau*, pike grey) with green collar, cuffs and turnbacks.
WAISTCOAT: Light blue grey (pike grey) or green.
BUTTONS: White then brass in 1762.
SHOULDER STRAP: None

1762
Bautzener

Feld-Jäger Korps
Donath (1970)

Feld-Jäger Korps

[183] Ottenfeld and Teuber (1895 rp 2003) II: 597
[184] Duffy (2008) 439

Commander
1757 *Captain Richard Christian*
1760 *Major Carl Enzenberg*

Campaigns
Seven Years War
Distinguished in the defence of Dresden (1760),
Nieder-Arnsdorf and Torgau.

1762
Albertini

Jäger Casket c1762

Deutsches
Feld-Jäger
Korps

Deutsches Frei-Jäger-Korps Otto

Raised in 1759 by Lieutenant (later Major) Michael Otto in his native Saxony. It had one company of 145 Jäger and a 120 strong detachment of Chevauleger and hussars. This was the nearest Austrian equivalence to a Prussian Freikorps.

Commander
1759-63 *Michael Ludwig Otto*

HEADWEAR: Tricorn hat with white edge.
COAT: Green long tailed coat with black cuffs and lapels. Yellow buttons.
WAISTCOAT : Green double breasted waistcoat.
LEGWEAR: Green, white or yellow breeches and black gaiters. Chevauleger wore heavy cavalry boots.
SIDEARMS: The Jäger were armed with rifles.

Campaigns
Seven Years War
Engaged in many actions as part of the *Reichsarmee* in Saxony and Thuringia involved mainly in the *Kleine Krieg*. In 1760 suffered many casualties.

Deutsches Jäger
Korps Otto

Chapter 20
Engineers

The French and the Dutch were the leading experts in fortress construction during the second half of the 17th century. Sebastian Vauban, chief engineer to Louis XIV, created a professional engineer corps with a comprehensive education and pay structure. He produced an almost complete chain of fortress to secure the borders of France. In comparison, the Habsburg fortresses at this time were created by architects and draftsmen. Engineers were poorly respected within the Austrian Army despite their important contribution to the war and were treated very badly by noble born field officers. Despite all the influence and power of Liechtenstein, he had not been able to win over the nobles to the artillery and there was little prospect for the engineer.

An aristocrat with an income of 30-40,000 florins will be unwilling to consign his son to a corps where courage and hard work are your own reward.[185]

Engineer Corps

Engineering Academies were finally set up by *Prince Eugene* in 1718 in Laimgrube near Vienna, another in Brussels and Prague. The first principle of the Academy near Vienna was the Italian born Leander Anguissola (1653-1720) who was the Vienna city engineer. The deputy-director from 1733 was the court mathematician Giovanni Giacomo Marinomi (1676-1755). Between 1718 and 1743, more than 300 pupils attended the Academy. The *Savoyische Ritterakademie* (Savoy Noble Academy) was opened in 1749 and gave increasing attention to science and engineering. After the death Marinoni in 1755, his Engineering Academy was merged with the Savoy Noble Academy to create a new state-run school of engineering in 1756. In 1760 it was fully militarised under the corps of engineers. The best pupils entered the corps of engineers with the others joining the infantry and cavalry.[186]

Engineer to 1761

In 1732, two Engineer Brigades were founded in the Austrian Netherlands in Brussels and Mecheln each with only 30 officers. On 6 February 1747, Maria Theresa agreed to a proposal of the council of war to form engineer corps consisting of four brigades (German, Hungarian, Italian and the Austrian Netherlands). Prince Charles of Lorraine, Governor General of the Netherlands, was appointed the Director General of Engineers. Paul Ferdinand Bohn became his Deputy Director. Each brigade consisted of an Obrist and some engineers. From 20 July 1747, engineer officers were now equal to those in the field army. They were responsible for the inspection of fortresses and defensive works and drew up plans for new

---

[185] Armfeld, 20
[186] Hochedlinger (2003) 124 and 306-7

arrangements. Officers were also assigned to field armies to organise the construction of field works. In 1758, only 30 engineer officers out of 98 were capable of active service.

During the War of Austrian Succession, the campaigns were in areas devoid of many fortresses. Following the loss of Silesia, it became important to protect Bohemia. The critical gateways were east of Prague along the Elbe towards Silesia. In the 1750s, Olmütz in Moravia was considerably reinforced and successfully withstood a Prussian siege in 1758.[187]

This situation changed at the beginning of the Seven Years War when the theatre of operation shifted to Prussian Silesia and Saxony. The Austrian Army had no suitable officer that could have lead the siege of Schweidnitz which had been blockaded in September. In consequence, Maria Theresa decided to entrust the Brigadier Riverson sent by the French king with this job. This humiliated the Austrian engineer corps.

In 1758 sent Louis XV sent Jean Baptiste Gribeauval[188] to the Austrians and was promoted to GFWM (brigadier-general). He undertook radical steps to improve the Austrian engineer corps. In 1759, Obrist Bohn died and was succeeded by GFWM Ferdinand Philipp Harsch.[189]

**Major
1761**

**Lieutenant
1761**

1761 Engineer Corps Uniform
HEADWEAR: Tricorn with thin gold border.
STOCK: Black cloth neck stock.
COAT: Light blue long tailed coat with carmine red small collar, cuffs and lapels. Gold aiguillette was worn on the right shoulder on parade.
WAISTCOAT: Light blue waistcoat with 12 buttons, gold buttonholes and border.
LEGWEAR: Carmine red breaches were worn on parade. Leather or white cloth breeches were worn in the field.

In January 1760, Unterlieutenant Nicolas-Joseph Cugnot (1725-1804) of the Austrian engineer corps who later designed the steam driven artillery transporter,[190] wrote a letter of resignation to the *Hofkriegsrat* (Austrian War Ministry) that claimed the Austrian engineer corps

[187] Hochedlinger (2003) 308

[188] **Gribeauval, Jean Baptiste Vacquette de (1715-89)** transferred into Austrian service in 1758 with the rank of *Obrist* (Mar 1758) then *GFWM* (1 Nov 1758), *Marechal de Camp* in the French Army (17 July 1762), *FML* (22 Oct 1762 in his absence).

[189] **Harsch, Ferdinand Philipp Graf (1704-92)** was appointed Deputy-Director of Engineers (1 Feb 1760) upon the death of *Deputy-Director Bohn. Inhaber* of IR50.

[190] **Nicolas-Joseph Cugnot (1725-1804)** was a 2nd Lt in the Austrian Engineer Corps who resigned in 1760 and had started thinking of steam locomotion in the 1750s. In 1765, *Gribeauval* and *Duc de*

was spoilt by favouritism.[191] On 20 January 1760, Gribeauval and Prince Charles of Lorraine (Director of Engineering from 1758) were tasked to investigate these claims.

Gribeauval's report dated 2 February informed the *Hofkriegsrat* that the faction riven engineer corps had overlooked merit in promotions, was little regarded by the rest of the army and the engineers were poorly trained. He proposed that the aged officers be purged and that Austria should set up a Corps of Sappers to provide a skilled labour force for the engineers as well as draughtsmen and cartographers.

I (Gribeauval) do not know what system has been followed … But I can assert that a number of officers, even among those how have reached high rank, are devoid of the aptitudes needed for the profession and have never been equal to meeting their responsibilities. In junior officers who have ideas and abilities that fit them for a successful career in the high reaches of their profession, but they nearly all complain of having been passed over repeatedly for promotion, and a number of them – including some of the best – up to 12 or 15 times. They say that it is because of favouritism.

The (Austrian) Engineer Corps is filled with factions, intrigues and cabals without end, but little evidence of enthusiasm, and not at all ambition. Most of them have shunned effort on the excuse that their goodwill has been abused – and here they are not entirely wrong. However, by dint of making promises (which we are admittedly not sure we can keep), and by pricking their vanity, we have begun to bring them into a better way of thinking."

(Engineers) are treated in a way that is harsh and even indecent. A number of generals know only how to convey their orders in terms of threats, holding out the prospect of confinement in chains as if they were criminals. When an officer, no matter how junior, is dispatched on some mission, he invariably takes a couple of engineers with him to see to the hard and uncongenial parts of the task; they load the blame on them if it anything goes wrong, but take the credit if turns out well. Just look at the state of the engineers to the middle of any campaign – you will see that most of them have lost their horses and money, and that they are worn out by exhaustion and maltreatment.

The soldiers and even their officers … just wish to exist until nightfall or the end of their duty overtakes them. New troops arrive, and with them a new crop of difficulties. The remedy must be to raise companies of sappers that will be distributed along the works to support the efforts of the soldiers and they can carry out demonstrations for the benefit of the officers of the engineer corps, which at the moment has neither the structure nor the training for this kind of warfare.

The engineers should employ four or five auxiliary draftsmen… A further body of civilian cartographers could be attached to the General Staff to produce maps of terrain and campsites… As this will be their sole occupation, they will soon acquire the necessary accuracy and facility – something that is impossible for an officer who can attend to such work for only a little while before he has to pass on. They will not be coming under fire, and will therefore have no right to military honours, which will put a limit to the cost and to any inconvenient pretensions on their part. They will be given rank equivalent to junior officers and be respected in their work by the soldiers and the local peasants. We have 80 such people in France (the Ingénieurs Géographes) divided into 1st and 2nd class.

Gribeauval (2 Feb 1760), Dresden

Choiseul supported his experiments and in March 1770 the first working model of a steam driven artillery tractor was demonstrated. The full scale prototype was ready in June 1771 but both *Duc de Choiseul* and *Gribeauval* were not in office so no further funds were available. (Duffy (2000) 189-191)
[191] Duffy (2000) 189-90

Engineer Officer, c1761
Ottenfeld (1895)

It is interesting to note that many of his observations could be made of most armies including Britain, France, Prussia and Russia. This report was sent to the newly appointed General Pro-Director of Engineering, GFWM Harsch who had been in office for only a few days. The proposals received his full support and in his report added that the education of engineers should be modelled on that of France.

On 27 February 1760, Maria Theresa decided that the Gumpendorf School was to be put under the complete control of Deputy-Director of Engineers, GFWM Harsch.[192]

On 7 March, Prince Charles of Lorraine replied defensively against the accusations of Gribeauval on the poor state of Austrian Engineering on his directorship.

He defended the late Deputy-Director Paul Ferdinand Bohn by writing:

> *A Deputy-Director* (of Engineering) *is not like a regimental commander, who has the opportunity to become acquainted with every officer detail. He must rely on reports….. All advancement of this kind* (ignoring seniority) *engenders resentment even among senior officers, for this part of human nature to have an inflated and unrealistic opinion of oneself.*
>
> *Charles of Lorraine to Maria Theresa* (7 Mar 1760)[193]

The latter was a pointed reference to Gribeauval's intervention in a couple of promotions. Despite this, he broadly supported the positive recommendations of both reports but requested that Gribeauval name the individuals at fault.[194] Both agreed that Unterlieutenant Cugnot should be permitted to resign.[195]

---

[192] SS (2011) 264
[193] Duffy (2000) 295
[194] Duffy (2000) 293
[195] Duffy (2000) 190

Miner Corps

In 1716, Prince Eugene v. Savoy formed the first permanent Miner Company for siege work against the Turks. Under Maria Theresa, two Miner companies attached to the artillery had 119 officers and men. Every company was commanded by a major and a captain with 3-4 sergeants. The demands on the men were very high and they should come from a mining background with robust health. The officers had to master mathematical knowledge, above all that which dealt with the mining and fortress construction. It should not be forgotten the achievement of the Miners in the defence of the Schweidnitz Fortress between the 4 August and 9 October 1762. The commander of the Miner-Detachments was Captain Joseph Pabliczek. By a series of mines and countermines, he waged a desperate fight under the glacis of the fortress. The fortress surrendered only after the explosion of a powder magazine.

Sapper Corps

In the 2 February report by GFWM Jean Baptiste de Gribeauval recommended the need for companies of sappers based on his first-hand experience of the inadequate field fortifications set up in the defence of Dresden in the winter of 1759-60. On 16 February 1760, Gribeauval submitted his proposals to the *Hofkriegsrat*. On 23 March, the *Hofkriegsrat* informed the infantry regimental commanders that a Sappers Corps of three companies was being set up. They were expected to send a draft of 4 men who were healthy, strong and of at least 174cm. One of these men was to be literate and suitable for promotion to NCO.

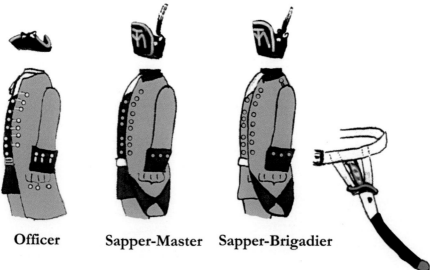

Officer   Sapper-Master   Sapper-Brigadier

By 20 April, the strength had grown to 186 men with another 60 on their way. They were stationed in Dresden under Major Johann Bechardt where they remedied the failings of the field defences.[196] According to Duffy (2000: 298), the Corps of Sappers was the most important contribution by Gribeauval to Austrian engineering service.

---

[196] Ottenfeld (1895) I: 169-70

~ 204 ~

Commander
1760-63 *Major Johann v. Bechard*

The Sapper Corps had originally of 3 companies each split into six brigades of 12 men plus 4 volunteers.

Staff –   *Hauptmann* (Captain),
               Oberlieutenant (1st Lieutenant),
               Unterlieutenant (2nd Lieutenant)

NCOs –   3 *Sappeurmeister* (sapper master),
               6 *Brigadiers* (NCOs)

Men –   32 *Obersappeur* (senior sappers),
               36 *Untersappeur* (junior sappers),
               36 *Gemeine* (men), 1 drummer.

Equipment   50 picks and shovels, 10 long coils of ropes, 6 large picks, 4 great saws, 14 large cauldrons, and 42 flasks.

1762
Albertini

Sapper

Uniform
HEADWEAR: Black casket with brass border and "MT" cipher, white over red feather.
STOCK: Black cloth neck stock.
COAT: Light blue grey (*Hechtgrau*, pike grey) long-tailed coat with poppy red collar and cuffs.
LEGWEAR: Light blue grey (*Hechtgrau*, pike grey) breeches, black gaiters and black shoes.
ARMOUR: In sieges, Sappers wore leather clothing, cuirass and a steel helmet.
EQUIPMENT: Carbine with a long bayonet, a short robust sabre as well as a cartridge pouch with 45 cartridges.

Officers
HEADWEAR: Black tricorn with gold braid edging.
COAT: Light blue grey (*Hechtgrau*, pike grey) with poppy red cuffs.
WAISTCOAT: Poppy red.
SASH: Officer's gold and black sash.
LEGWEAR: and black leather cavalry boots.

The newly raised Sappers Corps established their reputation during the storming of Glatz on the 26 July. Captain Jakob Enghel of the Sappers was awarded the Military Order of Maria Theresa [197] and their commander, Major Bechardt was promoted to Obrist-Lt (Lt-Colonel) when he had the honour given to him by FZM Loudon to take the 33 captured colours to Vienna.[198] Glatz surrendered on 26 July.[199]

In 1761, the corps was reduced to 2 companies. At the defence of Schweidnitz, 10 out of the 24 sappers were killed with a further 11 wounded. Three officers were distinguished with the Maria Theresa Order. In 1772, the Sapper Corps was combined with the Engineer and the Miner Corps.

Sapper, c1761
Ottenfeld (1895)

---

[197] The Knight Cross and Grand Cross of the **Maria Theresa Military Order** (*Militär-Maria-Theresien-Orden*) was founded on 18 June 1757 for meritorious and valorous acts by commissioned officers.
[198] Duffy (2000) 298
[199] Duffy (1985) 119

Pontoneer Corps

In 1749, two companies of Pontoneer were formed. In the Seven Years War, the first company commanded by Bruckhauptmann J.C. Paumann was attached to the Austrian Main Army. The second company commanded by Bruckhauptmann P.S. Gastl was attached to the *Reichsarmee*.

Officer   Pontooneer

HEADWEAR: Black tricorn with silver edging and silver cockade strap.

STOCK: Black cloth neck stock.

COAT: Ultramarine blue long-tailed coat with poppy red green lapels, Brandenburg cuffs with three buttons and turnbacks. White buttons.

WAISTCOAT: Ultramarine blue double breasted waistcoat.

DISTINCTIONS: Officers had black tricorn with gold edge.

LEGWEAR: Ultramarine blue breeches, long white stockings and black long cavalry boots.

EQUIPMENT: White leather sword belt.

SIDEARMS: Grenadier sabre with brown leather scabbard. Brass metalwork.

Each company had:

> **Staff–**
> 1 *Bruckhauptmann,*
> 1 *Brucklieutenant,*
> 1 *Feldpoter,*
> 1 *Felscher* (surgeon),
>
> **Men–**
> 1 *Feldwebel* (sergeant major),
> 2 corporals,
> 1 drummer,
> 15 *pontoneers,*
> 10 *Wasserer* (watermen)
>
> **Equipment –**
> 60 wooden pontoons.
> 40 copper pontoons.

1762
Albertini

Pontooneer

Pioneer Corps

The pioneers performed their work at the head of the marching columns, removing obstacles, repairing roads, and building bridges. GFWM Lacy in 1757 suggested that such a unit should be formed. The pioneers were recruited from skilled craftsmen, miners, fishermen and carpenters.

Commanders
1758 *Major Carl Frhr v Schmidburg*
1759 *Obrist-Lt. Carl Ludwig Montmartin*
1760 *Major Carl Frhr v Enzenberg*
1763 Disbanded

In January 1758, the *Pionierkorps* had four companies of 111 officers and men. Each Company had one corporal and 50 Jäger attached. The Jäger were recruited from hunters and gamekeepers.

Pioneer Company (1758)
　　Staff – 1 Captain, 1 1st Lt, 1 2nd Lt,
　　Men – 1 *Feldwebel* (sergeant major), 4
　　Corporals, 3 drummers, 25 *Zimmerman*
　　(sappers) and 76 pioneers.

In 1759, each company was increased to 261 officers and men.
　　Staff – 1 Major, 1 Adjutant,
　　1 *Proviantmeister* (quartermaster),
　　1 *Feldscher* (surgeon), 1 *Unterfeldscher*
　　(assistant surgeon), 2 *Fourier* (clerks),
　　Four Companies – 1 Captain,
　　1 1st Lt, 1 2nd Lt, 1 *Feldwebel* (sergeant major), 4 Corporals,
　　3 drummers, 25 *Zimmerman* (Sappers) and 125 men.

Uniform
HEADWEAR: Plain black casket.
STOCK: Black cloth neck stock.
COAT: Light blue grey (*Hechtgrau*, pike grey) long-tailed coat with apple green collar, cuffs and turnbacks.
WAISTCOAT: Light blue grey (*Hechtgrau*, pike grey).
BUTTONS: White then brass by 1762.
DISTINCTIONS: Black tricorn with gold edge and black leather cavalry boots.
LEGWEAR: White breeches, black gaiters and black shoes.

1762
Albertini

Pioneer

Pioneer Officer

Pioneer

Sapper of the Pioneer Corps, 1756-63

Watercolour by Ottenfeld, Courtesy of Dr. J. Sissak

Campaign

The pioneers proved themselves in 1758 at Hochkirch, in 1760 before Glatz, in 1761 at the siege and storming of Schweidnitz. The bridges were assigned to the Pontoneer. In 1762, the corps was dissolved by Kaunitz for reasons of cost against the will of the generals for cost reasons. An independent pioneer regiment was not again formed until 1867.

Pioneer and Pontoneer NCO in 1762
Ottenfeld (1895)

Jean Baptist Vicomte de Gribeauval (1715-89)

He was born in Amiens on 15 September 1715 to a middle class Amiens lawyer. In 1732 aged of 17, he entered the garrison Artillery School at La Fère where Bernard Forest de Belidor (1698-1761) famous for being the founder of the science of modern ballistics taught him. In 1735, he was promoted into the officer only *Corps-Royale de l'Artillerie* as *officier-pointeur*.[200] His first campaign experience was with the siege train in the 1743 campaign in Germany. Between 1744 and 1747, he served in Flanders with Marshal de Saxe's army and obtained the rank of *commissionaire ordinaire in the Corps Royal de l'Artillerie.*

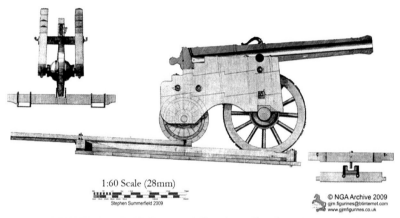

1:60 Scale (28mm)

Stephen Summerfield 2009

© NGA Archive 2009
gjm.figurines@btinternet.com
www.gjmfigurines.co.uk

M1749 16-pdr Gribeauval Garrison Carriage (prototype)
(After De Scheele 1777)

In September 1748, whilst in the garrison duty in Cherbourg, he proposed a design for a Garrison Carriage based upon a modified naval carriage. In March 1749, the M1749 Garrison Carriage was constructed in Douai and tested.[201] This had a medium sized solid trailing wheel on the fixed trail end of the high carriage cheeks which were built-up in a series of steps. This carriage had the advantage of being able to fire over flat embrasures that were less likely to be damaged by fire from enemy siege guns. *Vallière* decided not to accept it for production so only one prototype was constructed.[202]

In 1752, he was promoted to *Capitaine* (First Captain) in the Corps of Miners.[203] In 1755, still only a Captain in the Corps of Miners, he was chosen by Comte Marc-Pierre D'Argenson, the Secretary of State for War, to study the condition of the borders and fortresses whilst collecting a scale model of the new M1754 3-pdr Prussian battalion gun design by Dieskau. On 20 May 1755, Gribeauval arrived in Berlin and on 29 May was given full access to the battalion gun. On 9 June, *Gribeauval* returned to Paris with the model that had previously been requested. In

---

[200] Hennebert (1896) 22
[201] Fave (1871) IV: 144-5, Dollaczek (1887) 335
[202] Naulet (2003) 128-130
[203] Nardin (1982) 44

211 ~

his official report of the mission to Prussia, he liked the manoeuvrability but lacked sufficient hitting power.[204]

The Royal Ordinance dated 20 January and February 1757 introduced one "Swedish" 4-pdr and one M1757 1-pdr Rostaing gun to each French infantry battalion. *Gribeauval* attributed the humiliating defeat at Rossbach (5 Nov 1757) to regimental artillery.[205]

Soon after the outbreak of the Seven Years War, Maria Theresa realised that the Austrian Corps of Engineers lacked expertise especially in conducting sieges so asked the King of France for the services of good engineer officers. As a consequence in June 1757, Gribeauval was promoted directly to *Lieutenant-Colonel* from *Capitaine* and was sent to join the French Ambassador, César Gabriel de Choiseul, Duc de Praslin (1712 –1785) in Vienna. Gribeauval had been recommended for this task by his patron Victor-François, 2nd Duke de Broglie (1718-1804) According to Passac (1816: 100) Gribeauval and Choiseul-Praslin advised Marie Theresa that the ineffectual FM Charles-Alexander of Lorraine (1712-80) should be replaced by FM Leopold Joseph Daun (1705-66) as commander in chief of the Austrian Army. As a consequence, Daun was able to arrange the transfer of Gribeauval to Austrian service.

On 10 March 1758, Gribeauval entered the Austrian engineers as Obrist. At the camp of Neustadt in Moravia, he demonstrated the latest siege methods. He initiated a much needed investigation and reform of Austrian engineering.[206] He was attached to FZM Ferdinand Philip Graf Harsch. Gribeauval supervised the failed Austrian siege of Neisse whose key position was the modern star-fort named Fort Preussen during which he was promoted to GFWM (equivalent to brigadier-general in the British Army).[207]

In October 1759, Gribeauval wrote a memorandum in response to Daun's request for the improvement of the defences of the City of Dresden in order to allow it to hold out for 10-12 days. By 26 October, the programme of works had been agreed and the Saxon envoy, Graf Flemming, consented to provide the necessary labour, transport and materials. However, these were inadequate due to the parapets being excavated from inside rather than outside the works so making it an obstacle for the defenders as well as a high parapet.

In July 1760, he was attached to FZM Gideon Ernst Frhr. von Loudon who at the start of the campaign was in Königgrätz. Gribeauval was the technical director of the siege of Glatz which started on 21 July and was taken by storm on 25 July.[208]

---

[204] Nardin (1981) 43-7
[205] Hennebert (1896a) 30
[206] Duffy (2000) 293
[207] Duffy (2008) 148-9
[208] Duffy (1985) 119

Whilst still in the Austrian Army in March 1762, Gribeauval was instructed by Dubois of the War Office to answers to his 18 questions on the Austrian Artillery. The answers so pleased Duc de Choiseul (who was Secretary of State for War) that Gribeauval was breveted *Marechal de Camp* (equivalent *FML* in the Austrian or to major-general in the British Army) on 25 July 1762.[209]

In August 1762, *GFWM* Gribeauval commanded the technical troops in the defence of Schweidnitz. Under his was Major Frierenberger of the artillery, Obrist-Lt Steinmetz of Engineers, Captain Pabliczek of miners and Captain Eghels of the newly raised Corps of Sappers.[210]

Whilst still in captivity on 26 October 1762, Gribeauval was promoted by the Austrians to *FML* (equivalent to major-general in the British Army) and awarded the Grand Cross of the Maria-Theresa Order.

The Peace of Hubertusburg was signed on 15 February 1763 that ended the Seven Years War. In April 1763, he was released from captivity and returned to Vienna where he informed the Austrians that he wished to return to French service.

In 1763, Gribeauval wrote a response to the French Secretary for State for War's requesting suggestions for the improvement of the French Artillery. In April 1764, Duc de Choiseul chose Gribeauval as an *inspecteur de l'artillerie*. In 1764, he undertook tests at Strasbourg on the 18 calibre guns produced by Maritz II.[211]

However, on 24 December 1770, the Choiseul Ministry ended at the height of the Falklands Crisis between Britain and Spain. Gribeauval had lost all his political support with Choiseul's fall from grace. On 26 January 1771, Marquis de Monteynard (1720-82) replaced Choiseul as Secretary of State for War and decided to revert to the Vallière system by the Decree of 23 August 1772.

On 10 May 1774, *Louis XV* died. On 3 October 1774, the committee of the four Marshals of France after reviewing both systems recommended the re-instating of Gribeauval System. In 1 January 1777, Gribeauval was appointed *First Inspector-General of the Artillery* and died on 9 May 1789.[212] See (Dec 2010) *Smoothbore Ordnance Journal* Issue 2 for fuller biographical details on Gribeauval and a discussion of his Garrison Carriage.

---

[209] A copy of the Warrant dated 25 July 1762 can be found reproduced in Hennebert (1896) 511-2.
[210] Duffy (2008) 369-271
[211] Picard (1906) 71-73
[212] Fave (1871) IV: 160

Order of Battles

OOB 12: FM Browne's Army at Lobositz (1 Oct 1756)[213]

34 Bns, 34 grenadier coys, 69 squadrons, 12 combined elite squadrons

ADVANCE GUARD (*GFWM Hadik*) – In front of Lobositz
> 8 coys/Combined Carabiniers, 4 coys/Combined Horse Grenadiers
> I-IV/HR6 Baranyay Hussars, I-V/HR12 Hadik Hussars
> I-IV/Combined Grenadiers (34 coys)
> Detachment of Grenz from GIR Carlstädt & GIR Banal (100 men)

FIRST LINE (*General Lucchesi* assisted by *GL E. Kollowrat*)
> **Right Wing Cavalry** (*GL Radicati* & *GFWM O'Donnell*) deployed in the centre
>> I-VI/DR1 Erzherzog Joseph Dragoons, I-VI/KR6 Cordova Cuirassiers,
>> I-VI/KR15 Ansbach-Bayreuth Cuirassiers
>
> **Centre Infantry** (*General C. Kollowrat* assisted by *GL W. Starhemberg*)
> *GFWM Wied Infantry Brigade*
>> I-II/IR1 Kaiser Franz I, I-II/IR10 Jung-Wolfenbüttel, I-II/IR50 Harsch
>
> *General Perony Infantry Brigade*
>> I-II/IR29 Alt-Wolfenbüttel, I-II/IR27 Baden-Durlach
>
> *General McGuire Infantry Brigade*
>> I-II/IR11 Wallis, I-II/IR47 Harrach
>
> **Left Wing Cavalry** (*GFWM Löwenstein*)
>> I-VI/KR5 Serbelloni Cuirassiers, I-VI/KR8 Trautmansdorff Cuirassiers,
>> I-VI/DR2 Liechtenstein Dragoons

SECOND LINE
> **Right Wing Cavalry** (*GFWM Lobkowitz*) deployed in the centre
>> I-VI/KR1 Erzherzog Ferdinand Cuirassiers,
>> I-VI/KR4 Stampach Cuirassiers
>
> **Infantry Centre**
> *GFWM Krottendorf Brigade*
>> I-II/IR8 Hildburghausen, I-II/IR17 Kollowrat,
>> I-II/IR33 Esterhazy, Nicolas, I-II/IR37 Esterhazy, Joseph
>
> *GFWM Wolfersdorff Brigade*
>> I-II/IR49 Kheul, I-II/IR35 Waldeck
>
> **Left Wing Cavalry** (*GFWM Hedwiger*)
>> I-VI/KR3 Carl Pálffy Cuirassiers, I-VI/KR14 Brettlach Cuirassiers

ARTILLERY (*General Feuerstein* with 94 pieces and a pontoon train)
> Position batteries: 6x 12-pdrs guns, 12x 6-pdrs guns, 6x 7-pdr howitzers
> Battalion guns: 70x 3-pdrs battalion guns

DETACHMENTS (Graf von Lacy) along the Elbe up to Schreckenstein
> 4 coys/Converged Horse Grenadiers
> DR1 Erzherzog Joseph Dragoons, DR2 Liechtenstein Dragoons,
> DR3 Batthyányi Dragoons, DR10 Kollowrat Dragoons,
> GIR Carlstädt Grenz (400 men) (Oguliner or Ottochaner)
> I-II/IR36 Browne, I-II/IR20 Alt-Colloredo

CORPS DE RESERVE (GFWM Draskovich)
> I-II/GIR Carlstädt Oguliner (or Ottochaner), I-II/GIR Banal

---

[213] After Project 7YW (Aug 2008)

OOB 13: The Austrian at Breslau (22 Nov 1757)
Commanded by Prince Charles of Lorraine assisted by Graf Leopold Daun[214]

FIRST LINE
Right Wing Cavalry (*GdC Graf Lucchesi* assisted by *Marquis de Spada*)
Marquis de Ville Brigade: I-VI/DR1 Erzherzog Joseph Dragoons, I-VI/KR1 Erzherzog Leopold Cuirassiers
Graf Aspremont Brigade: I-VI/KR17 Lucchesi Cuirassiers
First Line Infantry (*General Kheul*)
Andlau Division
Duke d'Ursel Brigade: I-II/IR1 Kaiser Franz I, I-II/IR7 Neipperg
Unruhe Brigade: I-II/IR12 Botta, I-II/IR59 Leopold Jung-Daun
Graf Macguire Division
Marquis Los Rios Brigade: I-II/IR26 Puebla, I-II/IR21 Arenberg
Graf Browne Brigade: I-II/IR29 Alt-Wolfenbüttel, I/IR37 Esterhazy, Joseph
Graf D'Arberg Division
Graf Lacy Brigade: I/IR33 Esterházy, Nicolaus, I-II/IR25 Thürheim, I/IR49 Kheul
Left wing cavalry (*GdC Graf Serbelloni*)
Prince Hohenzollern Brigade (assisted by *Graf Stampach*): I-V/KR15 Ansbach-Bayreuth and I-VII/KR16 Gelhay Cuirassiers
Buccow Brigade (assisted by *Hedwiger*): I-VI/KR9 Kalckreuth and I-VI/KR2 Erzherzog Ferdinand Cuirassiers, I-IV/DR7 Hessen-Darmstadt Dragoons
Extreme Left Wing Infantry (Graf Puebla)
von Mayern Brigade: I-II/IR47 Harrach, I-II/IR13 Moltke
Marquis d'Aynse Brigade: I/IR8 Hildburghausen, I-II/IR2 Erzherzog Carl
ARTILLERY (220 artillery pieces and a Pontoon train)
Position batteries 14x 12-pdrs, 32x 6-pdrs, 14x 7-pdr howitzers
Battalion guns   160x 3-pdrs battalion guns
SECOND LINE
Second Line Right Wing Cavalry (*Prince Esterházy*)
Graf Benedict Daun Brigade
I-V/DR9 Benedict Daun Dragoons (Graf Lanthieri)
I-IV/DR11 Herzog Württemberg Dragoons (Graf Argenteau)
Graf Trautmansdorff Brigade
I-VI/KR5 Serbelloni Cuirassiers, I-VII/KR11 Anhalt-Zerbst Cuirassiers
Second Line Infantry (*General Kheul*)
Graf Starhemberg Division
Wulffen Brigade
I/IR3 Carl von Lothringen, I/35 Waldeck
Buttler Brigade
I/IR11 Wallis, I/IR15 Pallavicini
Haller Division
Graf Kinsky Brigade
I-II/IR17 Kollowrat
Graf Siskovics Brigade
I/IR27 Baden-Durlach, I/IR4 Deutschmeister, I/*Rot Würzburg*
Angern Division
Graf Würben Brigade
I/IR36 Browne, I/IR52 Bethlen

---

[214] 56 bns, 67 grenadier coys, 103 squadrons, (38,276 infantry and 8,292 cavalry) (After *Project 7YW* (Aug 2008))

Marquis de Clerici Division
    Baron Gemmingen Brigade
        I-II/IR50 Harsch, I/IR23 Baden-Baden
    O'Kelly Brigade
        I/IR42 Gaisruck, I-II/IR10 Jung-Wolfenbüttel
Second Line Left Wing Cavalry (*GdC Graf Stampach*)
    Graf Ludwig Starhemberg Brigade (assisted by *Graf Martigny*)
        I-VII/KR6 O'Donnell Cuirassiers,
        I-VI/KR7 Schmerzing Cuirassiers
    Graf Kollowrat Brigade
        I-VI/KR10 Birkenfeld Cuirassiers (*Lefebvre*)
        I-IV/DR10 Kollowrat Dragoons (*Prince Lobkowitz*)
RESERVE CORPS
Graf Nicolaus Esterházy Division
    Otterwolf Brigade
        I/IR57 Andlau, I/IR28 Wied, I/IR22 Sprecher, I/IR56 Mercy
Graf Wied Division
    Blanquet Brigade
        I/IR9 Los Rios, I-II/IR20 Alt-Colloredo, I/IR55 d'Arberg,
        I/IR31 Haller
    Wolff Brigade
        I/*Kurmainz IR*, I/IR16 Königsegg, I/IR30 Sachsen-Gotha,
        I/IR36 de Ligne
Grenadiers and Carabiniers Corps (*Sprecher*)
    Prince Löwenstein Brigade
        4 coys/Converged Horse Grenadiers, 8 coys/Converged Carabiniers
    Reichlin Brigade
        35 coys/Converged Grenadiers

OOB 14: Nádasdy Corps at Breslau (22 November 1757)[215]

FIRST LINE
Right Wing Cavalry
        Batthyányi Dragoons, Zweibrücken-Birkenfeld Dragoons
Infantry Centre (Austrian)
    FML Prince von Arenberg Division
        I/IR2 Erzherzog Carl, I-II/IR45 Alt-Daun, Heinrich, I/IR12 Botta,
        I/IR48 Luzan, I/IR25 Thürheim, I/IR44 Clerici, I/IR32 Forgách,
        I/IR34 Batthyány, I/IR39 Johann Pálffy, I/IR31 Haller,
        I/IR59 Leopold Daun, I/IR13 Moltke, I/IR7 Neipperg,
        I/IR55 Arenberg, I/IR46 Maguire, I/IR19 Leopold Pálffy
    Grenz Light Troops (*Nádasdy*)
        Grenz (8,729 men) and Hussars (2,696 men)
    Württemberg Corps (*GL von Spiznass*) of 5,237 men
        I-II/*Truchsess Fusilier Regiment*, I-II/*Roeder IR*, I-II/*Spiznass IR*,
        I-II/*Prinz Louis*, I-II/*Leib-IR*, *1st-3rd Grenadier Battalions*
Left Wing Cavalry (Saxon Cavalry)
        I-IV/*Prinz Albrecht Chevauleger*, I-IV/*Prinz Karl Chevauleger*

---

[215] 24,205 infantry, 8729 Grenz (40 Bns + 26 grenadier coys) and 4,198 cavalry, 2,696 hussars (38 sq)

SECOND LINE
Right Wing Cavalry
> I-VII/DR5 Jung-Modena Dragoons,
> I-VII/DR8 Sachsen-Gotha Dragoons,

Infantry Centre
> *Bavarian Corps* (*GFWM Graf Seyssel d'Aix*) of 5,119 men
> > II-III/*Leib-Regiment*, I/*Preysing IR*, II/*Kurprinz IR*, I-II/*Herzog Clemens IR*,
> > I-II/*Minucci IR*, I-II/*Morawitzky IR*

Left Wing Cavalry (Saxon Cavalry)
> I-VI/*Graf Brühl Chevauleger*

OOB 15: FM Daun Main Army at Torgau (3 Nov 1760).

FIRST LINE[216]
Left Wing of Cavalry: GdC. O'Donnell
> *Brigade Lobkowitz:* I-V/KR2 Ferdinand, I-V/KR11 Anhalt, I-V/DR7 Hessen-Darmstadt

Infantry Centre
FZM Herzog von Arenberg
> *Brigade Pellegrini:* I-II/IR26 Puebla, I-II/IR28 Wied
> *Brigade Hartenegg:* I-II/IR1 Kaiser, I-II/IR7 Neipperg, I-II/IR42 Gaisruck

FZM Sincère
> *Brigade Elmendorf:* I-II/IR17 Kollowrat, I-II/IR27 Baden-Durlach
> *Brigade Migazzi:* I-II/IR2 Herzog Karl, I-II/IR8 Hildburghausen

Right Wing Cavalry: GdC Buccow assisted by von Schallenberg
> *Brigade Voghera:* I-V/KR1 Leopold, I-V/KR13 Benedict Daun, I-V/DR4 Savoyen

SECOND LINE[217]
Left Wing of Cavalry: *von Pellegrini*
> *Brigade Zollern:* I-V/KR6 O'Donnell, I-V/KR12 von Portugal

Infantry Centre: *FML Graf Wied*
> *Brigade Browne:* I-II/IR3 Lothringen, I-II/IR12 Botta, I-II/IR21 Arenberg, I-II/IR56
> > Mercy
> *Brigade Brinken:* I-II/IR47 Harrach, I-II/IR50 Harsch, I-II/IR54 Sincère, I-II/IR59
> > Leopold Daun

Right Wing Cavalry: *von Schallenberg*
> *Brigade Wiese:* I-V/DR3 Batthyányi, I-V/KR17 Buccow

Grenadier Corp: *FML D'Ayasasa*
> *Brigade Ferrari:* I-III/Grenadiers, I-V/Converged Carabiniers/Horse Grenadiers
> *Brigade von Normann:* I-III/Grenadiers, I-V/Converged Carabiniers / Horse Grenadiers

RESERVE CORPS: *GdC. Prinz Lowenstein*
> *Brigade Bettoni:* I-V/KR4 Stampach, I-V/KR5 Serbelloni
> *Brigade St Ignon:* I-V/DR9 St-Ignon
> *Brigade Bibow:* I-II/IR36 Tillier, I-II/IR40 Jung Colloredo,
> *Brigade Dambach:* I-II/IR51 Gyulai, I-II/IR41 Bayreuth

CORPS LACY:[218] *FZM Lacy*
Light Troops
> I-VI/HR1 Kaiser, I-III/Grenz Hussars, I-III/GIR Warasdiner-Kreutzer

FML Buttler
> *Brigade Zigan:* I-II/IR20 Alt Colloredo, I-II/IR22 Lacy, I-II/IR45 Daun

---

[216] 23,546 infantry (48 Bns), 10,000 cavalry (75 Sq)
[217] 23,546 infantry (48 Bns), 10,000 cavalry (75 Sq)
[218] 11,541 infantry (19 Bns) and 6,908 cavalry (41 Sq)

FML Meyern
  Brigade Pfuhl: I-II/IR10 Jung-Wolfenbüttel, I-II/IR25 Thürheim, I-II/IR31 Haller,
    I-II/IR38 Ligne, I-II/IR52 Bethlen
FML Zeschwitz
  Brigade Lichtenstein: I-VI/KR10 Birkenfeld, I-VI/DR2 Liechtenstein
  Saxon Cavalry Brigade von Goesnitz: I-V/*Karabiniergarde*, I-V/*Graf Brühl*, I-V/*Prinz Albrecht*,
    I-V/*Prinz Karl*
ARTILLERY (275 artillery pieces and a Pontoon train)
  Position batteries: 8x 24-pdr, 30x 12-pdrs, 50x 6-pdrs, 20x 7-pdr howitzers
  Battalion guns: 167x 3-pdrs battalion guns

CORPS RIED[219]: *GFWM Ried*
  I-III/Stabs IR, Deutsches Feld-Jäger Corps (8 coys), I-III/GIR Slavonische Broder,
    I-V/HR7 Széchenyi, I-V/Stabsdragoner

OOB 16: Austro-Imperial Army at Strehla (20 August 1760)

Karl Friedrich Graf Palatine Zweibrücken-Birkenfeld commanded 9,500 Austrians (10 Bns,
12 grenadier coys and 26½ sq) plus 16,000 Reichsarmee (27 Bns, 20 grenadier coys and 12
sq). Austrian allies in *italics*.

MAIN CORPS:[220] *Palatine Zweibrücken-Birkenfeld*
Kreis Infantry: I-II/*Mainz Lamberg*, I-II/*Rot Würzburg*, I-II/*Kreis IR Baden-Baden*,
  I-II/*Kreis IR Fürstenberg*, I/*Kreis IR Württemberg*, I-III/*Kreis IR Kurbayern*,
  I-II/*Kreis IR Kurpfälzisch Effern*, I/*Kreis IR Kurkölnisch Nothaft*, I/*Kreis IR Kurkölnisch
  Wildenstein*, I-IV/*Kreis IR Kurmainz*, I/*Kreis IR Hessen-Darmstadt*, II/*Kurfalz Garde zu Fuss*
Cavalry (*Obrist Zettwitz*): I-V/*Kreis Bayreuth Cuirassiers*, I-III/*Kurfalz Cuirassiers*, Austrian I-
  V/Brettlach Cuirassiers and I-V/De Ville Cuirassiers

RESERVE CORPS:[221] *Prince Stolberg*
Austrian Infantry: GFWM *Würzburg*: I/IR46 Maguire, I-II/IR33 Nicolaus Esterházy,
  I/IR48 Luzan, Grenadier Bn (4 coys) (Luzan/Maguire/N. Esterházy),
  I-II/*Kreis IR Pfalz-Zweibrücken*, I/*Kreis IR Kurtrier*
Cavalry Brigade: Austrian I-V/Zweibrücken-Birkenfeld Chevauleger,
  I-V/*Kurfalz Leib-Dragoner*
Austrian Artillery: 2x 6-pdr guns

AUSTRIAN AUXILIARY CORPS:[222] *GFWM von Kleefeld*
Austrian and Allied Infantry: I-II/*Blau Würzburg*, I/GIR1 Banal, I/GIR Carlstädter-
  Szluiner, Converged Grenadier Bn (4 coys from *Blau Würzburg* and Grenz)
Attached Cavalry: Austrian I-V/Baranyay Hussars

GRENADIER and CARABINIER CORPS:[223] *FML Guasco*
Austrian Infantry: I-II/IR30 Sachsen Gotha, I-II/IR15 Pallavicini, 6 Bns of Converged
  Austrian Grenadiers
Cavalry Brigade: I-IV/*Kreis Hohenzollern Cuirassiers*, I-III/Converged Horse Grenadiers and
  Carabiniers

---

[219] 3,686 men (6 Bns, 10 sqns, 8 independent Coys)
[220] 13,000 men in 22 bns, 18 sqns
[221] 4,000 men in 7 bns, 1 grenadier Bn, 10 sqns
[222] 3,000 men in 4 bns, 1 grenadier Bn, 5 hussar sq
[223] 5,000 men in 4 bns, 6 grenadier bns and 5½ sq

OOB 17: Adelsbach (6 July 1762) under FML Brentano.

CORPS BRENTANO at Adelsbach

    Infantry (1,800 fusiliers, 900 grenadiers, about 2,750 Grenz, 256 Jäger)
    Converged Grenadiers Bn, I-II/IR52 Bethlen, I/IR55 d'Arberg,
    2 coy of Jäger, I-III/GIR Warasdiner-St Georges Grenz
    I-II/GIR Warasdiner-Creutzer Grenz
    Cavalry (about 2,000 men)
    I-V/HR4 Kálnoky Hussars, I-V/DR9 St-Ignon Dragoons,
    I-V/HR7 Hessen-Darmstadt Dragoons

REINFORCEMENT under Soutien

    Infantry
    Converged Grenadiers Bn I-II/IR23 Baden-Baden, I-II/IR27 Baden-Durlach,
    Cavalry
    I-V/KR1 Erzherzog Leopold Cuirassiers, I-V/*Prinz Albert Chevauleger* (Saxon)
    I-VI/HR1 Kaiser Franz I Hussars

"For prayer" from the 1749 Drill Book
Courtesy of Dr. J. Sissak

References

Adye RW and Eliot GW (1813 rp2010) *Bombardier and Pocket Gunner*, Ken Trotman Ltd.

Albertini-Handschrift (1762) *Dessins des Uniformes des Troupes I.I. et R.R. de l'Année 1762*, (Depicts 102 different uniforms.)

Anon (1885) *Mittheilungen des k. k. Kriegs-Archivs*, Vienna

Anon (1974) *Austrian Uniforms of the Seven Years War*, Greenwood and Ball Publication.

Asprey R.B. (1999) *Frederick the Great: The Magnificent Enigma*, History Book Club,

Becher, Johann Christian (1757-60) *Wahrhaftige Nachricht derer Begebenheiten, so sich in dem Herzogthum Weimar by dem gewaltigen Kriege Friedrichs II., Königs von Preußen, mit der Königin von Ungarn, Marien Theresen, samt ihren Bundesgenossen zugetragen*, Weimar

Brauer, Hans (1926-62) *Heeres-Uniformbogen*, Uniformbogen No. 7 and 23, Berlin.

Schmidt-Brentano, Antonio (2006), *Kaiserliche und k.k. Generale (1618-1815)*, Österreichisches Staatsarchiv (Austrian State Archive.)

Camille Rousset, (1868) *Le comte de Gisors 1732–1758, Études Historiques*, Paris

Chandler, D. (1976) *The Art of War in the Age of Marlborough*, B.T. Batsford Ltd, London.

Cogniazzo J. (1780) *Freymüthiger Beytrag zur Geschichte des österreichischen Militärdienstes* (Frank remarks to the history of Austrian military service), Frankfurt and Leipzig.

Dawson AL & PL, and Summerfield, S (2007) *Napoleonic Artillery*, Crowood Press.

Dawson DL and Summerfield S (2008) *French Artillery to 1824*: *Gribeauval, AnXI System and Manual*, DP&G Publishing.

Dolleczek, Anton (1896 rp1970) *Monographie der k.u.k. österr.-ung. blanken und Handfeuer-Waffen, Kriegsmusik, Fahnen und Standarten seit Errichtung des stehenden Heeres bis zur Gegenwart*, Kreisel & Groger, Vienna, (reprinted by Akademische Druck- u. Verlagsanstalt, Graz)

Donath, Rudolf (1970) *Die Kaiserliche und Kaiserlich-Königliche Österreichische Armee 1618-1918*, Simbach

Dorn, G. and Engelmann, J.
- (1989) *The Infantry Regiments of Frederick the Great 1756-63*, Schiffer Publishing Ltd.
- (1989) *The Cavalry Regiment of Frederick the Great 1756-63*, Schiffer Publishing Ltd.

Duffy, Christopher
- (1974) *The Army of Frederick the Great*, David & Charles, London
- (1975 rp 2006) *Fire and Stone: The Science of Fortress Warfare 1660-1860*, Castle Books, (1977) *The Army of Maria Theresia*, David & Charles, London.
- (1985) *The Fortress in the Age of Vauban and Frederick the Great 1660-1789*, Routledge and Kegan Paul, London
- (1996) *The Armies of Frederick the Great*, 2nd Edition, Emperor's Press
- (2000) *Instruments of War*, Volume I of the Austrian Army in the Seven Years War, Emperor's Press
- (2003) *Prussia's Glory; Rossbach and Leuthen*, Emperor's Press.
- (2008) *By Force of Arms*, Volume II of the Austrian Army in the Seven Years War, Emperor's Press

Drant, Will & Ariel
- (1965) *The History of Civilisation*, Volume IX: The Age of Voltaire, Simon and Schuster,
- (1967) *The History of Civilisation*, Volume X: Rousseau and Revolution, Simon and Schuster,

Dwyer, P.G. (2000) *The Rise of Prussia 1700-1830*, Longman, London

Frederic, Jacques Andre (1759) *Des Troupes de sa Majesté Imperiale Royale comme elles se trouvent effectivement l'an 1759*, Augsbourg

Funcken, Liliane and Fred (1976), *The Lace Wars*, Volume 1 & 2, Ward Lock Ltd, London

Graeffer, C. (1797) *Oesterreichischer Militaer-Almanach: für das Jahre 1797*, Vienna

Grant, Charles Stewart (1987) *From Pike to Shot 1685 to 1720*, Wargames Research Group.

Grosser Generalstab (1901). *Die Kriege Friedrichs des Großen. Dritter Teil: Der Siebenjährige Krieg 1756–1763, Volume 1 Pirna und Lobositz*, Berlin.

Hausen, Heinrich Freiherr von (1861) *Allgemeine Militär-Encyclopädie*, Volume IV, p182

Haythornthwaite, Philip
- (1994a) *The Austrian Army 1740-80: Vol 1 Cavalry*, Osprey Publishing
- (1994b) *The Austrian Army 1740-80: Vol 2 Infantry*, Osprey Publishing
- (1995) *The Austrian Army 1740-80: Vol 3 Specialist Troops*, Osprey Publishing

Hennebert
- (1896a) *Gribeauval, lieutenant-général des armées du roy*, Paris
- (1896b) "Gribeauval: premier inspecteur général du corps de l'artillerie. Quelques pages inedites relatives a son se jour en autriche," *Revue d'Artillerie*, **47**, 598-623.

Hochedlinger, Michael (2003) *Austria's Wars of Emergence 1683-1797*, Longman.

Hollins, David (2005) *Austrian Frontier Troops 1740-98*, Osprey Publishing

Kemp A (1980) *Weapons and Equipment of the Marlborough Wars*, Blandford Press. Dorset.

Knötel, R. (1890-1921) *Uniformkunde*, Plates: IV:43; V:10; V:30; V:51; VI:12; VI:13, VI:44; XII:4 and XIV:59.

Langins J. (2004), *Conserving the Enlightenment: French Military Engineering from Vauban to the Revolution*, The MIT Press, London

MacLennan, Ken (2003) "Liechtenstein and Gribeauval: 'Artillery Revolution' Political and Cultural Context," *War in History*, **10**(3), 249-264.

Mollo, John (1975) *Uniforms of the Seven Years War 1756-63*, Blandford Press

Nardin, Pierre (1981) *Gribeauval, Lieutenant Général des Armées du Roi (1715-1789)*, Paris

Ottenfeld, Rudolf von and Teuber, Oscar (1895 rp 2003) *Die österreichische Armee von 1700 bis 1867*, Verlag von Emil Berte, Vienna (reprint by Ken Trotman Ltd)

Passac, Chevalier de (1816) *Précis sur M. de Gribeauval, Premier Inspecteur de L'Artillerie de France*, In (May 1889), *Revue D'Artillerie*, 96-120.

Pengel R.D. and Hurt G.R.
- (1982) *Austro-Hungarian Infantry 1740-1762*, On Military Matters.
- (1983) *Austro-Hungarian Hussars, Artillery and Support Troops 1740-1762*, On Military Matters.

Raspe Manuscript (1762) *Der sämtlichen Kayserlich Koeniglichen Armeen zur eigentlichen Kentnis der Uniform von jedem Regimente. Nebst beygefügter Geschichte, worinne von der Stiftung, denen Chefs, der Staercke, und den wichtigsten Thaten jedes Regiments Nachricht gegeben wird.* Nürnberg.

Rickett, Richard (1983) *A Brief Survey of Austrian History*, 7th Edition, Georg Prachner Verlag.

Rothenberg, Gunther E. (1982) *Napoleon's Great Adversary: The Archduke Charles and the Austrian Armmy 1792-1814*, B.T. Batsford Ltd., London.

Rubli, F. von (1749) *Artillerie Exercitia, und Experimenten, welche zu Moldau Thein Anno 1749 in Beysein des Feldt Marchal Fürsten Ioseph Wenzel von Liechtenstein, unter der Direktion des Feldt Artillerie Comendanten und Feldt Marchal-Lieutenant von Feuerstein bewürcket worden.* KA, Kreigwissenschaftliche Memoiren, 13/465.

Scott H.M. (2000) "Prussia's emergence as a European great power, 1740-1763," in P.G. Dwyer (2000) *The Rise of Prussia 1700-1830,* Longman, London, pp153-176.

Seaton A.
- (1973a) *Frederick the Great's Army,* Osprey Publishing
- (1973b) *Austro-Hungarian Army of the Seven Years War,* Osprey Publishing

Schirmer, Friedrich, (1989) *Die Heere der kriegführenden Staaten 1756-1763*, Revised New Edition, KLIO-Landesgruppe.

Schultz, Johann Gottfried (1757-60) *Abbildung Preußischer Kayser und Französischer Soldaten aus dem siebenjährigen Kriege.*

Showalter, D.E. (1996) *The Wars of Frederick the Great,* London.

Smith, Digby
- (Aug 2010) "Wurzbach's Biography of Jean Baptist Viscomte de Gribeauval (1715-1789) written in 1859," *Smoothbore Ordnance Journal,* **1** (03)
- (2012) *Armies of the Seven Years War,* Spellmount.

Summerfield, Stephen
- (2009) *Saxon Artillery 1733-1827,* Partizan Press.
- (Dec 2010) "Part 1-4: Gribeauval," *Smoothbore Ordnance Journal,* **2** (01-04), Ken Trotman Publishing
- (2011a) *Austrian Seven Years War Infantry and Engineers Uniforms, Organisation and Equipment,* First Edition, Ken Trotman Publishing.
- (2011b) *Austrian Seven Years War Cavalry and Artillery Uniforms, Organisation and Equipment,* First Edition, Ken Trotman Publishing.
- (2012) *Saxon Army of the War of the War of Austrian Succession and Seven Years War, Uniforms, Organisation and Equipment,* Ken Trotman Publishing
- (2013) *Prussian Musketeer Regiments of the War of Austrian Succession and Seven Years War, Uniforms, Organisation and Equipment,* 1st Edition Ken Trotman Publishing
- (2015), *Prussian Fusiliers and Garrison Regiments of the War of Austrian Succession and Seven Years War, Uniforms, Organisation and Equipment,* Ken Trotman
- (2015) *Prussian Musketeer Regiments of the War of Austrian Succession and Seven Years War, Uniforms, Organisation and Equipment,* 2nd Edition Ken Trotman Publishing

Susane, General (1874 rp 1992) *Histoire de L'Artillerie Francais,* Paris (Reprint by C. Terana)

Szabo, F.A.J. (2007) *The Seven Years War in Europe 1756-63,* Longman, London

Thümmler, Lars-Holger (1993) *Die Österreichische Armee im Siebenjährigen Krieg Die Bautzener Bilderhandschrift aus dem Jahre 1762*, Berlin

Thürheim, Andreas (Graf) (1880) *Gedenkblätter aus der Kriegsgeschichte der k. k. Österreichischen Armee,* Vol I-II, Vienna

Wilson P.H. (1998) *German Armies: War and German Politics 1648-1806,* UCL Press Ltd.

Wood, J. (2008) *Armies and Uniforms of the Seven Years War Volume 3 - The Coalition Forces: Austria, Sweden and Russia,* Partizan Press, Nottingham.

Wrede, Alphons Freiherr von (1898-1905), *Geschichte der K. und K. Wehrmacht. Die Regimenter, Corps, Branchen und Anstalten von 1618 bis Ende des XIX. Jahrhunderts,* Volume I-V, Vienna

Wurzbach, Constant von (1859-61), *Biographisches Lexikon des Kaiserthums Oesterreich, enthaltend die die lebensskizzen der denkwürdigen perosnen, wesche seit 1750 bis 1850 in den österreichischen kronländern geboren wurden oder darin gelebt und gewirkt haben,* K. K. Hof- und Staatsdruckerei, Vienna.

Regimental Index

In 1769, the Infantry and the Grenz were numbered sequentially for the first time. Below is given the regimental order as used in the book and in alphabetical order.

Infantry Regiments

1769	Regimental No.	Page	Alphabetical	1769	Page
IR1	Kaiser	90	Andlau	IR57	87
IR2	Erzherzog Karl	119	Angern (1758)	IR49	55
	Erzg Ferdinand (1760)	119	Arenberg	IR21	79
IR3	Lothringen	50	Baden-Baden	IR23	63
IR4	Deutschmeister	51	Baden-Durlach	IR27	64
IR7	Neipperg	91	Batthyány	IR34	124
IR8	Hildburghausen	92	Bayreuth	IR41	70
IR9	Los Rios	106	Bethlen	IR52	128
IR10	Jung-Wolfenbüttel	74	Botta	IR12	93
IR11	Wallis	75	Browne;	IR36	83
IR12	Botta	93	Clerici	IR44	102
IR13	Moltke	68	Alt-Colloredo, Anton	IR20	94
IR14	Salm	57	Jung-Colloredo, Karl	IR40	98
IR15	Pallavicini	76	d'Arberg	IR55	109
IR16	Königsegg	62	Alt-Daun, Heinrich	IR45	66
IR17	Kollowrat	77	Daun, Leopold	IR59	59
IR18	Marschall	78	de Ligne	IR38	108
IR19	Pálffy, Leopold	120	Deutschmeister	IR4	51
IR20	Alt-Colloredo	94	Erzherzog Ferdinand 1760	IR2	119
IR21	Arenberg	79	Erzherzog Karl;	IR2	119
IR22	Hagenbach	96	Esterhazy, Joseph;	IR37	125
	Sprecher (1757);	96	Esterhazy, Nicolaus	IR33	123
	Lacy (1758)	96	Forgách	IR32	122
IR23	Baden-Baden	53	Gaisruck (Gaisrugg)	IR42	84
IR24	Starhemberg	54	Gyulai	IR51	127
IR25	Piccolomini	80	Hagenbach;	IR22	96
	Thürheim (1757)	80	Haller	IR31	121
IR26	Puebla	63	Harrach	IR47	85
IR27	Baden-Durlach	64	Harsch	IR50	58
IR28	Wied-Runkel	81	Hildburghausen	IR8	92
IR29	Wolfenbüttel, Alt-	97	Kaiser	IR1	90
	Loudon (1760)	97	Kheul	IR49	55
IR30	Sachsen-Gotha	107	Kinsky (1761)	IR36	83
IR31	Haller	121	Kollowrat	IR17	77
IR32	Forgách	122	Königsegg	IR16	62
IR33	Esterhazy, Nicolaus	123	Lacy (1758)	IR22	96
IR34	Batthyány	124	Los Rios	IR9	106
IR35	Waldeck	82	Lothringen	IR3	50
IR36	Browne	83	Loudon (1760)	IR29	97
	Tillier (1759)	83	Luzan	IR48	103
	Kinsky (1761)	83	Maguire	IR46	71
IR37	Esterhazy, Joseph	125	Marschall	IR18	78
	Sikovics (1762)	125	Mercy	IR56	99
IR38	de Ligne	108	Moltke	IR13	68
IR39	Pálffy, John	126	Neipperg	IR7	91
IR40	Jung-Colloredo, Karl	98	O'Kelly (1761)	IR45	66
IR41	Bayreuth	70	Pálffy, John	IR39	126
IR42	Gaisruck (Gaisrugg)	84	Pálffy, Leopold	IR19	120
IR43	Platz	85	Pallavicini	IR15	76
IR44	Clerici	102	Piccolomini,	IR25	80

1769	Regimental No.	Page	Alphabetical	1769	Page
IR45	Alt-Daun, Heinrich	66	Platz	IR43	65
	O'Kelly (1761)	66	Puebla	IR26	63
IR46	Maguire	71	Sachsen-Gotha	IR30	107
IR47	Harrach	85	Salm	IR14	57
IR48	Luzan	103	Sikovics (1762)	IR37	125
IR49	Kheul	55	Simbschen	IR53	130
	Angern (1758)	55	Sincère	IR54	86
IR50	Harsch	58	Sprecher (1757);	IR22	96
IR51	Gyulai	127	Starhemberg	IR24	54
IR52	Bethlen	128	Thürheim (1757)	IR25	80
IR53	Simbschen	130	Tillier (1759);	IR36	93
IR54	Sincère	86	Waldeck	IR35	82
IR55	d'Arberg	109	Wallis	IR11	75
IR56	Mercy	99	Wied-Runkel	IR28	81
IR57	Andlau	87	Alt-Wolfenbüttel, Carl	IR29	97
IR59	Daun, Leopold	59	Jung-Wolfenbüttel	IR10	74

Grenz Infantry Regiments

	Regimental No.	Pg	Alphabetical		1769	Pg
GIR1	Likaner GIR	170	1st Banal GIR	GIR10	IR69	188
GIR2	Ottochaner GIR	172	2nd Banal GIR	GIR11	IR70	190
GIR3	Oguliner GIR	174	Broder GIR	GIR7	IR66	180
GIR4	Szluiner GIR	176	Grasdiscaner GIR	GIR8	IR67	184
GIR5	Kreutz GIR	178	Kreutz GIR	GIR5	IR64	178
GIR6	St. George GIR	180	Likaner GIR	GIR1	IR60	170
GIR7	Broder GIR	182	Oguliner GIR	GIR3	IR62	174
GIR8	Grasdiscaner GIR	184	Ottochaner GIR	GIR2	IR61	172
GIR9	Peterwardeiner GIR	186	Peterwardeiner GIR	GIR9	IR68	186
GIR10	1st Banal GIR	188	St. George GIR	GIR6	IR65	180
GIR11	2nd Banal GIR	190	Szluiner GIR	GIR4	IR63	176
-	Tschaikist Bn	192	Tschaikist Bn	-	-	192

Jäger-Korps (disbanded in 1763)

Regimental No.	Notes	Pg
Deutsches Feld-Jäger Korps	Est 1758 to accompany the Pioneers	198
Deutsches Frei-Jäger-Korps Otto	Est 1759	199

Freikorps (disbanded in 1763)

Regimental No.	Notes	Pg
Freikorps Bethüne	Netherland Freikorps est. 1757	197
von Böck Freikorps	Est. 1759: Voluntaires Silesiens, Voluntaire Böck or Vountaire Beck	195
Freikorps le Bon	Netherlands Freikorps est. 1762	197
Freikorps Kühlwein	Netherlands Freikorps est 1762	197
Company de Lacy	Est 1758	196
Green Loudon Freikorps	Est. 1758: also known as Freiwilligen-bataillon Loudon, Loudon Grenadiers, Grün Loudon	193
Korps Wurmser	Netherlands Freikorps est. 1762	197

Engineering Corps

Regimental No.	Notes	Pg
Engineer Corps		200
Miners Corps		204
Pioneer Corps		204
Pontoneer Corps		207
Sappers Corps		208